The Old ONTARIO CookBook

Dear Lizzy,

Hope your birth day was happy and may the coming year be the "best ever".

Love
Eleanor

1986

The Old ONTARIO CookBook

Over 420 delicious and authentic recipes from Ontario country kitchens

Collected, adapted and tested by Muriel Breckenridge

McGraw-Hill Ryerson Limited

Toronto   Montreal   New York   London   Sydney   Mexico
Panama   São Paulo   Johannesburg   Düsseldorf   New Delhi   Singapore
Kuala Lumpur   Auckland

This book is affectionately
dedicated to the memory of my mother,
Edna Magee Vannest,
who bequeathed to me her love of cooking
as well as most of the
recipes herein.

The Old Ontario Cookbook
Copyright © Muriel Breckenridge, 1976.

First published in paperback 1980

ISBN 0-07-092365-5

    2 3 4 5 6 7 8 9 10 THB 9 8 7 6 5 4 3 2 1

Printed and bound in Canada

Design/Peter Maher

Canadian Cataloguing in Publication Data
Breckenridge, Muriel, 1931-
   The old Ontario cookbook
Includes index.
ISBN 0-07-082422-3 bd
ISBN 0-07-092365-5 pa
1. Cookery, Canadian. I. Title.

TX715.B74   641.5'9713   C76-017151-3

CONTENTS

INTRODUCTION

BECAUSE OF THE fertile land and mild climate with which we are blessed, especially in Southern Ontario, we are able to grow and enjoy a wide variety of foods. We are also lucky to inherit a wide diversity in our cuisine from the people of many nations who settled our province, bringing with them their national dishes — the United Empire Loyalists who came up the Mohawk and Champlain Trails and brought with them their heritage of British and early North American cooking, as well as the Irish, Scottish, German, and Dutch settlers, with their own recipes. These people adapted quickly to the land, learning much in the process from the Indians in the use and preparation of new foods.

My paternal ancestors were Dutch United Empire Loyalists who came to Ontario in the late 1700s, and my maternal ancestors were Irish and Scottish immigrants who came to Ontario in the early 1800s. Our family recipes have been passed down from generation to generation. I come from a family of good cooks — indeed, of all my many aunts, I do not know of one who is not an excellent cook. I have grown up in an atmosphere of good food, and my sister and I

1

have inherited a love of cooking from our mother. The backbone of my recipe collection is taken from my mother's cookbook, just as hers was taken from her mother's, and so on through the generations.

In the 1800s cookbooks were few and far between. An 1883 cookbook by Mrs. Anne Clarke notes that she feels she is filling a real need for housewives because of the number of requests for her book even before it was published. In my book you will find many names attached to recipes which were gifts from friends and relatives to my forebears. Thus our grandmothers obtained most of their new recipes, pasting them in "receipt" books or files for future use. And so "family" cookbooks were begun and added to with each generation. Such is the book from which I have taken most of the recipes for use here.

In this age of "instant" and "prepackaged", we are apt to lose the age-old art of home cooking and, with it, the great satisfaction of turning out a dish, delicious to taste and appetizing to the eye. The recipes I have recorded are not complicated and use ingredients that are, on the whole, easily available in your local supermarket. They are economical. Most of the herbs and seasonings and many of the ingredients will be found commonly on your kitchen shelves. I have adapted the old recipes to new ingredients but have sometimes noted what the old ingredient might have been. One of the joys of cooking is experimenting with a recipe until it meets your own taste, and many of these recipes can be changed to do just that. Mine usually vary with whatever ingredients I happen to have on hand.

It is interesting to note some of the old terms used in measurement before the days of measuring spoons and cups. For example, butter the size of an egg, walnut or hickory nut; a pinch of . . . .; a granite cupful, teacup, coffee cup; a saltspoon, dessertspoon; "oiled paper" used instead of waxed paper to cover steamed puddings. Now we are in the process of changing measurements once more and so I have included metric ones.

I would like to thank my children, Margaret and John, and my husband, Al, for their constant encouragement and support while I have been working on this book. I have made every recipe in this book and my family has been a marvellous group of taste-testers.
M.E.B.

A GLIMPSE OF OLD ONTARIO
ITS HOMES AND ITS FOODS

THE EARLY SETTLERS, who came to Ontario in the late 1700s and early 1800s, were a rugged, strong, and determined group. Undiscouraged by tremendous hardships, they forged ahead, surmounting whatever difficulties lay in their paths. Although the first few years were extremely difficult, devoid of almost every comfort, their fortitude, courage, and ability to adapt to the land they found themselves in resulted in a kind of prosperity within six or seven years of their arrival — plenty to eat, good crops, larger stocks, and a surplus of produce to trade for some of the finer necessities of life.

The United Empire Loyalists were the first main group of settlers to come to Ontario. They came in great numbers after the American Revolution, when Britain could protect them no longer in America and so offered them new homes in Canada. They followed the waterways and so the first settlement, in 1784, was made up of a disbanded British regiment of Highlanders at Cornwall in an area that became known as Glengary. They were soon joined by other immigrants from Scotland. In the same year, settlements were begun at Kingston and Adolphustown, on the Bay of Quinte and Hay Bay. Immigrants were also entering Canada at the other end of Lake Ontario and were crowding into Fort Niagara. Toronto had been picked as the temporary site of the capital of Upper Canada and in 1793 the erection of Fort York was begun. (On August 26 of that year the Governor changed the name from Toronto to York, and it was not renamed Toronto until 1834.) Because the United Empire Loyalist settlers either stopped east of York when travelling up Lake Ontario or travelled on into the western areas, the population of York was mainly made up of officials and showed little growth until after 1810.

The settlements spread both east and west, along the shores of the lakes and gradually northwards up the rivers. Windsor was established as a stage-coach stop in 1828. Previously, it had been known as "The Ferry" because of a ferry service by log canoe to Detroit.

In the early 1800s thrifty and hard-working German and Dutch families from Pennsylvania came by covered wagon to take up a new life in Waterloo County around Berlin, now called Kitchener. They were later followed by Mennonite immigrants from Europe who were equally thrifty and deeply religious. These farmers and craftsmen have left a deep imprint on the manners, customs, and foods of the area to this day. They introduced such dishes as sauerkraut, kohl salad, carrot cakes and puddings, as well as double-crusted pie. By the 1830s these same nationalities had settled in Lincoln, Welland, and Haldimand Counties, bringing to these areas the same kind of cuisine. It was not until after the 1850s that settlement of the Georgian Bay counties, the Ottawa area, and the Muskoka district was begun.

A settler's first home was literally carved out of the woods. He built a house, about 8 X 10 X 6 feet high, of logs, notched to fit at the corners. The roof was made of thick overlapping slabs of basswood or strips of elm bark held down in layers by tied poles. Spaces were chinked with wood and moss and plastered inside and out with clay. Usually a fireplace was not built in this first home; the smoke from the cooking fire was allowed to escape through a hole in the roof. Later stone fireplaces were constructed. Cooking was usually done outside in good weather. If the cabin was being built in an already established settlement, neighbours would help to erect it at very little cost — about five English pounds. But if the family's land was back in the bush, they would have to hire help; then the cost was about twelve English pounds.

This story of Robert Turnbull's gives a little insight into the kind of wilderness life facing a pioneer housewife. In 1794, three Loyalist families, the Burkes, Trulls, and Conants came to settle in the Port Darlington area east of York. Because it was desolate they were worried about possible attacks by Indians who lived in the area. One day an Indian woman and her four children appeared at the door of Mrs. Trull's cabin and asked for flour. Since it was very difficult to obtain, Mrs. Trull had hidden the flour in the cabin and refused the woman's demand. The intruder pushed her aside and searched the cabin until she found it. She then proceeded to hand the flour out in double handfuls, one to Mrs. Trull and to each of her children, then to her own four children and herself, until the supply was equally distributed. She then departed with her own and her children's shares.

Pioneer families had to depend largely on their own resources for food, clothing, utensils, and furniture. Home-made tables, chairs, benches, cradles, and churns often had a simple beauty that reflected the settler's home. The pioneer woman accepted the main responsibility for organizing the household. Her days were spent in an endless round of cooking, churning, spinning, and weaving.

During the first years, especially in the winter, supplies were very meager. Pork, flour, potatoes, and corn were the mainstays of the diet, supplemented by fresh fish and game, which the settlers either caught themselves or obtained from the Indians by trading pork and flour. After shelters were built, settlers were able to keep cattle over the winter months, and so fresh milk, buttermilk, and cheese became available. Some of the products made at home were yeast, molasses, cider, vinegar, gelatin, maple syrup, and sugar. Fruits that could be dried and vegetables that could be pickled were preserved in this manner for use through the winter months.

Because of the immediate need for both flour and lumber, grist and sawmills began to spring up quickly. In 1783 the first grist mill in Upper Canada was built by Loyalists near Kingston and another at Niagara. In 1787 a third mill was built at Napanee. By 1818 a grist and sawmill had been built at Scott's Landing, renamed Peterborough in 1826 in honour of Peter Robinson who had the task of settling immigrants in the new land. In 1833 Mr. William Chisholm, of United Empire Loyalist stock, opened a store at Oakville, established a fleet of five schooners sailing the lake, and began making barrel staves from the white oaks that grew in abundance in the area (hence the name Oakville).

Food production made rapid progress in the first half of the 1800s. The settlements along the St. Lawrence and the lakes were older and consequently more prosperous and progressive. The French settlers who first came to the Canadian side of the Detroit River in the mid 1700s introduced plums, cherries, apples, pears, and grapes in great quantities. Almost every home had an orchard. By 1794 these very prosperous French settlements were supplying apples and cider to the Niagara area, where orchards of peaches, cherries, and apples were then being planted.

In Dundas County, John McIntosh experimented with transplanting wild apples and in 1796 was finally successful in producing an apple tree that was named after him — McIntosh Red. Melons were also grown in the Niagara area as well as along the Detroit River and, by the mid 1800s, in the Peterborough area. By 1840 the large settlement of Irish near Sandwich had turned a wet area into highly productive farm land. It was the most prosperous settlement in Western Upper Canada. By 1850 lettuce, cabbage, and various root crops that could be kept through the winter were being grown in most areas, and settlers were experimenting with new vegetables such as broccoli, parsley, and endive. Turnips were becoming a staple crop, for these were fed to cattle as well as to humans. Niagara vineyards had their start in the 1860s when the government encouraged the growing of grapes.

In the first half of the 1800s foods varied widely, depending upon the prosperity of the settler. By 1821 Perth had two bakeries and ice cream was being sold in York. In 1826 Joseph Pickering describes as excellent a meal he had in Whitby of eggs, fried pork, pancakes, and new potatoes. Mrs. Anna Jameson tells us that a breakfast in 1837 in Erindale of tea and coffee, cream, hot cakes, and fresh eggs was equally delightful. When Queen Victoria was married on April 2, 1840, a whole ox was roasted on a street in York, and the townspeople were invited to help themselves to a portion of it. During the 1840s, the food at raising bees in the Ottawa Valley consisted of

6

roast beef, veal or sheep, boiled potatoes, breads, buns, cakes, puddings, and pies, with tea, coffee, and whiskey in great quantities.

By 1867, the year of Confederation, Upper Canada, or Ontario as it was now known, was just emerging from the pioneer stage. Oranges and lemons were occasionally obtainable, but bananas, figs, or grapefruit were almost unknown. Raisins and nuts gradually became available. Staple country foods were still wheaten bread, pork, and potatoes. Turnips were being fed in quantity to cattle and sheep. Canned goods were almost unknown, patented cereals completely unknown until the turn of the century.

Manufacturing had begun in a few lines such as farm machinery, furniture, and cloth, but millions of yards of cloth were still made on spinning wheels and hand looms in homes. One of the earliest furniture companies was The Gibbard Furniture Co. in Napanee, established in 1835. People also generally made their own bread, soap, candles, and many of their own clothes. Table utensils were not much different from today's, but spoons of pewter, wood, or horn were still common.

Letters, and messages sent by word of mouth, were the main means of communication. The post was very irregular, and in the country there were still only weekly newspapers, although some of the larger cities had daily papers.

After 1867 transportation constantly improved and manufacturing was growing. Standards of living and eating changed quickly. A sugar refinery had been established in Lower Canada in 1854 and, as more cane sugar became available, the use of maple sugar declined, although the first cane sugar was dark and coarse in texture as well as expensive.

The abundance and richness of foods continued to increase through the latter half of the 1800s, and in fact the early years of the 1900s were sometimes known as the "age of over-abundance"; the measure of a man's girth was also the measure of his bank account. These were the days when a large portion of a housewife's day was spent in the kitchen preparing food. Today, with so many convenience foods available, no one *need* spend long hours in the kitchen. On the other hand, no ready-mix can really take the place of those truly home-baked loaves of bread, pies, and cakes of yesteryear.

BEVERAGES & APPETIZERS

TEA AND COFFEE were very expensive in Upper Canada, and so substitutes were found. Mountain-sweet leaves were commonly steeped for use as tea. The leaves were dried in the sun and then rolled. Maidenhair fern, cherry bark, sage, chocolate root, tansy, and hops were other tea substitutes. Hop tea was also used to induce sleep and dull pain, and several herb teas were drunk for their medicinal qualities.

Coffee substitutes were numberless, ranging from beans, barley, and corn to dried potatoes. I have heard my father speak of how my great-grandmother made coffee from toasted bread. Mrs. Susanna Moodie, in her book, *Roughing It in the Bush*, describes how dandelion roots were washed, cut into small pieces, roasted until brown, ground, and then boiled in water a few minutes to produce excellent "coffee". She suggested washing, cutting, and drying them in the sun; this way the roots were preserved for years and were then roasted just before use.

Raspberry vinegar, still known in some parts of Canada, was widely used. Raspberries were allowed to stand in vinegar for 24 hours and then the vinegar was drained off. This process was repeated twice more until sufficient raspberry juice had been mixed with the vinegar. A pound of lump sugar was added to each pot of boiling water, boiled for ten minutes, and bottled. It was allowed to cure for several months. To use it as a drink, one mixed a small amount of the vinegar with water in a cup.

One of the most popular beverages in old Ontario was apple cider. Apple juice from the pressed fruit was collected in casks or vats, some of which were set aside to be used at bees or other festivities. The cider thus laid by soon became "hard" and intoxicating.

Cocoa is native to South America and was domesticated and valued greatly by the Aztecs. The Spanish took the plant to Europe where it was extensively grown and later imported to North America.

By the late 1800s, lemons were imported, but expensive, and so tartaric acid and sometimes vinegar were partially substituted for it. An 1880 recipe for lemonade calls for one ounce tartaric acid, one pound loaf sugar, one pint boiling water, and 20 to 30 drops of essence of lemon. This mixture was kept in a bottle and mixed with cold water as desired. Early settlers steeped the flowers of the sumach in boiling water and produced a lemonade-like drink.

Cranberry Cocktail

This recipe originally called for the juice drained from cooked cranberries, but commercially canned juice is just as good. I like to add ginger ale as well.

cranberry juice   *5 cups (1.13 l)*
orange juice   *1 cup (225 ml)*
apple juice   *1 cup (225 ml)*
lemon juice   *½ cup (110 ml)*
ginger ale   *1¼ cups (280 ml)*

Mix all but the ginger ale, adding it just before serving. Chill well.

Yield: 8½ cups (2 litres)

Rhubarb Punch

We used to have a long, thick row of rhubarb at home. How I loved the flavour of my mother's preserved rhubarb and pineapple! That same flavour comes through beautifully in this punch, which may also be used as a beverage appetizer. It is a delicate pink if made with red rhubarb. Make it ahead of time and freeze it for later use.

> rhubarb, chopped   10 cups (2.26 l)
> water   8 cups (2 l)
> grated lemon rind   1 tablespoon (15 ml)
> lemon juice   2 tablespoons (30 ml)
> sugar   1¾ cups (395 ml)
> pineapple juice, fresh or canned   4 cups (1 l)

Place the rhubarb and water in a large kettle, bring to a boil, and simmer until tender. Strain the pulp through a fine sieve or in a colander, gently pressing the pulp. There will be approximately 10 cups (2.26 l) of juice. Add the lemon juice and rind. Mix the sugar with 2 cups (450 ml) of juice and bring to a boil to dissolve the sugar. Stir into the remaining juice. Add the pineapple juice. Chill well and serve.

Yield: 14 cups (3.5 litres)

Pineapple Shrub

> pineapple juice
> egg white, slightly beaten
> lime sherbet
> sugar

Dip the rim of each glass in egg white. Spread some sugar on a plate and turn the moistened glass rims in it to frost the rims. Chill glasses. Chill sufficient sweetened pineapple juice for required number of servings. Immediately before serving, add one small scoop of lime sherbet to each filled glass.

Lemonade

My children love this lemonade, and it's a handy syrup to keep on hand for hot summer days.

> sugar   2 cups (450 ml)
> water   2½ cups (560 ml)

oranges, juice and grated rind   2
or
orange juice   *1 cup (225 ml)*
lemon juice concentrate   *12 tablespoons (180 ml)*

Mix the sugar and water and boil for 5 minutes. Cool and add the remaining ingredients. Store in the refrigerator. To mix lemonade, use one part syrup to two parts water.

Yield: 4½ cups (1 litre) syrup

Percolated Coffee

My father-in-law taught me the secret of making good coffee in a percolator. For 8 cups (2 l) of coffee, use 8 coffee measures of ground coffee, 1/8 teaspoon (0.5 ml) salt, 1/8 teaspoon (0.5 ml) dry mustard, 8 cups (2 l) cold water. Percolate as usual.

Cocoa Syrup

This syrup will keep indefinitely in your refrigerator.

cocoa   *1 cup (225 ml)*
sugar   *1½ cups (335 ml)*
salt   *¼ teaspoon (1 ml)*
boiling water   *2 cups (450 ml)*
vanilla   *1 teaspoon (5 ml)*

Mix the cocoa, salt, and sugar. Add the water and stir until the sugar is dissolved. Boil 5 minutes. Add the vanilla. Cool and store in a cool place. To use as beverage, mix 2 tablespoons (30 ml) of cocoa syrup to one 8-ounce (225 ml) glass of cold milk, or add to the same quantity of hot milk to make delicious cocoa.

Yield: 3 cups (675 ml) syrup

earthenware pitcher c. 1895

MEAT, POULTRY, FISH, AND SAVORY SAUCES

EARLY SETTLERS IN Upper Canada obtained much of their meat from the land and rivers about them. Fish — salmon-trout, maskinonge (muskellunge), whitefish and black bass — were plentiful in our Ontario waters and were used fresh, dried, and salted. Maskinonge and salmon were the varieties most commonly dried; after being treated with salt, the fish was dried in the sun, then smoked over red cedar bark and corn cobs to give it flavour. Thus treated it would keep practically indefinitely, needing only to be soaked in warm water as needed then fried or boiled. Quite often fish was salted away in barrels. In the Bruce Peninsula around 1830, Alexander MacGregor found that the waters north of Sauble Beach teamed with fish. He agreed to supply a firm in Detroit with all the fish he could catch at one dollar a barrel and so he made his fortune during the next few years.

Venison could easily be obtained from the Indians, or the settlers could shoot their own. It could be preserved by several methods: corned (rubbed with salt), smoked in the smokehouse, or cut into strips and hung outside to dry. Often it was roasted, made into pot-pies, or fried, the method of cooking depending on the age and fat-

12

ness of the animal; young or fat animals could usually be roasted. Today, tougher cuts should be marinated first and moist-cooked, as for a beef pot roast or stew.

Bear meat, if cured like ham, is delicious, although it tends to be tough, so that long, slow cooking is necessary. If you should happen to acquire some, marinate it for a day before cooking it.

Settlers considered black squirrels a delicacy. Rabbits were sometimes roasted, made into stew or pie, or fried. Mrs. Anna Jameson tells us, in her journal of 1837, that quails were caught in immense numbers near Toronto and were delicious eating.

Wild pigeons or carrier pigeons were abundantly plentiful and were one of the settler's staple sources of meat. They were fattest right after the harvest season, when they were often roasted. A favourite dish was pigeon pie. The breasts were placed with a little butter and salt on a crust that lined the bake-kettle. Water was added and then a crust was put over the top. It was baked in the usual fashion with hot coals under and on the lid, with the kettle turned periodically. Sometimes the breasts were salted down for later use. Often they were kept in the ice-house, fresh, for several weeks. The carrier pigeon became extinct in 1914.

By the mid 1800s chickens, geese, ducks, domestic turkey and guinea fowl were being raised on the older and cleared farms. (These fowl needed shelter at night to protect them from foxes, and so could not be grown until such shelter could be built.) At the same time beef, pork, and lamb were becoming more available.

• BEEF •

Cattle were first brought to the Western Hemisphere by Columbus on his second voyage but remained scarce because of difficulties encountered in raising them in the wilderness. By the 18th Century, cattle breeding was important in England and, consequently, there was a fair supply of fine animals to ship to new colonists in Canada. Originally it was intended that every two families in Upper Canada should share a cow, but the supply from England proved insufficient. Furthermore until farms developed, feed for cattle was scarce, and so beef was also in poor supply. However by the mid 1860s milk was plentiful enough to supply the few cheese factories which were being built.

Beef cattle, like hogs, were killed in the fall and salted down in casks or tubs for winter use. Sometimes, if cows were slaughtered in cold weather, the quarters were frozen and roasts cut off for use as needed. Some beef was also dried, as venison had been. A corned-beef recipe of the mid 1800s called for four gallons of fresh water, one half pound of coarse brown sugar, two ounces of saltpetre, seven pounds of common salt. This mixture was well boiled, "scummed", allowed to cool, then poured over the meat in the barrel. The meat was weighted down with stones or bricks; before it could be eaten, it was simmered slowly over the fire in an open pot — often with suet pudding. Fresh meat was usually served roasted, boiled, or fried, but by the mid 1800s "beef omelets" made from ground meat were common, as were stews.

After the beef and sheep were killed, tallow was prepared from the rendered fat to make candles.

Beef Loaf

This recipe originally called for ground salt pork, but I find sausage meat is a good substitute. It is as good the second day, cold, as it is hot the first day and excellent, sliced thinly, with Worcestershire sauce, for sandwiches.

> ground beef   *1½ pounds (682 g)*
> bulk sausage meat   *½ pound (227 g)*
> cracker crumbs   *½ cup (110 ml)*
> egg   *1*
> pepper   *¼ teaspoon (1 ml)*
> sage   *1 teaspoon (5 ml)*
> salt   *1¾ teaspoons (9 ml)*
> lemon juice   *1 tablespoon (15 ml)*

Mix all ingredients together lightly, and form into a loaf. Place in a *shallow* pan and dust with cracker crumbs or corn flake crumbs. Roast at 350°F (175°C) for 1¼ hours. If drippings are not too fat, gravy may be made from pan juices and served over the meat.

Yield: 6 servings

Savory Herb Meat Loaf

Here is another version of meat loaf that we enjoy for a change. If you have any cottage cheese on hand, add ½ cup (110 ml) to the meat. It's good!

14

ground beef   *1 pound (455 g)*
fine bread crumbs   *1 cup (225 ml)*
oatmeal   *¾ cup (170 ml)*
egg   *1*
milk   *1/3 cup (75 ml)*
catsup   *½ cup (110 ml)*
prepared mustard   *2 tablespoons (30 ml)*
salt   *1 teaspoon (15 ml)*
garlic powder   *1/8 teaspoon (0.5 ml)*
oregano, savory, and marjoram   *dash*
green onions, chopped   *2*

Beat the egg, milk, and mustard. Then add all the other ingredients and mix lightly but thoroughly. Place in a loaf pan and bake at 350°F (175°C) for 1¼ hours. Bacon strips may be placed over the top before baking, if desired.

Yield: 6 servings

Oatmeal Meat Loaf

This recipe came from my aunt, Mrs. F. Wright, of Conway, Ontario. Several variations in ingredients are suggested.

ground veal, beef, etc. or mixture   *1 1/3 pounds (600 g)*
quick-cooking oats   *1 cup (225 ml)*
salt   *2 teaspoons (30 ml)*
celery salt   *½ teaspoon (2.5 ml)*
pepper   *¼ teaspoon (1 ml)*
egg, well beaten   *1*
milk, sweet or sour   *1¼ cups (280 ml)*
catsup   *1/3 cup (75 ml)*
chopped onion   *2 tablespoons (30 ml)*

Combine all the ingredients and pack into a loaf pan. Bake at 350°F (175°C) for 1¼ hours. One cup (225 ml) of stewed tomatoes and ¾ cup (170 ml) milk may be substituted for the milk and catsup called for in the recipe.

Yield: 6 servings

Meatballs In Tomato Sauce

I like to serve these balls over cooked spaghetti. When I do, I double the amount of sweetened tomato juice used in order to have enough sauce.

> ground beef   *1 pound (455 g)*
> chili sauce   *¼ cup (55 ml)*
> dry mustard   *½ teaspoon (2.5 ml)*
> salt   *1 teaspoon (5 ml)*
> pepper to taste
> onions, chopped   *2*
> tomato juice   *1 cup (225 ml)*
> sugar   *1 teaspoon (5 ml)*

Combine meat, chili sauce, mustard, onions, and seasonings. Shape into 12 round balls. Roll in flour. Heat 2 tablespoons (30 ml) fat in a frypan. Sear the balls on all sides. Add sweetened tomato juice and simmer for 30 minutes. Thicken sauce and serve over the meatballs.

Yield: 4 servings

Swedish Cakes

Any kind of cooked meat may be used for these — bologna is particularly nice.

> cooked meat, finely ground   *2 cups (450 ml)*
> cold mashed potatoes   *1 cup (225 ml)*
> medium onion, finely chopped   *1*
> sage   *1½ teaspoons (7.5 ml)*
> salt and pepper to taste
> egg, beaten   *1*
> cracker crumbs   *¾ cup (170 ml)*
> oil for frying

Lightly mix all ingredients except oil. Form into 8 cakes and fry in oil until well browned on both sides. Serve with catsup.

Yield: 4 servings

Bacon-wrapped Meatburgers

Appealing to the eye as well as to the appetite.

ground meat   *1 pound (455 g)*
egg   *1*
small onion, minced   *1*
salt   *1 teaspoon (5 ml)*
prepared mustard   *2 teaspoons (10 ml)*
fine bread crumbs   *½ cup (110 ml)*
mixed herbs or poultry seasoning   *1 teaspoon (5 ml)*
bacon   *6 slices*

Lightly mix all ingredients except the bacon. Form into 6 round cakes, 1 inch (2.5 cm) thick. Wrap each with a piece of bacon fastened with a toothpick. Bake at 350°F (175°C) for 1 hour.

Yield: 6 servings

Baked Meatballs

Mashed potatoes make these extra light.

cold mashed potatoes   *1 cup (225 ml)*
ground meat   *1 pound (455 g)*
salt   *1 teaspoon (5 ml)*
dry mustard   *1 teaspoon (5 ml)*
minced onion   *2 tablespoons (30 ml)*
egg, slightly beaten   *1*
Worcestershire sauce   *1 teaspoon (5 ml)*

Mix all the ingredients lightly. Form into 8 meatballs and place in a greased pan. Bake at 350°F (175°C) for 1 hour.

Yield: 4 servings

Japanese Meat Roll

Did you ever wonder what to do with that leftover roast? Here's a tasty way to stretch it.

cooked beef, finely chopped   *2 cups (450 ml)*
salt, pepper
Worcestershire sauce
gravy

flour   1½ *cups (335 ml)*
baking powder   1½ *teaspoons (7.5 ml)*
salt   ½ *teaspoon (2.5 ml)*
shortening   3 *tablespoons (45 ml)*
milk   ½ *cup (110 ml)*

Sift the dry ingredients together. With a pastry blender or two knives, cut in the shortening until the mixture resembles coarse meal. Add milk to make a fairly soft dough. Roll into a rectangle ¼ in. (6 mm) thick. Spread chopped beef evenly over dough. Sprinkle with salt and pepper and generously with the Worcestershire sauce. Roll up as a jelly roll and place, seam side down, on a baking sheet. Bake at 425°F (220°C) for 20 minutes. Serve at once, cut in slices, with hot leftover gravy.

Yield: 5 servings

Meat Pie

My mother preferred to make a meat pie in the oven, with a biscuit topping that came out golden and crispy, rather than a stove-top stew with dumplings.

stewing beef cut in 1″ (2.5 cm) cubes   2½ *cups (560 ml)*
flour, salt, and pepper
cooking oil   1/3 *cup (75 ml)*
water   2 *cups (450 ml)*
oregano, thyme, savory, and marjoram   *dash*
medium carrots   2
medium onions   2
medium potatoes   2
celery   1 *stalk*

Mix the flour, salt, and pepper, place in a bag, and shake the beef cubes in it. Brown the meat in a saucepan in cooking oil. Add the water and herbs, cover, and simmer for 1½ hours. Peel and cut vegetables in large pieces and cook until just tender. Add enough vegetable water to the stewing beef to make 2 cups (450 ml) of liquid, and thicken liquid with sufficient remaining seasoned flour to make a thin gravy. Gently mix cooked vegetables, meat, and gravy together in a 2 quart (2 l) casserole. Place in a 450°F (230°C) oven while making topping.

flour   1 *cup (225 ml)*
baking powder   2 *teaspoons (10 ml)*

salt   *½ teaspoon (2.5 ml)*
each oregano, savory, sage   *1/8 teaspoon (0.5 ml)*
milk   *½ cup (110 ml)*
cooking oil   *3 tablespoons (45 ml)*

Sift the flour, baking powder, and salt together. Stir in the herbs. Mix oil and milk together and stir with a fork into dry ingredients until barely combined. Place in 6 mounds on top of the hot stew. Return to the oven and bake at 450°F (230°C) for 20 to 25 minutes or until golden.

Yield: 4 servings

Braised Short Ribs

Start this cooking early in the afternoon, add the vegetables later, and sit back and relax while dinner simmers away, all in one pot.

short ribs   *2 pounds (910 g)*
flour   *½ cup (110 ml)*
salt   *1 teaspoon (5 ml)*
pepper
cooking oil   *2 tablespoons (30 ml)*
water   *1½ cups (335 ml)*
oregano, thyme, garlic powder
medium carrots, potatoes, onions   *2 each*
celery   *1 cup (225 ml)*

Cut ribs into pieces and dredge in flour seasoned with salt and pepper. Brown in the oil in a Dutch oven or heavy pot. Add the water, dash of oregano, thyme, and garlic powder. Cover and simmer 2 hours. Prepare the vegetables. Cut the carrots, potatoes, and onions in large chunks and the celery in 1-inch (2.5 cm) slices and add to the pot. Cook for 30 minutes, covered.

Yield: 4 servings

fireplace cooking utensils c. 1825-60

Beef Stroganoff

This is one of my favourite recipes to serve to large crowds. I just double or triple the recipe according to the amount I require. Use the largest platter you own. Cover it with the noodles, pour the stroganoff over, and let everyone help himself.

> beef tenderloin or tender steak   *2 pounds (910 g)*
> onion, finely chopped   *1/3 cup (75 ml)*
> garlic, minced   *1 clove*
> cooking oil   *4 tablespoons (60 ml)*
> sliced mushrooms   *2 cups (450 ml)*
> salt, mace, nutmeg
> condensed beef broth   *1¼ cups (280 ml)*
> tomato paste   *3 tablespoons (45 ml)*
> Worcestershire sauce   *1 tablespoon (15 ml)*
> flour   *2 tablespoons (30 ml)*
> sour cream   *1 cup (225 ml)*
> noodles   *12 ounces (340 g)*
> melted butter   *3 tablespoons (45 ml)*

Slice steak across grain into strips ¼ inch (6 mm) wide. Sauté onion and garlic in half the oil until tender. Remove from pan and sauté mushrooms. Remove from pan and add remaining oil. Add sliced beef and sauté until it is lightly browned on both sides. Return onions, garlic, and mushrooms to pan and sprinkle with salt, nutmeg, and mace. Add beef broth, Worcestershire sauce, and tomato paste and heat to boiling point. Combine the flour with the cream and stir in until sauce is thickened. Cook noodles until tender, draining well. Lightly stir butter into drained noodles. Serve stroganoff over noodles.

Yield: 6 to 8 servings

Mock Duck

A flavourful way to serve round steak.

> round steak   *2 pounds (910 g)*
> pepper, salt
> bread crumbs   *2 cups (450 ml)*
> poultry seasoning   *1 teaspoon (5 ml)*
> shredded carrots   *¼ cup (55 ml)*
> diced celery   *¼ cup (55 ml)*
> chopped onion   *1/3 cup (75 ml)*
> salt   *½ teaspoon (2.5 ml)*

butter, melted   *4 tablespoons (60 ml)*
flour
fat for browning
water   *1 cup (225 ml)*

Melt the butter and sauté the onion and celery until tender. Mix with the crumbs, poultry seasoning, carrots, and salt. Pound the steak well on both sides. Sprinkle with salt and pepper. Spread crumb mixture evenly over meat and roll up, beginning with the narrow side. Fasten the skewers and lace with string, tying each end. Sprinkle with flour and brown in fat on all sides in a dutch oven or similar utensil. Add water, cover, and bake in a 350°F (175°C) oven for 1½ to 2 hours. Remove the meat and make gravy.

Yield: 4 to 6 servings

Head Cheese

This recipe usually calls for pork but may be made with beef. I like to serve it as a cold meat in hot weather.

stewing beef   *1½ pounds (682 g)*
summer savory   *¾ teaspoon (4 ml)*
sage   *½ teaspoon (2.5 ml)*
salt   *½ teaspoon (2.5 ml)*
onion powder   *¼ teaspoon (1 ml)*
pepper

Simmer beef in lightly salted water to cover, until very tender, about 2½ hours. Remove meat and cool completely. Boil cooking liquid until reduced to 2 cups (450 ml) and cool. Skim off fat. Put meat through coarse blade of food grinder. Stir in seasonings and liquid. Press into flat-bottomed mould. Chill until well set. Slice and serve as cold meat.

Yield: 6 servings

Liver, Bacon, and Onions

An all time favourite of my husband!
Fry as many slices of bacon as desired for required number of servings. Drain on paper towels. Remove bacon fat from skillet, leaving about 4 tablespoons (60 ml). Place liver, cut in serving pieces, in skillet and add enough water to not quite cover. Sprinkle with a little salt, cover pan and simmer gently, turning once, for 15 minutes. Slice as many large onions as desired in thin slices. Spread over liver in pan. Remove cover from skillet and boil off water. Allow liver and onions to

gently brown in bacon fat, adding more fat if required. When the liver has browned sufficiently on both sides, return bacon to pan and cover, turning heat very low. Allow a few minutes for bacon to become thoroughly hot. Serve at once.

• LAMB OR MUTTON •

Sheep were first domesticated in Europe about 7000 years ago and the fleece was first used as wool about 4000 B.C. Herding of sheep is frequently mentioned in the Bible. Sheep were not introduced to Upper Canada until farms had progressed far enough to produce feed and shelter for them, for they had to be shut inside each night to protect them from wild animals. Once sheep became plentiful, the settlers soon learned to rely heavily on their wool for weaving and knitting into clothing at home. Tallow from their fat was used extensively in candle-making.

Oven-Baked Lamb Chops

lamb shoulder chops   6
onion, chopped   *½ cup (110 ml)*
catsup   *½ cup (110 ml)*
water   *½ cup (110 ml)*
Worcestershire Sauce   *1 tablespoon (15 ml)*
lemon juice   *1 tablespoon (15 ml)*
garlic powder   *¼ teaspoon (1 ml)*
dry mustard   *1 teaspoon (5 ml)*
butter   *1 tablespoon (15 ml)*

Brown the chops on both sides under the broiler. Drain off the fat. In the meantime sauté the onion in the butter until tender. Stir in the remaining ingredients and bring to a boil. Pour over the browned chops and cook at 350°F (175°C) for 40 minutes, basting occasionally.

Yield: 6 servings

Hogs were introduced into North America by the Spanish in the 16th century and were shipped to the American colonies from England. They soon became plentiful because they could root in the woods for their food. Customarily, pigs were slaughtered in the fall. After being cut up, they were rubbed with salt and packed away in a strong brine in covered tubs or barrels, to be gradually consumed throughout the winter. Settlers sometimes sold these barrels of pork, weighing about 200 pounds, to the British army in nearby forts. In the spring, any remaining meat was washed, rubbed, hung in the smokehouse until cured, then packed in cotton bags. Hams were also soaked in a salt brine for six to eight weeks, then smoked. Head cheese and jellied hock were prepared from the meat of the head and legs. Sausages were made by chopping and seasoning the meat, then stuffing it into the washed entrails or cotton bags. Bacon was smoked and cured.

When I was very young, my parents still salted away their winter's supply of pork. They used a wooden barrel and my mother had a supply of well-scrubbed flat stones that she placed on top of the pork to weigh it down below the surface of the brine. My grandmother has made a note, beside her recipe for salting away pork, to the effect that they tried to use up their pork before May each year.

Ham Pie

As pork was plentiful, even in the earliest days of Upper Canada, the settlers devised countless ways to use it in their daily diet. Here is a delicious variation for ham — a great way to use up leftovers.

    Filling:
    ham, ground   1¼ pounds (568 g)
    prepared mustard   ½ cup (110 ml)
    Dough:
    flour   2½ cups (560 ml)
    baking powder   2½ teaspoons (12.5 ml)
    salt   ¾ teaspoon (4 ml)
    shortening   ¼ cup (55 ml)
    milk, or enough to make a soft dough that can be rolled   ¾ cup (170 ml)

Mix together the ham and mustard. Sift the dry ingredients and cut in the shortening with a pastry blender or two knives until the mixture looks like coarse meal. Stir in milk. Turn out onto a floured surface, and roll quite thin and about 8 in. (20 cm) wide. Spread on ham filling, being sure to cover dough to edges. Roll up as jelly roll and slice into 16 slices. Place flat in a shallow 9 X 13″ (3 l) baking pan and cover with this sauce:

23

Sauce:
milk   *2 cups (450 ml)*
butter   *2 tablespoons (30 ml)*
flour   *2 tablespoons (30 ml)*
salt   *1 teaspoon (5 ml)*
shredded Cheddar cheese   *2 cups (450 ml)*

Melt butter, stir in flour and salt. Cook briefly over medium heat to cook flour. Remove from heat and slowly add milk, stirring until smooth. Return to heat and stir constantly until mixture comes to boil and is thickened. Remove from heat and stir in cheese until melted. Pour over ham biscuits and sprinkle buttered crumbs over top. Bake at 375°F (190°C) for 45 minutes.

Yield: 8 servings

Baked Pork Chops

My family are particularly fond of loin pork chops cooked this way. They're easy to fix and they come out juicy and golden brown.
Allow one pork chop per serving. Sprinkle both sides with a seasoned instant meat tenderizer. Place on a broiler pan and bake in a 350°F (175°C) oven for 45 to 50 minutes.

Crumb-Topped Pork Chops

Allow one loin pork chop per serving. Spread prepared mustard thinly over both sides. Then sprinkle both sides with fine corn-flake crumbs, garlic powder, salt, and pepper. Place on a rack in a baking pan. Cover and bake at 350°F (175°C) for 60 minutes.

Cranberry-Baked Ham Slice

This is quick to prepare and delicious to look at.

ham slice   *1" to 1½" thick (2.5 to 3.5 cm)*
cranberry sauce   *½ cup (110 ml)*
prepared mustard   *1 teaspoon (5 ml)*

Place ham slice in shallow baking dish. Spread with mustard and pour cranberry sauce over all. Bake at 350°F (175°C) for 30 minutes.

Here are two old-time recipes that were always used when the pig was killed. I always liked the head cheese better than the jellied hock when my mother made it. I have made the jellied hock myself, and it is a good cold meat in hot weather. Both recipes are typical of their time in that they do not specify quantities.

Jellied Hock

Scrub hocks well and soak in a medium brine overnight. Place in a large pot and pour boiling water over, just to cover. When tender, remove skin and gristle. Remove the meat from the bones and cut in large pieces. Season with salt and pepper to taste and place in a square mould. Allow liquor the meat was cooked in to cool. Skim off and discard fat. Pour just enough over the meat to cover. Allow to set. Serve chilled in slices, with catsup.

Head Cheese

Soak head and hocks in medium brine overnight. Cover with boiling water and cook until flesh drops from bones. Put through the coarsest blade of the meat chopper. Place it in a colander and weight down with a plate to press out fat. Save liquor in pot and allow to set and remove fat. Season meat, which has been mixed with just enough liquor to make soft, with sage, summer savory, pepper, and salt, to taste. Place in square mould and allow to set. Serve chilled, in slices.

Spareribs with Barbecue Sauce

A quick and easy way to prepare a company dish! The sauce seems to counteract the richness of the ribs.

    onion   1
    spareribs   3 pounds (1365 g)
    Sauce:
    prepared mustard   2 tablespoons (30 ml)
    vinegar   2 tablespoons (30 ml)
    brown sugar   4 tablespoons (60 ml)
    tomato soup   10-ounce can (280 ml)
    water   1 cup (225 ml)

Cut onion into small pieces and ribs into serving-size pieces. Scatter onions over ribs in a shallow baking dish. Mix sauce ingredients together and pour over ribs. Bake at 350°F (175°C) for 1 to 1½ hours.

Yield: 4 servings

Sausage Upside-Down Cake

An artful way to dress up sausages! Easy on the budget, too.

sausages   *1 pound (455 g)*
large onion, sliced   *1*
tomato soup   *10-ounce can (280 ml)*
sugar   *1 teaspoon (5 ml)*
water   *½ cup (110 ml)*

Brown the sausages on all sides under the broiler. Sauté the onion slices until tender. Place the sausages in a shallow 8″ (2 l) square pan. Arrange onion on top of meat and pour the soup, mixed with the sugar and water, over all. Place in 375°F (190°C) oven while you make topping.

TOPPING:

flour   *2 cups (450 ml)*
baking powder   *3 teaspoons (15 ml)*
salt   *2/3 teaspoon (3.5 ml)*
dry mustard   *1 teaspoon (5 ml)*
shortening   *¼ cup (55 ml)*
milk

Sift the dry ingredients together and cut in the shortening. Mix lightly with just enough milk to make a soft dough. Spread the topping over the sausages and return to oven for 15 to 20 minutes or until crust is golden. Turn upside down onto a serving platter.

Yield: 6 servings

• POULTRY •

Chickens and geese were domesticated over 3000 years ago. Chickens probably originated as a jungle fowl in South West Asia. They gradually spread westward and were brought by the colonists to North America and finally to Canada. Until the farms began to develop in Upper Canada, poultry could not be kept because they had to be sheltered from wild animals at night. But a flock of chickens was one of the first requirements, and eggs and poultry for eating were soon in good supply.

The North American wild turkey is the source of all today's domesticated turkeys, and the subspecies, the Eastern wild turkey, was plentiful in New

England when the Pilgrims arrived. The Pilgrims made the turkey a symbol of Thanksgiving. It was also found commonly in the woods of southern Ontario at the time of the first settlements. The Aztecs of southern Mexico had domesticated turkeys, which the Spaniards took to Europe about 1519. By 1541 they had been introduced to England, and thence back to North America where they were stocked along with the native wild turkey and today's varieties were gradually developed.

Chicken Fricassee

> chicken legs or breasts   6
> *or*
> stewing chicken, cut up   *5-pound (2.3 kg)*
> milk   *2 cups (450 ml)*
> flour   *½ cup (110 ml)*
> salt   *1½ teaspoons (7.5 ml)*
> paprika   *1/8 teaspoon (0.5 ml)*
> cooking oil   *1/3 cup (75 ml)*
> small onion, minced   *1*
> poultry seasoning   *¼ teaspoon (1 ml)*
> lemon juice   *1 teaspoon (5 ml)*
> water   *1 cup (225 ml)*

Dip pieces of chicken in milk, and dredge in mixture of flour, salt, paprika, and pepper. Brown chicken in oil in frying pan. Place pieces in casserole. Sauté onion in oil and stir in remaining flour mixture. Add the rest of the milk and water and stir until sauce thickens. Add poultry seasoning and lemon juice. Pour over the chicken, cover, and bake at 350°F (175°C) for 1¼ hours.

Yield: 6 servings

Roast Chicken

A recipe of the 1880s for roast chicken suggests that constant basting is the secret of a well-roasted fowl. Twenty minutes before the fowl is cooked, little balls of butter rolled in flour should be placed over it and allowed to melt. A little lemon juice should be added to the gravy when it is thickened. The recipe suggests serving sausages or rolled bacon and mashed potatoes with roast fowl.

Oven-Baked Barbecued Chicken

A delicious and easy way to serve chicken.

Allow one chicken leg and thigh or breast per serving. Brush with cooking oil and brown on both sides under the broiler. Place in shallow baking pan, sprinkle

27

with salt, cover, and bake at 350°F (175°C) for 55 minutes. Pour barbecue sauce over, cover, and continue to cook for 30 minutes more.

Sauce:
Sauté ½ cup (110 ml) chopped onion and ½ cup (110 ml) thinly sliced celery in 1 tablespoon (15 ml) butter.
Add:
catsup   *½ cup (110 ml)*
chili sauce   *1/3 cup (75 ml)*
brown sugar   *2 tablespoons (30 ml)*
Worcestershire sauce   *1 tablespoon (15 ml)*
salt   *¼ teaspoon (1 ml)*
lemon juice   *1 teaspoon (5 ml)*
dash of garlic powder

Bring to a boil and bubble 5 minutes. Pour over meat.

Fried Chicken

My mother preferred to do her fried chicken this way — crisp, golden, and delicious.

chicken   *4- to 5-pounds (1.8 to 2.3 kg)*
flour, salt, pepper, paprika, butter

Cut the chicken into serving pieces. Place in a large saucepan with 2 cups (450 ml) water. Sprinkle with salt and cover. Cook over medium heat until meat is just tender, adding more water if necessary. Drain and allow to cool before frying. About 40 minutes before serving time, mix the remaining ingredients in a covered container large enough to hold the individual pieces of chicken. Melt ¼ cup (55 ml) butter in a skillet. Shake pieces of chicken in flour mixture and fry in butter until golden on all sides. Add more butter as needed.

Yield: 5 servings

Stewed Chicken with Dumplings

Pile the chicken and dumplings high on a platter and pour steaming hot gravy over all.

stewing fowl   *4- to 5-pounds (1.8 to 2.3 kg)*
boiling water   *5 cups (1.13 l)*
salt   *2 teaspoons (10 ml)*
large carrot   *1*
onion   *1*

28

celery stalk   *1*
slice of turnip (if desired)   *1*
whole peppercorns   *2*

Cut the fowl into serving pieces. Pare and cut carrot into thick slices, quarter the onion, cut celery into large pieces, and cube the turnip. Place all the ingredients in a Dutch oven and simmer 2½ to 3 hours or until tender. Lift out chicken and strain the broth. Add water if necessary to make 4 cups (1 l). Return to heat.
Thicken broth with 1/3 cup (75 ml) flour and
                        ½ cup (110 ml) water
Return the chicken to the gravy and drop in dumplings.

DUMPLINGS:

flour   *2 cups (450 ml)*
baking powder   *4 teaspoons (20 ml)*
salt   *½ teaspoon (2.5 ml)*
dried onion powder   *¼ teaspoon (1 ml)*
shortening   *3 tablespoons (45 ml)*
milk   *1 cup (225 ml)*

Sift the dry ingredients and cut in the shortening. Lightly mix in the milk with a fork, stirring only until moistened. Drop dough into gravy by spoonfuls. Cover the pot and allow to simmer 15 to 20 minutes.

Yield: 8 servings

Roast Turkey Breasts

This is an easy way to have a turkey dinner without all the fuss of dressing and roasting a whole turkey.

large turkey breasts   *2*
bacon   *6 strips*
bread stuffing

Butter breasts well and place three strips of bacon on each. Place, side by side, in a large roasting pan and cover. Roast at 350°F (175°C) for 1½ hours. Make two mounds of the dressing on a heavy sheet of foil long enough to fit the roasting pan. Remove breasts from oven and place one breast over each mound. Lift whole into pan and cover. Roast 1 hour more or until done.

BREAD DRESSING:

    bread crumbs   *4 cups (1 l)*
    butter   *¼ cup (55 ml)*
    shredded carrots   *½ cup (110 ml)*
    celery, diced   *½ cup (110 ml)*
    onion, chopped   *1/3 cup (75 ml)*
    salt   *1 teaspoon (5 ml)*
    pepper
    mixed herb seasoning   *1 teaspoon (5 ml)*

Sauté the onion in the butter until tender. Stir into the bread crumbs with the carrots and seasonings.

Yield: 6 servings

• FISH •

Since the early days of Upper Canada, our lakes and rivers have been teeming with fish. Many of these fish have ended up being fried, and although fried fish are good, there are many more ways to prepare fish to provide variety. Here are a few of those ways.

Salmon Loaf

Nice to serve chilled in hot weather.

    milk   *1 cup (225 ml)*
    eggs   *3*
    bread crumbs   *1½ cups (335 ml)*
    salt   *¼ teaspoon (1 ml)*
    pepper   *1/8 teaspoon (0.5 ml)*
    salmon   *1-pound can (455 g)*

Beat the eggs well and add to the milk. Add the crumbs, salt, and pepper and mix well. Bone salmon and add to milk mixture. Beat well. Pour into a greased loaf pan. Bake at 350°F (175°C) for 50 minutes. Chill and slice before serving.

Yield: 6 servings

Salmon Patties

These patties fry to a golden brown and are especially good with tartar sauce.

> salmon   *1-pound can (455 g)*
> fine bread crumbs   *2 cups (450 ml)*
> eggs   *2*
> milk   *1/3 cup (75 ml)*
> salt and pepper

Mix all together throughly. Fry in butter in a hot pan. Serve at once.

Yield: 18 patties.

Salmon Croquettes

These turn into golden brown cakes, good to look at and delicious to eat.

> salmon   *1-pound can (455 g)*
> milk   *1 cup (225 ml)*
> butter   *4 tablespoons (60 ml)*
> lemon juice   *1 tablespoon (15 ml)*
> flour   *½ cup (110 ml)*
> salt   *½ teaspoon (2.5 ml)*
> fine, dry bread crumbs   *1 cup (225 ml)*
> egg (optional)   *1*
> fat for frying

Melt the butter and stir in the flour. Cook for a moment to cook the starch in the flour. Add the milk and beat over medium heat until smooth and thick. Add the salt and lemon juice. Bone the salmon, flake it, and add to the cream sauce. Set aside and allow to cool. When mixture is firm, shape it into small cakes, dip in the dry bread crumbs and, if desired, into the egg beaten with 2 tablespoons (30 ml) water. Cook in very hot fat until golden brown, turning once. Serve hot.

Yield: 12 croquettes

Baked Fillet of Perch

Stuffing makes the difference. Try this method with other kinds of fish too.

    fresh perch fillets, or frozen ones, thawed   *1 pound (455 g)*
    fresh bread crumbs   *1 cup (225 ml)*
    butter   *3 tablespoons (45 ml)*
    chopped onion   *¼ cup (55 ml)*
    finely shredded carrot   *2/3 cup (150 ml)*
    salt   *1/3 teaspoon (2 ml)*
    mixed herb seasoning   *½ teaspoon (2.5 ml)*
    lemon juice

Sprinkle fillets with pepper and a little lemon juice. Sauté the onion in the butter until tender, then mix with the carrot, crumbs, and seasonings. Butter a shallow casserole. Lay half the fillets, skin side down, close together in the bottom of the casserole. Spread dressing evenly on the fillets, top with the remaining fillets, and sprinkle with crumbs. Cover and bake at 400°F (205°C) for 50 to 55 minutes.

Yield: 4 servings

Poached Fish Fillets

Special dressing on top, broiled to a golden brown, makes this dish appealing both to eye and appetite.

    fresh fish fillets, or frozen ones, thawed   *1 pound (455 g)*
    milk   *½ cup (110 ml)*
    lemon juice   *1 tablespoon (15 ml)*
    salt
    shredded old Cheddar cheese   *2/3 cup (150 ml)*
    mayonnaise   *¼ cup (55 ml)*

Place fillets in a greased, shallow baking dish. Pour milk over and sprinkle lightly with salt and lemon juice. Cook at 375°F (190°C) for 35 minutes. Mix the shredded cheese with the mayonnaise and spread over the fillets. Brown under the broiler. Serve at once.

Yield: 4 servings

Creamed Fish Fillets

So simple and yet so good!

fresh fillets, or frozen ones, thawed   *1 pound (455 g)*
cream of shrimp soup   *10-ounce can (280 ml)*

Place the fillets in a greased shallow pan. Pour the soup over and bake at 350°F (175°C) for 40 to 50 minutes.

Yield: 4 servings

Tuna Cakes

Try serving these with tomato sauce.

canned tuna   *1 cup (225 ml)*
fine bread crumbs   *½ cup (110 ml)*
mashed potatoes   *1 cup (225 ml)*
egg, beaten   *1*
salt and pepper
butter or margarine

Mix the potatoes and fish together until well blended. Add the crumbs, egg, salt, and pepper. Shape into 9 cakes. Melt butter in skillet. Slowly fry cakes on both sides to golden brown.

Yield: 4 servings

Fish Loaf

We like cod in this fish loaf, but try tuna, too. It's good served hot or cold.

flaked, cooked fish   *2 cups (450 ml)*
fine bread crumbs   *1½ cups (335 ml)*
baking powder   *½ teaspoon (2.5 ml)*
chopped celery   *2/3 cup (150 ml)*
chopped onion   *1/3 cup (75 ml)*
lemon juice   *1 tablespoon (15 ml)*
chopped green pepper   *1 tablespoon (15 ml)*
chopped pimiento   *1 tablespoon (15 ml)*
milk   *1 cup (225 ml)*
egg   *1*
salt   *1 teaspoon (5 ml)*
pepper

Combine the baking powder and the crumbs. Stir in the remaining ingredients, adding the milk last. Pack firmly in a greased loaf pan and bake at 375°F (190°C) for 1¼ hours. Serve with white sauce.

Jellied Apples

I like to use Talman Sweets or Russets and leave the skins on.

    apples   8
    sugar   *1 cup (225 ml)*
    water   *1½ cups (335 ml)*
    ground almonds   *1 tablespoon (15 ml)*
        OR
    slivered almonds   *½ pound (227 g)*
    lemon juice   *1 teaspoon (5 ml)*
    unflavoured gelatin   *1 tablespoon (15 ml)*

Core the apples, and put them in a bowl of water to prevent their turning brown. Boil sugar and water together for 5 minutes, then cook apples in this syrup, covered, until soft, turning every 2 to 3 minutes. Watch carefully so that they cook through but remain firm — total cooking about 6 minutes. Place in a flat pan and, if using slivered almonds, stick in apples to form a decorative pattern. If using ground almonds, scatter some over the tops of the apples. Sprinkle the apples with sugar and place under the broiler for a few minutes until lightly browned. Add water to syrup in which the apples were cooked to make 2 cups (450 ml). Soften gelatin in 1 tablespoon (15 ml) cold water and dissolve it in the hot juice. Add lemon juice. Put apples on serving dish and pour syrup around them. Serve cold with plain or whipped cream if for dessert or plain if served with meat dishes.

Steamed Sweet Apples

I find Talman Sweets the best apples to steam as they don't fall apart and are sweet to taste.

    Wash, halve and core as many apples as desired. Boil ¾ cup (170 ml) sugar and ¾ cup (170 ml) water in a large flat saucepan for 2 minutes. Lay the apples, cut side down, in one layer in the syrup and baste with syrup. Cover and allow to simmer for approximately 10 minutes or until the apples are starting to become tender. Turn and baste again with syrup and continue to steam, covered, until the apples are tender. Lift into a dish and boil down the syrup for a few minutes until it begins to thicken. Pour over the apples. Chill before serving. These apples may be frozen for later use.

Baked Apples

We used to have Russet apple trees at home, so my mother usually had a good supply of baked apples on hand.

Remove stem and bud ends from as many apples as required. Peel a ring of skin from each apple to help prevent skin from bursting when baking. Place in a flat casserole and sprinkle each apple with 1 teaspoon (5 ml) sugar. Fill the dish half full with water and for every 1 cup (225 ml) water used, add ½ cup (110 ml) sugar. Bake at 350°F (175°C) for 40 minutes or until tender. Remove apples to a dish and pour the syrup from the pan over them. Drizzle with corn syrup just before serving. Serve chilled.

Cranberry Sauce from the Female Emigrant's Guide, 1854, by Mrs. Catharine Parr Traill

1 quart ripe picked berries, stewed with as much water as will keep them from drying to the pan, closely covered. A pound of soft sugar must be added when the fruit is burst; boil ½ hour after you add sugar, and stir them well. When quite stewed enough, pour them into a basin or mould: when cold they will be jellied so as to turn out whole in the form of the mould. Serve with roasted venison, mutton and beef. Makes rich "open-tarts" or "can be served at tea-table in glass plates, to eat with bread".

Cranberry Sauce

This sauce, made with pectin crystals, is thick and delicious. Freeze it for later use.

cranberries   *4 cups (1 l)*
large, tart apples   *2*
oranges   *2*
lemon   *1*
sugar   *3 cups (675 ml)*
pectin crystals   *2 ounces (58 g)*

Pare and core the apples. Put cranberries and apples through the food chopper, using the fine cutter. Quarter the unpeeled oranges and lemon, remove seeds, and put through chopper. Mix fruits, add sugar, and bring slowly to boil. When boiling vigorously, add pectin crystals. Boil vigorously for 1 minute. Remove from heat and store in a cool place or freeze.

Yield: 6 cups (1.5 l)

Yorkshire Pudding

An old pioneer favourite in Upper Canada. In the mid 1800s it was often made with Indian meal and poured into the roasting pan with the beef, pork, or mutton.

```
eggs    2
flour   1 cup (225 ml)
salt    ¼ teaspoon (1 ml)
milk    ¼ cup (55 ml)
water   ¼ cup (55 ml)
```

Beat all the ingredients together until smooth. Allow to stand at room temperature for 1 hour. Lightly oil muffin tins and heat in oven until very hot. Fill 2/3 full with batter. Bake at 400°F (205°C) for 30 minutes. Serve hot with roast beef and gravy.

Yield: 8 puddings

• SAVORY SAUCES •

Never underrate the importance of a sauce in cooking. It can turn an everyday vegetable into something special or add variety to meat dishes.

Tomato Sauce

This is a tangy and creamy sauce. The original recipe called for stewed tomatoes, and a whole onion stuck with a clove. It was then rubbed through a strainer.

```
tomato juice    2 cups (450 ml)
minced onion    2 tablespoons (30 ml)
salt    1/3 teaspoon (2 ml)
dash ground cloves
sugar    1 teaspoon (5 ml)
bay leaf    ½
butter    2 tablespoons (30 ml)
flour    2 tablespoons (30 ml)
```

Simmer all the ingredients together, except butter and flour, for 15 minutes. Melt butter, blend in the flour. Stir in liquids until thickened and smooth.

Yield: 2 cups (450 ml)

Barbecue Sauce

This is a good sauce to pour over meats cooked in the oven, especially spareribs that have been precooked about 30 minutes.

Sauté 1 chopped onion in 1 tablespoon (15 ml) butter.
Add: catsup   *½ cup (110 ml)*
chili sauce   *½ cup (110 ml)*
brown sugar   *2 tablespoons (30 ml)*
prepared mustard   *1 tablespoon (15 ml)*
Worcestershire sauce   *1 tablespoon (15 ml)*
celery salt   *¼ teaspoon (1 ml)*
salt   *¼ teaspoon (1 ml)*
vinegar   *1 teaspoon (5 ml)*
dash of garlic

Bring to boil and let bubble 5 minutes.

Yield: Approximately 1 cup (225 ml)

White Sauce for Fish

butter   *1 tablespoon (15 ml)*
flour   *1 tablespoon (15 ml)*
milk   *1 cup (225 ml)*
salt   *1/3 teaspoon (2 ml)*
dried marjoram   *¼ teaspoon (1 ml)*

Melt the butter and add the flour. Stir in the milk until smooth and creamy. Add the salt and marjoram.

Yield: 1 cup (225 ml)

McLary copper kettle,
1903

MAIN DISHES
CASSEROLES

"The casserole is a one-dish meal they say,
But Oh! how many dishes does it take to get
that way."

THAT BIT OF verse surely describes how many of us feel on surveying the kitchen counter after we've put together a casserole. Nevertheless, the casserole is one of the commonest methods of bringing variety into our diets and of using up odds and ends, often in combination with rice or one of the pastas.

Rice cultivation goes back 4000 years in China. Rice was introduced to the American colonies in the mid-17th century. Settlers used it quite commonly, as it could be imported very cheaply. Wild rice, an entirely different plant, grows in shallow lakes with mud or sand bottoms. The settlers sometimes bought it from the Indians, who were the real rice gatherers, and boiled or baked it. There used to be great areas of wild rice growing just north of Kingston and in the Peterborough area.

Macaroni, in the form of flour and pastes, similar to our modern ones, has been known in Asia for several thousand years and may have been introduced into Germany as early as the 13th Century by Mongolian invaders. It early spread to Italy where it soon became a staple diet item and was manufactured for export. It was only in the 19th century that macaroni became widely used in North America. Today there are over five hundred different kinds and shapes available.

To Butter Crumbs

Here is a quick way to butter crumbs for the top of a casserole. Melt the butter in a casserole dish in the oven. Stir in crumbs for topping and set aside in a saucer for later use. With this method, both your casserole dish and your crumbs are buttered.

Creamed Salmon Casserole

A delicious luncheon dish! Try substituting tuna, adding green pepper, and topping with cheese and crumbs.

    canned salmon, boned   1 pound (455 g)
    milk   3 cups (675 ml)
    flour   4 tablespoons (60 ml)
    eggs, well beaten   2
    butter   1 tablespoon (15 ml)
    pepper, salt
    fine bread crumbs   1½ cups (335 ml)

Make a smooth paste of the flour with a little of the milk. Stir smoothly into the milk. Add the eggs, salmon, butter, pepper, and salt. Bring to a boil and add the bread crumbs. Turn into a greased casserole dish and top with buttered crumbs. Set in a dish of hot water and bake at 350°F (190°C) for 30 minutes.

Yield: 8 servings

Salmon Vegetable Casserole

Salmon and creamed peas are a good combination in this casserole. Serve it with a salad for a complete dinner.

    salmon   1-pound can (455 g)
    eggs   2
    milk   ½ cup (110 ml)
    salt   ½ teaspoon (2.5 ml)
    poultry seasoning   ¼ teaspoon (1 ml)
    crushed cracker crumbs   ½ cup (110 ml)

Beat together the eggs, milk, salt, and seasoning.
Stir in the crumbs and the flaked salmon. Pour into a greased 2-quart (2 l) casserole. Top with creamed peas or corn and corn-flake crumbs.

Creamed Sauce:

> milk   *2 cups (450 ml)*
> butter   *3 tablespoons (45 ml)*
> flour   *4 tablespoons (60 ml)*
> salt   *½ teaspoon (2.5 ml)*
> cooked peas or corn   *1 cup (225 ml)*
> corn-flake crumbs   *¼ cup (55 ml)*

Melt the butter, blend in the flour. Cook for a moment to cook the flour. Stir in the milk and continue to stir until thick and smooth. Add the peas. Pour over the salmon mixture and sprinkle with crumbs. Bake at 375°F (190°C) for 45 minutes.

Yield: 6 servings

Creamed Salmon

Serve this over hot rice, toast, or for a special luncheon, warm patty shells.

> canned red salmon   *1 cup (225 ml)*
> butter or margarine   *3 tablespoons (45 ml)*
> flour   *2½ tablespoons (38 ml)*
> milk plus the drained juice from salmon   *1½ cups (335 ml)*
> salt to taste
> pimiento

Melt the butter or margarine and stir in the flour. Cook for a moment, then slowly add the liquids, stirring until smooth. Add the salmon in chunks and chopped pimiento. Heat thoroughly.

Yield: 4 servings

Tuna A La Queen

A colourful mixture to serve over hot rice, toast, or warm patty shells.

> butter, melted   *3 tablespoons (45 ml)*
> flour   *2½ tablespoons (38 ml)*
> milk   *1½ cups (335 ml)*
> canned mushrooms, drained   *1 cup (225 ml)*
> canned tuna, drained   *1 cup (225 ml)*
> chopped pimiento strips
> peas, cooked   *2/3 cup (150 ml)*

Add the flour to the melted butter, cook for a moment, then slowly stir in the milk to make a smooth sauce. Add the mushrooms, peas, and pimiento strips. Heat thoroughly.

Yield: 6 servings

Corned Beef Casserole

Nice for a change! Serve it with a fresh salad.

> medium carrots   8
> medium potatoes   5
> large onions   4
> stalk celery, cut in large pieces   *1*
> green pepper, cut in large pieces   *1*
> cooked corned beef, sliced   *1 pound (455 g)*
> milk   *1¾ cups (395 ml)*
> prepared mustard   *1 teaspoon (5 ml)*
> salt, pepper

Boil potatoes, carrots, and onions, whole, about 10 minutes. Place meat in a large greased casserole and place vegetables around meat. Mix mustard with milk and pour over all. Bake in a 350°F (175°C) oven for 1½ hours.

Yield: 4 servings

Casserole Dinner

Quickly put together if you use canned vegetables.

> fresh mushrooms, sliced   *1 cup (225 ml)*
> chopped onion   *¾ cup (170 ml)*
> chopped green pepper   *½ cup (110 ml)*
> butter   *2 tablespoons (30 ml)*
> ground beef   *1 pound (455 g)*
> salt   *1 teaspoon (5 ml)*
> eggs   *2*
> catsup   *½ cup (110 ml)*
> cooked corn   *1½ cups (335 ml)*
> cooked green beans   *2 cups (450 ml)*
> buttered fine bread crumbs   *¾ cup (170 ml)*

Sauté onion, green pepper, and mushrooms in the butter until tender. Lightly mix together the beef, salt, eggs, and catsup. Spread half the corn in a greased 2-qt. (2 l) casserole, then half the meat mixture and half the beans mixed with the sautéed vegetables. Repeat layers. Sprinkle with crumbs. Bake at 350°F (175°C) for 1¼ hours.

Yield: 6 servings

Pork Pie

This casserole is labelled "excellent" in my cookbook.

cold roast pork, diced   *2 cups (450 ml)*
diced, cooked vegetables (potatoes, carrots, onions, etc.)   *1½ cups (335 ml)*
diced green pepper   *½ cup (110 ml)*
cream soup   *10-ounce can (280 ml)*
milk   *1 cup (225 ml)*
flour   *2 tablespoons (30 ml)*
biscuit topping

Dilute the soup with milk and thicken with flour. Combine the meat, vegetables, and sauce and pour into a greased baking dish. Heat through in a 375°F (190°C) oven while making the biscuit topping.

Topping:

flour   *1½ cups (335 ml)*
baking powder   *1½ teaspoons (7.5 ml)*
salt   *½ teaspoon (2.5 ml)*
shortening   *3 tablespoons (45 ml)*
milk

Sift the dry ingredients and cut in the shortening. Add enough milk to make a soft dough. Roll out to the size of the baking dish. Place on top of meat mixture and brush with butter. Cut a slit in top to let steam escape. Return to oven for 20 to 25 minutes.

Yield: 5 servings

Sausage Corn Casserole

Corn and sausages complement each other for a unique flavour in this recipe.

sausages   *1¼ pounds (568 g)*
medium onions, separated into rings   *2*
flour   *1 tablespoon (15 ml)*
milk   *½ cup (110 ml)*
canned cream-style corn   *2½ cups (560 ml)*
fine bread crumbs   *1 cup (225 ml)*

Lightly brown sausages in frypan and place in a shallow casserole. Fry onion rings till tender in sausage drippings and scatter over the sausages. In the frypan blend in the flour in 2 tablespoons (30 ml) of sausage drippings. Cook for 1 minute over medium heat. Stir in the milk, cooking until thickened and smooth. Add the corn and pour over sausages and onions. Lightly mix crumbs with 2 tablespoons (30 ml) drippings and sprinkle over the casserole. Bake at 350°F (175°C) for 30 minutes.

Yield: 6 servings

Creamy Macaroni

Cook 1 cup (225 ml) macaroni in boiling, salted water for 20 minutes or until tender.
In the meantime prepare the following sauce:

butter   *1½ tablespoons (22.5 ml)*
flour   *1½ tablespoons (22.5 ml)*
salt   *½ teaspoon (2.5 ml)*
milk   *1 cup (225 ml)*
Worcestershire sauce   *1 teaspoon (5 ml)*
cheese, grated   *1 cup (225 ml)*
cooked bacon strips if desired

Melt the butter in a saucepan and blend in the flour and salt. Cook for a moment over medium heat. Stir in milk and cook until mixture boils and thickens. Add Worcestershire sauce. Pour over well-drained macaroni and stir in cheese. Serve with strips of cooked bacon.

Yield: 4 servings

Beef Macaroni Casserole

Serve this with your favourite hot muffins and a salad.

          macaroni   *2 cups (450 ml)*
          minced beef   *1 pound (455 g)*
          medium onion, chopped   *1*
          chopped green pepper   *½ cup (110 ml)*
          finely crushed corn-flake crumbs   *½ cup (110 ml)*
          tomato soup   *10-ounce can (280 ml)*

Cook macaroni in boiling salted water until tender. Drain well.
Brown the meat in frying pan. Remove from pan and set aside. Sauté the onion
and pepper until tender. Drain the fat. Add the soup and the meat. Alternate
layers of macaroni and meat mixture in a greased casserole. Top with crumbs.
Cook in a 350°F (175°C) oven for 40 minutes.

Yield: 6 to 8 servings

Chicken Noodle Scallop

Serve a salad along with this and your dinner is complete.

          finely chopped onion   *¼ cup (55 ml)*
          cream soup, any kind   *10-ounce can (280 ml)*
          milk   *1 cup (225 ml)*
          noodles, cooked   *6 ounces (170 g)*
          cooked corn   *1½ cups (335 ml)*
          cooked chicken   *2 cups (450 ml)*
          grated cheese   *½ cup (110 ml)*
          butter
          fine bread crumbs

Mix together the onion, soup, and milk. Place in layers the cooked noodles, corn,
chicken, cheese, and sauce in greased baking dish. Melt butter and mix crumbs
with it. Sprinkle over the top. Bake in a 400°F (205°C) oven for 35 to 40 minutes.

Yield: 6 servings

Rice and Tomatoes

This is a tasty and easy way to prepare rice.

          rice   *½ cup (110 ml)*
          boiling water, with ½ tsp (2ml) salt added   *2 cups (450 ml)*
          cooked tomatoes   *1 cup (225 ml)*
          chopped green pepper   *½ cup (110 ml)*

small onion, chopped   *1*
milk   *1/3 cup (75 ml)*
buttered crumbs   *¾ cup (170 ml)*
salt   *¼ teaspoon (1 ml)*

Cook the rice in boiling, salted water. Drain well. Mix together the tomatoes, green pepper, onion, salt, and milk and add the rice. Turn into greased casserole. Cover with buttered crumbs and bake about 30 minutes or until browned in a 350°F (175°C) oven.

Yield: 4 servings.

Tuna Rice Casserole

butter   *3 tablespoons (45 ml)*
flour   *2 tablespoons (30 ml)*
milk   *2 cups (450 ml)*
salt   *½ teaspoon (2.5 ml)*
oregano   *¼ teaspoon (1 ml)*
Worcestershire sauce   *1 teaspoon (5 ml)*
grated cheese   *1½ cups (335 ml)*
cooked rice   *2 cups (450 ml)*
cooked tuna   *2 cups (450 ml)*
chopped green pepper   *½ cup (110 ml)*
mushroom pieces   *1 cup (225 ml)*
chopped green olives   *½ cup (110 ml)*
buttered bread crumbs   *¾ cup (170 ml)*

Melt butter, stir in flour, cook for 1 minute over medium heat. Add milk and stir until smooth and thick. Add the cheese, salt, oregano, and Worcestershire sauce and stir until cheese is melted. Butter a 2-qt. (2 l) casserole. Place alternate layers of rice, tuna, green pepper, mushrooms, and olives with sauce in casserole. Top with buttered bread crumbs. Cook at 375°F (190°C) for 35 to 40 minutes or until crumbs are golden and sauce is bubbling.

Yield: 8 servings

Spanish Rice

I usually make this in double quantity and freeze half of it.

cooked tomatoes   *3 cups (675 ml)*
grated cheese   *1 cup (225 ml)*
rice, cooked   *1 cup (225 ml)*
onions, chopped fine   *2*
butter   *¼ cup (55 ml)*
salt, pepper

Mix together all the ingredients, put in a well-greased casserole and bake, covered, at 325°F (165°C) for 2 hours.

Yield: 4 servings

Tomato, Egg, and Spaghetti Casserole

Eggs add interest in this casserole.

spaghetti   *½ pound (227 g)*
butter   *2 tablespoons (30 ml)*
flour   *2 tablespoons (30 ml)*
medium onion, chopped   *1*
cooked tomatoes or juice   *2 cups (450 ml)*
salt   *½ teaspoon (2.5 ml)*
dried parsley   *1 teaspoon (5 ml)*
sugar   *2 teaspoons (10 ml)*
hard-boiled eggs   *4*
buttered crumbs   *¾ cup (170 ml)*
Parmesan cheese

Cook spaghetti in salted boiling water until tender. Drain well. Melt butter and sauté the onion until tender. Add flour and stir until blended. Add tomatoes and stir until smooth. Add the salt, parsley, and sugar. Blend well. Place half the spaghetti in a buttered casserole. Slice the eggs lengthwise and place, cut side up, over the spaghetti. Pour on half the sauce. Add the rest of the spaghetti and pour remainder of sauce over all. Top with crumbs and cheese. Bake at 375°F (190°C) for 35 minutes.

Yield: 4 servings

46

SANDWICHES, SOUPS, EGGS, & CHEESE

SANDWICHES CAN BECOME terribly monotonous fare, but with a little imagination and effort they can be both an interesting and nutritious part of our diet. The secret of a moist sandwich is in buttering the bread right to the crust, not leaving even a small morsel unbuttered. For variety, try different kinds of bread, buns, and rolls. Use mayonnaise sometimes instead of butter. Prepared mustard can also be used on half of the sandwich, instead of butter, if the filling is meat.

• SANDWICHES •

Salmon and Egg Salad Sandwich

    canned salmon   ½ cup (110 ml)
    hard-boiled eggs   2
    pickle relish   2 teaspoons (10 ml)
    salt, pepper, and mayonnaise

Chop the eggs and mix with the salmon, relish and seasonings. Add enough mayonnaise to moisten.

Yield: 1¼ cups (280 ml)

47

Egg Cream Sandwich

    cottage cheese   3 tablespoons (45 ml)
    hard-boiled eggs   2
    mayonnaise   1½ tablespoons (22.5 ml)
    chopped pimiento   1 tablespoon (15 ml)
    salt and pepper

Chop the eggs and mix thoroughly with other ingredients. Spread on thinly sliced, buttered bread with leaves of lettuce.

Yield: 1½ cups (335 ml)

Chicken Sandwich

    butter   2 tablespoons (30 ml)
    flour   1½ tablespoons (22.5 ml)
    milk   1 cup (225 ml)
    salt   ½ teaspoon (2.5 ml)
    dash pepper
    finely chopped cooked chicken   1 cup (225 ml)
    celery seed   ½ teaspoon (2.5 ml)
    chopped stuffed olives   2 tablespoons (30 ml)

Melt the butter and stir in the flour. Cook for 1 minute over medium heat. Add the milk, stirring constantly until the sauce is thickened and smooth. Remove from heat and add the salt, pepper. Chill. Just before using, stir in the remaining ingredients.

Yield: 2 cups (450 ml)

Cheese Sandwich

Grate cheese and moisten with mayonnaise so it will spread easily. This is one of our favourites.

Beef Loaf Supreme Sandwiches

Watch everyone go for seconds of this one! Make the beef loaf on page 14. Chill thoroughly. Slice thinly for sandwiches. Sprinkle with a little Worcestershire sauce.

Cheese Spread

    grated cheese   *1 cup (225 ml)*
    melted butter   *2 tablespoons (30 ml)*
    tomato catsup   *2 tablespoons (30 ml)*
    Worcestershire sauce   *1 teaspoon (5 ml)*
    salt

Mix well. Place cress or lettuce leaves on thinly sliced, buttered bread and spread mixture.

Yield: 1¼ cups (280 ml)

Cheese and Egg Salad Sandwich Spread

    hard-boiled eggs   *2*
    sweet cucumber relish   *2 tablespoons (30 ml)*
    finely chopped onion   *2 teaspoons (10 ml)*
    grated old cheese   *½ cup (110 ml)*
    mayonnaise

Chop the eggs and mix with all the remaining ingredients, using enough mayonnaise to make filling of spreading consistency.

Yield: 1¼ cups (280 ml)

• SOUPS•

Soups are probably one of the oldest ways of cooking food and endless recipes can be found for almost any kind of soup. There are clear soups or broths, and when strips of vegetables are added they are called julienne soups. There are thick soups such as cream soups and chowders. A purée is one thickened with vegetable or meat pulp; when made with fish, it becomes a bisque. Gumbo is a soup thickened with okra.

    Because of the ease of making soups over an open fire with minimum equipment, soup was a staple in the diet of early explorers and settlers alike. Around 1780, the voyageurs, when they were transporting trade goods in return for furs from the Indians and trappers, had two meals a day, breakfast and supper. Both meals consisted of a monotonous fare of dried peas cooked in a communal kettle with a small quantity of grease, pork or bacon, into a kind of dried pea soup. Sometimes cornmeal was used instead of the peas. They helped themselves from the pot with wooden spoons, as they had no plates.

When our grandmothers used large iron cook stoves, it was a very common sight to see the soup kettle bubbling away at the back. My mother had a kettle that she kept frozen up in the winter, and into it went all the left-over vegetables, bits of meat, gravy, etc. from the week. It produced marvellous soups and never were they the same twice running.

We rely heavily on spices and herbs for flavouring in soups and stews. They have been important in cooking ever since ancient times. Our pioneer forefathers grew their own and preserved them for use all year 'round.

Mrs. Catharine Parr Traill, in her *Female Emigrant's Guide* of 1854, tells us that, "All seasoning herbs, as savory, thyme, marjoram, and the like, should be gathered green, dried for a few minutes in the oven, and preserved in bottles for winter use. Horseradish scraped down into vinegar and bottled, is very useful."

Mrs. Anne Clarke, in her *Mrs. Clarke's Cookery Book* of 1883, tells how to dry parsley for winter use. "Take fresh bunches of parsley and plunge into boiling water slightly salted, boiling for 3 or 4 minutes. Remove from the water, and drain. Dry very quickly before the fire and put in bottles for use. Soak in tepid water 5 minutes when required for cooking."

A household guide of 1894 suggests it is best to store dried herbs in tin cans and not bottles, perhaps to preserve better the colour and dryness of the herbs.

Vegetable Soup

A good way to make use of bones from a roast. Quantities may be adjusted to suit supplies on hand. This recipe is based on the bones from a 4-pound (1.8 kg) short-rib roast.

Bones from roast — cut off any remaining meat into pot
water   *6 cups (1.5 l)*
salt   *1½ teaspoons (7.5 ml)*
chopped chives   *¾ teaspoon (4 ml)*
dried sweet-pepper flakes   *1 tablespoon (15 ml)*
oregano   *½ teaspoon (2.5 ml)*
pepper, garlic powder and sage   *dash*
medium onion, sliced   *1*
sliced carrots   *1 cup (225 ml)*
celery sliced on the diagonal
(adds to the appearance of the soup)   *1 cup (225 ml)*

Bring all ingredients to a boil and simmer, covered, about 1½ hours. During the last half hour, add 1 cup (225 ml) canned tomatoes, 1 teaspoon (5 ml) sugar, and short lengths of spaghetti. Taste for seasoning. I like to serve this soup on a cold blustery day with hot sourdough or buttermilk herb biscuits and Cheddar cheese. Homemade oatmeal bread is also delicious with it. This soup freezes well for future use.

Yield: 8 cups (2 litres)

50

Vegetable Chowder

If you have any leftover gravy from roast beef or chicken, add it to this soup as part of the liquid.

Place in a dutch oven or heavy saucepan:
>   bacon fat or cooking oil   *2 tablespoons (30 ml)*
>   Sauté until brown:
>   thinly sliced tender beef or lamb   *¼ pound (113 g)*
>   Then add:
>   water   *4 cups (1 l)*
>   pepper   *1/8 teaspoon (0.5 ml)*
>   salt   *1 teaspoon (5 ml)*
>   medium carrots, diced   *3*
>   medium potatoes, diced   *3*
>   medium onions, diced   *2*
>   undrained canned corn   *1 cup (225 ml)*
>   Bring to a boil and simmer 40 minutes.
>   Add:
>   shredded cabbage   *1 cup (225 ml)*
>   chopped parsley   *1 tablespoon (15 ml)*
>   poultry seasoning   *dash*

Simmer 20 minutes. Serve piping hot with Herb Fingers (page 209).

Yield: 8 servings

Tomato Soup

A creamy and filling soup.

>   tomatoes, fresh or canned   *1½ cups (335 ml)*
>   sugar   *½ teaspoon (2.5 ml)*
>   baking soda   *¼ teaspoon (1 ml)*
>   milk   *1 cup (225 ml)*
>   butter   *½ tablespoon (7.5 ml)*
>   flour   *1½ tablespoons (22.5 ml)*
>   salt   *½ teaspoon (2.5 ml)*
>   onion salt   *dash*
>   small bay leaf

Cook the peeled tomatoes, covered, with the sugar, salt, and bay leaf until quite tender. Remove bay leaf and either blend tomatoes in a blender or mash the pulp through a sieve or colander. Melt the butter in a saucepan, blend in the flour and salt, cook for 1 minute, and slowly add the milk, stirring constantly until thick and smooth. Reheat tomatoes, add the soda, and while it is still effervescing, add the pulp to the cream sauce. Reheat a moment, season to taste, and serve at once.

Yield: 3 large servings

Bean Soup

A hearty soup, good for a cold night or for lunch.

> navy beans   *2 cups (450 ml)*
> cold water   *8 cups (2 l)*
> stalks celery   *2*
> carrot   *1*
> onion   *1*
> meaty ham bone
> marjoram   *½ teaspoon (2.5 ml)*
> summer savory   *½ teaspoon (2.5 ml)*
> salt   *1 teaspoon (5 ml)*
> mace   *dash*

Soak the beans overnight in the water. Put beans and liquid into a large pot and add the vegetables cut into large pieces, the ham bone and the seasonings, except the mace. Bring to a boil and simmer for 2 hours or until the beans are tender. Remove the vegetables and purée them with a cupful of the beans in a blender. Remove the bone, returning any meat to the pot. Add the vegetable purée and bring to a simmer. Serve hot with a dash of mace.

Yield: 9 to 10 cups (2 to 2.25 l)

Cream of Potato Soup

> medium potatoes, cubed   *3*
> onion, chopped   *1*

Cook the potatoes and onion until tender. Drain, reserving liquid. Season cooked vegetables and mash well. Stir into cream sauce.

CREAM SAUCE:

> milk   *4 cups (1 l)*
> butter   *2 tablespoons (30 ml)*
> flour   *2 tablespoons (30 ml)*
> hot potato water   *1 cup (225 ml)*

salt   *1 teaspoon (5 ml)*
fresh minced parsley   *1 tablespoon (15 ml)*
garlic powder

Melt the butter and stir in the flour. Cook for 1 minute over medium heat. Add the potato water, stirring until smooth and thickened. Add mashed potatoes and milk, stirring continuously until soup comes to a boil and is thickened. Add dash of garlic powder and sprinkle with minced parsley just before serving. Good served with Cheese Straws (page 208).

Yield: 6 servings

Oyster Stew

By the latter half of the 1800s, fresh oysters were being brought regularly by water into the ports of the Great Lakes, and a goodly number of recipes for oysters can be found in early cookbooks. Here is a recipe for stew that our family was fond of.

milk   *8 cups (2 l)*
butter   *2 to 3 tablespoons (30-45 ml)*
fresh oysters   *¾ quart (48 to 50) (848 ml)*
pepper and salt

Heat the milk and butter to boiling point. Season with pepper and salt. Add the oysters and liquid. Heat until liquid is boiling slightly or until edges of oysters curl. Remove from heat and serve at once.

Yield: 10 servings of 5 oysters each

Cream of Carrot Soup

When you serve carrots for dinner, prepare a few more and save the vegetable water to make this soup for lunch the next day.

butter   *1 tablespoon (15 ml)*
flour   *1½ tablespoons (22.5 ml)*
milk   *1 cup (225 ml)*
vegetable water   *1 cup (225 ml)*
carrot pulp   *½ cup (110 ml)*
salt, pepper,
fresh chopped parsley

Melt the butter and stir in the flour. Cook for a minute over medium heat. Slowly add the milk, stirring to a smooth sauce. Add the vegetable water and the pulp, mixing until smooth. Season to taste and serve, when reheated, sprinkled with parsley.

Yield: 4 servings

Split Pea Soup

Easy to prepare and delicious to taste, split pea soup was one of the mainstays of the voyageurs of early Canada.

split peas   *1 cup (225 ml)*
cold water   *3 cups (675 ml)*
strips bacon, diced   *4*
potato water   *8 cups (2 l)*
salt   *1½ teaspoons (7.5 ml)*
pepper   *1/8 teaspoon (0.5 ml)*
celery salt   *½ teaspoon (2.5 ml)*
onion, chopped   *1*

Soak the peas overnight in the cold water. Drain. Mix the potato water, peas, bacon, and onion together. Bring to a boil and simmer, covered, for 2 to 3 hours, stirring often to prevent sticking. Add seasonings during last hour of cooking.

Yield: 5 to 6 cups (1.13 to 1.35 l)

Corn Chowder

This recipe originally called for corn pulp, which had to be prepared first. Serve this chowder with hot whole-wheat muffins and a tuna salad for a Saturday night supper.

½″ (1.3 cm) cubed raw potatoes   *2 cups (450 ml)*
medium onion, sliced   *1*
boiling water   *2 cups (450 ml)*
cream-style corn   *2½ cups (560 ml)*
butter   *1 tablespoon (15 ml)*
milk   *1 cup (225 ml)*
salt and pepper to taste

Cook the potatoes in the boiling water for 5 minutes. Add the sliced onion and cook until the potatoes are tender, about another 5 minutes. Add milk, corn, and seasonings. Heat thoroughly. Serve hot.

Yield: 5 servings

Cream of Corn Soup

    cooked corn   1 cup (225 ml)
    milk   2 cups (450 ml)
    butter   1 tablespoon (15 ml)
    flour   1½ tablespoons (22.5 ml)
    salt   ½ teaspoon (2.5 ml)
    pepper, garlic powder   dash

Blend the corn in a blender or use cream-style corn. Melt the butter and stir in the flour. Cook for 1 minute. Add the milk and salt and stir over medium heat to make a smooth sauce. Add the corn, pepper, and garlic. Heat thoroughly and serve at once.

Yield: 3 cups (675 ml)

• EGGS AND CHEESE •

Corn Omelet

Golden brown and more filling than a traditional one.

    eggs, separated   4
    milk   ¼ cup (55 ml)
    drained, cooked corn   ½ cup (110 ml)
    fine bread crumbs   2/3 cup (150 ml)
    salt   1 teaspoon (5 ml)
    pepper
    butter   3 tablespoons (45 ml)

Beat egg yolks until thick. Add milk, corn, bread crumbs, pepper, and salt. Beat the egg whites until stiff but not dry. Fold first mixture gently into the beaten whites. Heat frying pan, if electric, to 300°F (150°C) and add butter. Pour in omelet and let cook 15 minutes, covered, until set. Fold omelet in half, cut into four portions, and serve at once, garnished with parsley.

Yield: 4 servings

Baked Cheese Omelet

This will provide a change in pace for your luncheon menu and is filling besides.

slices stale bread   *4*
slices Cheddar cheese   *4*
eggs   *2*
milk   *1½ cups (335 ml)*
salt   *½ teaspoon (2.5 ml)*

Butter a 1½-quart (2 l) shallow casserole. Place half the bread slices in the bottom, side by side. Top with half the slices of cheese. Repeat layer. Beat eggs well and mix thoroughly with milk and salt. Pour over all. Bake at 350°F (175°C) for 30 to 35 minutes, until the omelet puffs and the cheese melts.

Yield: 4 servings

Foamy Omelet

grated cheese   *½ cup (110 ml)*
eggs, separated   *4*
milk   *2 tablespoons (30 ml)*
water   *2 tablespoons (30 ml)*
salt   *½ teaspoon (2.5 ml)*
butter   *2 tablespoons (30 ml)*

Beat the egg whites stiff. Mix all the remaining ingredients except the butter and fold into the whites. Melt the butter in a frypan and heat very hot. Pour in omelet and turn down heat to medium. Cover and cook slowly for 8 to 10 minutes. Serve at once.

Yield: 4 servings

English Monkey

A cheese omelet with a difference.

milk   *¾ cup (170 ml)*
grated cheese   *¾ cup (170 ml)*
butter   *1 tablespoon (15 ml)*
fine bread crumbs   *¾ cup (170 ml)*
salt   *¼ teaspoon (1 ml)*
eggs   *2*
pepper

Soak the crumbs in the milk. Melt the butter, add cheese and melt. Mix the crumb mixture, eggs, and seasonings and add to the butter and cheese. Cook over low heat 3 to 5 minutes or until thick.

Yield: 3 servings

Our ancestors did not seem to differentiate between the words "soufflé" and "fondue" as we know them today. Although some of their recipes for soufflés are based on a cream sauce, others had a custard-type base with bread crumbs mixed in. The latter type was sometimes called "fondue". It is quite different from the Swiss fondue as we know it today.

Cheese Soufflé

Its colour is golden, its aroma delicious!

> butter   *2 tablespoons (30 ml)*
> flour   *2 tablespoons (30 ml)*
> milk   *1 cup (225 ml)*
> grated cheese   *1 cup (225 ml)*
> salt   *½ teaspoon (2.5 ml)*
> eggs, separated   *3*

Beat the egg whites until stiff. Melt the butter and stir in the flour. Cook for a minute over medium heat. Add the milk slowly, stirring until sauce comes to a boil and is smooth. Add the cheese and salt, stirring until creamy. Beat the egg yolks and stir into them a little of the hot cheese mixture. Then stir the yolks into the cheese sauce until smooth. Gently fold the whites into the sauce and pour into a 1½-quart (2 l) buttered casserole. Cook, with a pan of hot water in the oven, at 450°F (230°C) for the first 10 minutes and then 400°F (205°C) for 25 minutes. Serve at once before it deflates.

Yield: 4 servings

Cheese Fondue

A golden mound of fluffy eating that tastes as good as it looks.

> scalded milk   *1 cup (225 ml)*
> soft bread crumbs   *1 cup (225 ml)*
> shredded cheese   *1 cup (225 ml)*
> egg yolks, well beaten   *3*
> egg whites   *3*
> salt   *¼ teaspoon (1 ml)*

Mix all but the egg whites. Beat whites well and fold mixture in. Pour into a 1½-

57

quart (2 l) buttered dish and bake at 325°F (165°C) for 30 to 40 minutes. Put a pan of hot water in oven while baking.

Yield: 4 servings

Ham Fondue

Cheese and ham team up to make this a tasty luncheon dish for family or friends.

    ground cooked ham   *1 cup (225 ml)*
    grated cheese   *1 cup (225 ml)*
    flour   *4 tablespoons (60 ml)*
    milk   *2 cups (450 ml)*
    eggs, separated   *3*
    salt   *1 teaspoon (5 ml)*
    pepper

Thicken the milk with the flour and cook a few moments until thick and smooth. Beat the egg whites stiff. Add the ham, cheese, slightly beaten yolks, and seasonings. Fold in the egg whites. Pour into a greased 2½-quart (3 l) casserole and set in a pan of hot water in a 325°F (165°C) oven. Bake for 1 hour or until firm.

Yield: 6 servings

Rice Soufflé

A good dish for lunch or supper.

    uncooked rice   *¼ cup (55 ml)*
    butter   *3 tablespoons (45 ml)*
    flour   *3 tablespoons (45 ml)*
    milk   *¾ cup (170 ml)*
    grated cheese   *2 cups (450 ml)*
    eggs, separated   *4*
    salt   *½ teaspoon (2.5 ml)*
    pepper
    chopped pimiento   *1 tablespoon (15 ml)*
    oregano   *¼ teaspoon (1 ml)*

Cook the rice in boiling, salted water until tender. Drain well. Beat the egg whites until stiff, set aside. Melt the butter and blend in the flour. Cook for 1 minute over medium heat. Add milk gradually and stir until thickened and smooth. Add the cheese, mixing until melted. Remove from heat and add the egg yolks, salt, pepper, pimiento, and oregano, stirring until smooth and creamy. Add the rice and fold in the well-beaten egg whites. Pour into a 1½-quart (2 l) unbuttered casserole and bake at 350°F (175°C) for 60 minutes. Place a pan of hot water in the oven while baking. Serve at once when baked.

Yield: 4 servings

Old-Fashioned Omelet

This recipe came from the recipe book of the late Mrs. E.H. Wright of Conway, Ontario. It is a soft-textured omelet, nice for a change.

eggs, separated   *4*
milk   *1¾ cups (395 ml)*
cornstarch   *4 teaspoons (20 ml)*
baking powder   *2/3 teaspoon (3.5 ml)*
salt   *¼ teaspoon (1 ml)*
butter   *1 tablespoon (15 ml)*

Beat the egg whites until stiff but not dry. Beat the yolks and add the cornstarch, baking powder, salt, and milk. Fold the whites into the yolk mixture and cook in the butter in a hot pan until set.

Yield: 4 servings

Baked Cheese

This is another recipe from the book of the late Mrs. E.H. Wright. It is a good dish to bake for lunch, served with your favourite bread or muffins.

fine bread crumbs   *2 cups (450 ml)*
grated cheese   *1¾ cups (395 ml)*
butter the size of an egg
hot milk   *2 cups (450 ml)*
salt   *½ teaspoon (2.5 ml)*
pepper
eggs, beaten   *2*

Butter a casserole dish and stir together the crumbs, cheese, hot milk, and seasonings. Stir in the eggs and dot with butter. Place dish in a pan of hot water and bake at 350°F (175°C) for 40 to 50 minutes.

Yield: 4 servings

Potato Omelet

This omelet rises high and bakes golden brown under the broiler. It's nice for lunch along with a salad and rolls. For a change, try 1 cup (225 ml) cooked rice, instead of the potatoes.

mashed potatoes   *1 cup (225 ml)*
milk   *½ cup (110 ml)*
eggs, separated   *4*
salt   *½ teaspoon (2.5 ml)*
pepper   *1/8 teaspoon (0.5 ml)*
butter   *2 tablespoons (30 ml)*

Beat the whites of the eggs until stiff. Mix together the other ingredients, except the butter, and fold in the whites. Turn into a hot 10″ (25 cm) skillet in which the butter has been melted. Cook over medium heat until the bottom is browned then place under broiler to brown the top. Serve immediately.

Yield: 4 servings

Scrambled Rice

A good luncheon dish. Try sprinkling Parmesan cheese over it.

uncooked rice   *1 cup (225 ml)*
eggs   *6*
salt   *½ teaspoon (2.5 ml)*
butter   *2 tablespoons (30 ml)*
pepper

Cook the rice in boiling salted water. Drain, leaving a little moisture on it. Beat the eggs and stir into the rice along with the salt and pepper. Fry in a skillet in butter like scrambled eggs.

Yield: 6 servings

VEGETABLES

AMONG THE MANY varieties of vegetables available nowadays, it is interesting to note, many originally came from Europe and Asia, but a great many were also native to North and South America and were known to the Indians, long before America was colonized by outsiders. Settlers were quick to adopt these new vegetables in their diets.

The vegetable garden formed an essential part of every pioneer household. Early housewives, whose job it was to care for these gardens, took great pride in the raising of vegetables and flowers as well as in caring for fruit trees. By the mid-1850s squash, turnips, vegetable marrow, cucumbers, and melons were grown, as well as beans, beets, broccoli, corn, cauliflower, cabbage, carrots, celery, hops, asparagus, tomatoes, and potatoes.

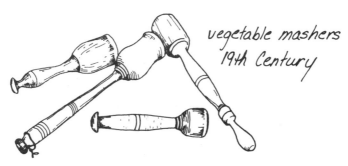

vegetable mashers
19th Century

These three vegetables have come to us from Europe or Asia. Asparagus grew wild in the salt marshes of Europe and Asia and has been used as a food since antiquity. There are several species of onion, but all are believed to have been native to southwest Asia and have been cultivated since ancient times. The Egyptians grew large crops of onions and their cultivation was spread westward by the Spanish colonists. Since they could be dried for winter use, they became an important part of early diets.

Peas are probably native to Asia and were grown for food several thousand years before Christ. Although it was not until the Middle Ages that peas were used as a fresh vegetable, they had been used dried or in meal form or as food for cattle. In New England, it was customary to plant peas on April 19, which is the anniversary of the Battle of Lexington. With luck, they would then be ready to serve on the Fourth of July with the traditional salmon.

Asparagus, Peas, and Green Onions

A great way to make a little asparagus go a long way. Adjust the amounts of any of the vegetables to suit the quantity required.

> fresh asparagus   *½ pound (227 g)*
> fresh or frozen peas   *1½ cups (335 ml)*
> green onions   *1 bunch*

Slice the asparagus on the diagonal in ¼″ (6 mm) slices. Slice the onions, keeping the green tops separate. Cook the asparagus in boiling salted water for approximately 3 minutes or until not quite tender. Add the peas and sliced onion bulbs. Bring to a boil and cook 1 to 2 minutes. Lastly add the green onion tops and boil 1 minute more. Serve at once with butter and seasonings.

Yield: 6 servings

The Indians had developed most of the bean varieties used today by the time America was discovered by Europeans. Lima beans, kidney beans, string and shell beans, as well as pea beans, were all commonly used in their diet. Early sailors obtained white beans from the Indians and took them to sea; consequently they became known as "navy beans". Because they were nourishing, filling, and easily portable, beans were carried by new settlers and explorers. Fur trappers regarded them as a necessity; armies consumed them in large quantities. Also beans became a staple crop of the settlers and were preserved for winter use by drying. The pioneers brought with them to Upper Canada the recipe for traditional New England baked beans with salt pork and molasses.

Old Fashioned Baked Beans

Bacon adds a delicious flavour to these beans.

    navy beans   *2 cups (450 ml)*
    bacon, cut in small pieces   *4 slices*
    salt   *1¾ teaspoon (8 ml)*
    brown sugar   *¼ cup (55 ml)*
    molasses   *3 tablespoons (45 ml)*
    dry mustard   *½ teaspoon (2.5 ml)*
    onion, quartered   *1*

Wash the beans and sort them, culling out broken and discoloured ones. Soak them overnight in water to cover, then simmer in the soaking liquid until just tender. Drain and save liquid. Combine all the remaining ingredients but the bacon and onion. Place half the beans in a bean pot. Bury half the bacon bits and onion in the beans. Pour on half the mustard-sugar mixture. Repeat layer. Cover with bean liquid, cover the pot, and cook at 300°F (150°C) for approximately 6 hours. Add more liquid if necessary.

HERE IS A story of baked beans and salt pork from *Canada: The Story of Ontario*, by Robert Turnbull:

> Lumbermen of the 1880's lived in log lodges called camboose camps, and ate three meals a day — breakfast at 5 a.m. of beans, fried salt pork, bread and strong tea; a noon dinner described by one old-timer: "You dropped the meat, cold salt pork, into a long linen bag, tied it with a string in the centre, then put a loaf of bread in the top half. In the other hand you took a pail containing blackstrap, and away you went. At dinnertime you made tea. When you ate your meal you gouged a large hole into the bread and poured the blackstrap into it, unless the weather was too cold, and then you cut out a hunk of blackstrap and put it into the hole. Then you took your fat salt pork in one hand, and your bread and molasses in the other, and ate them bite about." At 6 p.m. dinner, same as the breakfast menu, was served.

Harvard Beets

Beets have been cultivated in Europe since pre-Christian times. Here is a pleasing way to serve them for a change.

butter   *1 tablespoon (15 ml)*
flour   *1 tablespoon (15 ml)*
boiling water   *3 tablespoons (45 ml)*
pepper, ground cloves
brown sugar   *3 tablespoons (45 ml)*
vinegar   *2 tablespoons (30 ml)*
salt   *¼ teaspoon (1 ml)*
cooked, diced beets   *2 cups (450 ml)*

Melt the butter, blend in the flour, and let bubble for 3 minutes. Add boiling water, stirring until thick. Add brown sugar, vinegar, and seasonings, blend well. Add beets and let stand over boiling water until very hot.

Yield: 4 servings

• CABBAGE •

Our early settlers used cabbage as food for both man and stock; it was cooked as a fresh vegetable as well as being made into sauerkraut and slaw. Cabbage is probably a descendant of the wild sea cabbage that grew along the coasts of Europe. Broccoli and cauliflower are of the same family.

Scalloped Vegetables

Use any one of broccoli, cabbage, cauliflower, beans, or carrots in this casserole. It's an easy way to dress up a vegetable.

cooked vegetables   *2½ cups (560 ml)*
white sauce (see below)   *1½ cups (335 ml)*
fine bread crumbs   *1 cup (225 ml)*
melted butter   *2 tablespoons (30 ml)*

WHITE SAUCE:
butter   *2 tablespoons (30 ml)*
flour   *2 tablespoons (30 ml)*
salt   *½ teaspoon (2.5 ml)*
milk   *1½ cups (335 ml)*
celery salt   *pinch*

Melt the butter and blend the flour into it. Add the salt and milk, stirring until smooth and thick. Stir in the celery salt. Place the cooked vegetables in a greased casserole and cover with the sauce. Mix the butter with the crumbs and scatter over top. Bake at 350°F (175°C) about 30 minutes or until crumbs are golden.

Yield: 4 servings

• CARROTS •

Before settlers brought carrots to North America, they had been used in Europe mainly for soups and stews, as well as for some medicinal purposes, but the Germans who arrived in Waterloo County around 1800 introduced the making of cakes and puddings with raw carrots.

Celery, a carrot relative, was also used mainly in soups and stews in the early days. It, too, is of European origin.

Carrots

A quick way to dress up carrots for company.

cooked, diced carrots   *2½ cups (560 ml)*
diced onions   *¼ cup (55 ml)*
butter   *1 tablespoon (15 ml)*
flour   *1 tablespoon (15 ml)*
liquid drained from carrots, heated   *3 tablespoons (45 ml)*

Brown the onions lightly in the butter. Add the flour and blend in well. Add hot liquid and stir until thick. Stir in the carrots and set over hot water until very hot.

Yield: 4 servings

VARIATION:

Try using canned small whole carrots in the above recipe. Put them in a shallow casserole dish and pour the sauce over them. Heat, covered, at 350°F (175°C) for 40 minutes.

Carottes (Glacées)

from *Mrs. Clarke's Cookery Book* by Anne Clarke. Cook these carrots over a medium heat, stirring frequently to prevent burning.

"Trim up to resemble little pears in shape some new red carrots and soak a few minutes in water. Then fry in butter with the addition of some white powdered sugar and a little good stock. When the pieces are sufficiently cooked, increase the heat of the fire so that evaporation goes on rapidly; let the carrots glaze and then serve."

• CORN •

The grain referred to as "corn" in North America is Indian corn or maize, cultivated in America long before Europeans reached the New World and used to feed both animals and people. In fact, the Indians grew several varieties of corn — sweet corn, popcorn, corn for corn meal; white, yellow, red, and blue corn were grown as distinct strains. Settlers contrived endless ways to use Indian corn or maize, fresh, dried, as corn meal or corn flour.

Corn Custard Pudding

Cheese adds real zest to this golden pudding.

> cooked whole-kernel corn   *2 cups (450 ml)*
> sugar   *1 tablespoon (15 ml)*
> salt   *1 teaspoon (5 ml)*
> pepper   *dash*
> eggs, slightly beaten   *2*
> melted butter   *2 tablespoons (30 ml)*
> scalded milk   *2 cups (450 ml)*
> grated cheese   *2/3 cup (150 ml)*

Mix all the ingredients and pour into a buttered 1½-quart (2 l) casserole. Place in a pan of hot water and bake, uncovered, at 350°F (175°C) for 40 minutes.

Yield: 8 servings

Corn and Cheese Casserole

> eggs, separated   *2*
> hot milk   *2 cups (450 ml)*

cooked corn   *1 cup (225 ml)*
fine bread crumbs   *1¼ cups (280 ml)*
grated cheese   *1 cup (225 ml)*
salt   *½ teaspoon (2.5 ml)*
chopped pimiento   *2 tablespoons (30 ml)*
chopped green pepper   *¼ cup (55 ml)*
chopped onion   *2 tablespoons (30 ml)*

Beat egg whites until stiff. Set aside. Beat the yolks into the milk and combine with remaining ingredients. Fold in the egg whites. Pour into a buttered casserole, set dish in a pan of hot water and bake in a 350°F (175°C) oven for about 40 minutes or until firm.

Yield: 6 servings

Succotash

The Indians called this *misickquatash* and combined meat, lima beans, and corn. In early times each locality had its own version of this dish based on local availability of ingredients. All kinds of beans, including navy and lima, may be used, and some versions also call for tomatoes. Salt pork is sometimes added.

cooked lima beans   *2 cups (450 ml)*
cooked corn   *2 cups (450 ml)*
butter   *2 tablespoons (30 ml)*
salt   *½ teaspoon (2.5 ml)*
nutmeg   *1/8 teaspoon (0.5 ml)*

Mix all ingredients together and heat in a double boiler over hot water until thoroughly hot.

Yield: 8 servings

Corn and Tomato Succotash

This is a simple but tasty version of this Indian dish.

fresh tomatoes   *1 cup (225 ml)*
or
canned tomatoes   *1½ cups (335 ml)*
fresh or frozen corn   *2 cups (450 ml)*
cooked baby lima beans   *1 cup (225 ml)*
fine bread crumbs   *½ cup (110 ml)*
butter   *3 teaspoons (15 ml)*
salt and pepper to taste
sugar   *1 teaspoon (5 ml)*

67

Cook the corn and tomatoes together over medium heat until corn is tender — about 20 minutes. Add bread crumbs, lima beans, butter, and seasonings. Allow to heat until tomato juice is almost boiled away.

Yield: 6 servings

Stuffed Green Peppers

large green peppers   *4*
stale bread   *3 slices*
medium onion, finely chopped   *½*
butter   *1 tablespoon (15 ml)*
salt   *¼ teaspoon (1 ml)*
pepper   *¼ teaspoon (1 ml)*
paprika   *¼ teaspoon (1 ml)*
finely chopped ham   *1 cup (225 ml)*
buttered crumbs   *½ cup (110 ml)*

Cut the tops from peppers and carefully scoop out seeds and membrane. Parboil (boil in water to cover) for 5 minutes and drain well. Rub the stale bread into very fine crumbs. Saute the onion in butter until tender, then mix with the bread crumbs, seasonings, and ham. Fill the peppers with stuffing. Top with buttered crumbs. Set upright in a shallow casserole containing 1 cup (225 ml) hot water. Bake at 350°F (175°C) for 25 to 30 minutes.

Yield: 4 servings

• POTATOES •

Native to the Andes, the potato was a staple food for the Indians in pre-Columbian times. Spanish explorers took it to Europe in the sixteenth century, and European settlers brought it to North America around 1600. Sometimes the white potato is called the Irish potato; it formed the major food in eighteenth century Ireland to such a degree that when the crop failed in the mid 1800s, thousands of Irish starved to death. One of the results of this famine was a great influx of starving Irish immigrants into Upper Canada, particularly Toronto, where the city for the winter of 1847 became like one large hospital, with most of its public buildings being turned into hostels and relief centres for the penniless new arrivals. These new immigrants gradually spread out into southern Ontario forming new communities.

Oven-Brown Potatoes

A quick way to dress up leftover potatoes.

large cold boiled potatoes   2
butter   *2 tablespoons (30 ml)*
milk   *2/3 cup (150 ml)*
salt   *½ teaspoon (2.5 ml)*
egg, beaten   *1*

Butter a 6 X 10″ (1.5 l) shallow casserole dish. Shred the potatoes into the dish and spread evenly. Mix together the milk, salt, and egg and pour over the potatoes, stirring slightly. Dot with butter. Place in a 350°F (175°C) oven for 40 minutes or until browned.

Yield: 4 servings

Potato Puff

A nice change from mashed potatoes that can be prepared a couple of hours ahead, put into muffin tins and refrigerated, then baked just before dinner. The quantities may be adjusted to suit numbers.

mashed potatoes   *2 cups (450 ml)*
butter   *2 tablespoons (30 ml)*
milk   *1 cup (225 ml)*
eggs   *2*
salt and pepper

Mix all ingredients except eggs with potatoes. Beat eggs and then stir in lightly. Bake in buttered muffin tins until well puffed and golden brown, about 35 minutes at 375°F (190°C). (Allow another 15 minutes if previously refrigerated.) Allow 1 large puff or 2 small ones per serving.

Yield: 4 large or 8 small puffs

Pillsburgh Potatoes

An easy way to prepare a company-style potato.

raw, cubed potatoes   *2 cups (450 ml)*
medium onion, chopped   *1*
butter   *2 tablespoons (30 ml)*
grated cheese   *2/3 cup (150 ml)*
flour   *1 tablespoon (15 ml)*
milk   *1 cup (225 ml)*
salt   *½ teaspoon (2.5 ml)*

69

Boil cubed potatoes in salted water 5 minutes. Drain and turn into a greased casserole. Sauté onion in 1 tablespoon (15 ml) butter. Spread over potatoes along with the cheese. Melt remaining butter and stir in flour. Add milk and salt, stirring to make a smooth sauce. Pour over casserole contents. Bake at 350°F (175°C) for 35 minutes.

Yield: 4 servings

Potato Risotto

Serve this with pork.

> large potatoes   2
> canned corn   *2 cups (450 ml)*
> milk   *1 cup (225 ml)*
> salt, pepper, butter

Peel and slice the potatoes and arrange in alternate layers with the corn in a buttered dish. Add seasoning and butter to layers. Pour in the milk. Bake at 325°F (165°C) for 1¾ hours.

Yield: 4 servings

Mountain Fritters

Fry these potatoes slowly to a golden brown to fancy up an ordinary meal.

> large potatoes   3
> egg   1
> garlic powder   *1/8 teaspoon (0.5 ml)*
> *or*
> onion, finely chopped   ½
> salt   *½ teaspoon (2.5 ml)*
> paprika   *¼ teaspoon (1 ml)*
> pepper

Pare and grate the potatoes. Beat the egg and mix thoroughly with the potato. Add seasonings. Drop by large spoonfuls on a well-greased griddle or pan. Cook slowly until brown, turning once. Allow 30 to 35 minutes cooking time.

Yield: 9 fritters or 4 servings

Skillet Potatoes

When you're boiling potatoes for dinner, cook a double quantity and save half for this dish.

        cold boiled potatoes   4
        butter   3 *tablespoons (45 ml)*
        chopped onion   *½ cup (110 ml)*
        salt, pepper, milk

Melt the butter in a skillet. Cut the potatoes into small pieces or shred on a coarse shredder and add to the skillet along with the onion and seasonings. Stir gently until well blended. Add enough milk to just show through the potatoes. Cover and heat slowly for 15 to 20 minutes until the milk is absorbed and the bottom is browned.

Potato Balls

This was a favourite way for my mother to dress up leftover mashed potatoes.

        cold mashed potatoes, seasoned   2 *cups (450 ml)*
        finely chopped onion   *1/3 cup (75 ml)*
        summer savory   *1 teaspoon (5 ml)*
        butter   4 *tablespoons (60 ml)*

Mix all the ingredients and form into 8 balls or round cakes. Melt 2 tablespoons (30 ml) butter in a skillet large enough to hold all the balls or cakes. Cook potatoes over medium heat, turning gently until browned on all sides and cooked through. Add remaining butter as needed. Allow about 25 minutes total cooking time, being careful to keep heat low enough so as not to over-brown the balls. If made into cakes, brown slowly on one side, add more butter, and turn and brown on second side.

Yield: 4 servings

Hungarian Rice

This recipe came from Mrs. Alfreda Plewes of Mississauga, Ontario. The mushrooms on top look extra good. Serve for a company meal instead of potatoes.

        raw rice   2 *cups (450 ml)*
        margarine   *½ pound (227 g)*
        beef consommé   *10-ounce can (280 ml)*
        mushrooms, undrained   *2 10-ounce cans (560 ml)*
        water   *2½ cups (560 ml)*

In skillet, brown the rice in the margarine until golden in colour. Add consommé and let bubble a few minutes. Place in a 2-quart (2.5 l) greased casserole. Add undrained mushrooms and water. Cook, covered, at 350°F (175°C) for about 1 hour.

Yield: 10 to 12 servings

• SWEET POTATOES •

Sweet potatoes are native to the New World tropics, introduced in Europe in the 16th century and to North America by early settlers. Although the sweet potato was not a widely grown crop, it did succeed in the milder sections of southern Upper Canada.

Sweet Potato Casserole

Try serving this with ham.

> medium sweet potatoes, cooked and halved   *4*
> butter
> sweetened applesauce   *1 cup (225 ml)*
> cinnamon   *1 teaspoon (5 ml)*

Place the sweet potatoes in a buttered shallow casserole. Dot with butter. Stir the cinnamon into the applesauce and spread over potatoes. Cook in a 350°F (175°C) oven for 25 to 30 minutes.

Yield: 6 servings

• SQUASH •

Squash is native to North and Central America and was grown and used in large quantities by the Indians. Settlers quickly learned to adopt it, once again learning methods of using it from the Indians.

Squash Casserole

This can be prepared ahead of time, refrigerated, and heated before dinner.

    cooked squash   3 cups (675 ml)
    sweetened applesauce   1 cup (225 ml)
    egg   1
    melted butter   3 tablespoons (45 ml)
    corn syrup   1/3 cup (75 ml)
    salt   ¼ teaspoon (1 ml)

Mix all the ingredients together, beating in the egg. Pour into greased casserole.
Top with: Crumb Topping:

    Combine:
    melted butter   2 tablespoons (30 ml)
    fine bread crumbs   ½ cup (110 ml)

Bake at 375°F (190°C) for 45 minutes.

Yield: 8 servings

Oven-Baked Acorn Squash

The dressing imparts a good flavour to the squash.

    medium acorn squash   4
    fresh bread crumbs   3 cups (675 ml)
    medium onion, chopped   1
    chopped celery   ½ cup (110 ml)
    butter   ¼ cup (55 ml)
    salt   ¾ teaspoon (4 ml)
    poultry seasoning   ¾ teaspoon (4 ml)

Wash the squash and cut in half; remove seeds and membrane. Bake, cut side
down, in 350°F (175°C) oven for 50 minutes. In the meantime, prepare dressing.
Sauté the celery and onion in the butter until tender. Combine with the crumbs,
salt, and seasoning. Turn the squash after 50 minutes and brush with melted
butter. Fill loosely with the dressing. Cover with foil and continue to bake 40
minutes longer.

• TOMATOES •

The tomato was cultivated in Mexico and Peru for centuries before the European
invasion. Long regarded as poisonous by settlers, the "love apple" was not
recognized as a food until around 1800 in North America. Now it is the most

73

widely used canned vegetable. The settlers dried tomatoes into cakes for preservation in the same manner as they dried fruit. Tomato butter was used both as a spread for bread and as a relish with meat.

Early books suggest taking up the plants before frost and hanging upside down in a cool place. This will prolong the life of the fruit for a short time. Allow the fruit to ripen, as needed in a sunny window.

Scalloped Tomatoes

My family ask for seconds of this!

    onion, chopped fine   *1*
    butter   *2 tablespoons (30 ml)*
    fresh bread crumbs   *2½ cups (560 ml)*
    canned tomatoes, or fresh, sliced   *2 cups (450 ml)*
    salt   *½ teaspoon (2.5 ml)*
    brown sugar   *1 tablespoon (15 ml)*

Sauté the onion in butter until tender. Mix in bread crumbs. Heat the tomatoes, salt and sugar together. Grease a casserole dish and place alternating layers of tomatoes and crumbs, ending with crumbs on top. Bake in a 350°F (175°C) oven for 40 minutes or until crumbs are browned.

Yield: 4 servings

• TURNIPS •

Turnips also came from Europe, where they were grown as a root crop to feed animals as well as humans. The turnip was not at first grown by our Ontario settlers, but by the 1850s it was being cultivated in the Peterborough area. Since it could be fed to cattle in large quantities, farmers could consequently enlarge their herds inexpensively, thus increasing milk, cheese, butter, and beef supplies.

Turnips were used sparingly in stews, usually being served as a vegetable course, boiled and mashed with butter, salt, and pepper. They were often served with mutton.

Buttered Turnips

The lemon butter adds an unusual but delicious flavour to this dish.

¾" (2 cm) cubed turnips   *3 cups (675 ml)*
small onion, chopped   *1*
butter   *3 tablespoons (45 ml)*
lemon juice   *2 teaspoons (10 ml)*

Cook the turnips in boiling salted water until tender. Drain well. Sauté the onion in the butter until tender. Add the lemon juice and the turnips. Serve hot, garnished with snipped parsley.

Yield: 4 servings

Scalloped Turnips

The cheese bakes to a golden top.

sliced turnips   *3½ cups (785 ml)*
medium onion, sliced   *1*
milk   *1½ cups (335 ml)*
flour   *1½ tablespoons (22.5 ml)*
butter   *2 tablespoons (30 ml)*
salt   *1 teaspoon (5 ml)*
grated cheese   *¾ cup (170 ml)*

Butter a baking dish and put in it half the turnips and onions. Scatter half the flour and salt over. Repeat layer. Pour milk over all and top with cheese. Bake at 350°F (175°C) for 1¾ hours.

Yield: 5 servings

Zucchini Skillet

Use fresh zucchini for this combo in the summer or frozen zucchini in the winter.

butter   *2 tablespoons (30 ml)*
thinly sliced zucchini   *4 cups (1 l)*
medium onions, thinly sliced   *2*
large tomatoes, peeled and quartered   *2*
salt, garlic powder
Parmesan cheese

Melt the butter in a 10" (25.40 cm) skillet. Add the rest of the ingredients except the cheese. Sprinkle with salt and garlic powder. Cover and simmer, stirring often but gently to avoid breaking the vegetables, until squash is tender-crisp, about 8 minutes. Remove cover and allow some of the liquid to evaporate before serving. Serve with Parmesan cheese sprinkled over top.

Yield: 4 servings

SALADS & DRESSINGS

GREEN SALADS HAVE been used since ancient times. The early settlers served raw vegetables dressed with vinegar, sugar, and seasonings. In the mid-1800s, Susanna Moodie tells of blanching dandelions to a cream colour by covering them with a cloth as they grew. The greens were used as a salad, rather like endive, or they were boiled and served with pork instead of cabbage. Cabbage and potato, as well as meat salads, were commonly used by the early settlers. Both Dutch and German peoples claim to have originated hot potato salad. The use of sour cream reflects a German tradition.

Frozen and jellied salads are a modern development. Early in the 1900s, the use of gelatin for salads was introduced, although a kind of gelatin was being made as early as the 1840s by grinding the bones and cartilage of animals and mixing it with boiling water. This liquid, when cooled, would set meat or dessert dishes. As early as 1850 recipes can be found for a dessert made with this same gelatin, milk, and sugar.

Cottage Cheese and Pineapple Jelly

This is a pretty green salad dotted with bits of red pimiento.

> lime gelatin   *3-ounce package (85 g)*
> drained crushed pineapple   *2½ cups (560 ml)*
> juice from pineapple plus water to make 1 cup (225 ml)
> cottage cheese   *1 cup (225 ml)*
> finely sliced celery   *2/3 cup (150 ml)*
> chopped pimiento   *2 tablespoons (30 ml)*

Heat the pineapple juice and water to boiling. Dissolve the gelatin in it and chill until syrupy. Add remaining ingredients and pour into a 9″ square (2 l) cake pan. Chill until firmly set before turning out onto a serving plate. Frost top and sides with:

> Cream Cheese Frosting:
> cream cheese   *4 ounces (113 g)*
> salad dressing   *1½ tablespoons (22.5 ml)*

Whip the softened cheese and dressing together.
   Garnish frosted jelly with sliced olives. Cut in squares to serve.

Yield: 16 servings

Individual Lime Pineapple Salads

A colourful addition to any luncheon table.

> lime gelatin   *3-ounce package (85 g)*
> pineapple juice plus water   *1¾ cups (395 ml)*
> pineapple   *6 slices*
> cottage cheese   *¾ cup (170 ml)*
> stuffed olives, halved   *3*

Dissolve the gelatin in 1 cup (225 ml) hot pineapple juice and water. Add the remaining cold liquid. Place one slice of pineapple in the bottom of each individual mould. Place ½ olive in center of each ring, cut side down. Spoon a little of the dissolved gelatin over each, and allow to set. In the meantime, chill the remaining gelatin mixture and when syrupy, stir in cottage cheese. Spoon into each and chill well. Unmould onto lettuce on individual serving plates.

Yield: 6 servings

77

Applesauce Jelly

Good served with pork dishes.

>   strawberry gelatin   *3-ounce package (85 g)*
>   sweetened applesauce   *1¼ cups (280 ml)*
>   fresh, grated orange rind   *2 teaspoons (10 ml)*
>   lemon juice   *3 tablespoons (45 ml)*
>   water   *¼ cup (55 ml)*
>   orange juice   *½ cup (110 ml)*

Heat the applesauce and dissolve the gelatin in it thoroughly. Stir in the remaining ingredients. Pour into a 2½ cup (560 ml) mould. Chill well before serving.

Yield: 6 servings

Cherry Jelly Supreme

My mother used to take a quart jar of preserved cherries, measure the syrup, and use enough unflavoured gelatin to set. When it became syrupy, she stirred in the cherries and poured it into a large glass bowl. Just before serving, she would whip a cup (225 ml) of cream with a little sugar and cover the top of the jelly It was completely delicious.

Yield: 8 servings

Rhubarb and Strawberry Mould

A combination of flavours that's guaranteed to please.

>   sweetened stewed rhubarb   *1 cup (225 ml)*
>   water   *½ cup (110 ml)*
>   pineapple gelatin   *3-ounce package (85 g)*
>   frozen strawberries   *15-ounce package (425 g)*

Heat the rhubarb and water to boiling. Stir in the gelatin until dissolved. Pour over the strawberries and stir until liquid begins to thicken. Pour into a 3 cup (675 ml) mould. Chill well.

Yield: 6 servings

Lime Vegetable Jelly

Set this jelly in a flat-bottomed mould so the colour will show.

> lime gelatin   *3-ounce package (85 g)*
> water   *1¾ cups (395 ml)*
> drained asparagus tips   *1 small can*
> small whole beets   *6*

Dissolve the gelatin in 1 cup (225 ml) boiling water. When completely dissolved, add the rest of the water and chill until syrupy. Lay the asparagus tips gently in the bottom of the mould and arrange the beets in a pattern. Pour the gelatin mixture over. Allow to chill until very firm. Unmould on lettuce.

Yield: 6 servings

Chicken Salad

A good luncheon salad or summer-night supper dish on the patio. Serve it on crisp shredded lettuce.

> cubed chicken or turkey   *1 large cup (225 ml)*
> hard-cooked eggs, diced   *2*
> diced celery   *½ cup (110 ml)*
> chopped green pepper   *½ cup (110 ml)*
> lemon juice   *1 tablespoon (15 ml)*
> chopped chives   *1½ teaspoons (7.5 ml)*
> mayonnaise   *1/3 cup (75 ml)*
> crushed potato chips   *1 cup (225 ml)*

Toss together all the ingredients, but the chips which should be added just before serving. Chill at least 1 hour before serving.

Yield: 3 to 4 servings

Bean Salad

This is a tasty vegetable combination and good for a summer night.

To cooked green beans (canned, fresh, or frozen), add any or all of the following: chopped onions, celery, apples, or cooked potato. Add pimiento, one or two hard-boiled eggs, chopped, salt and pepper to taste. Mix in just enough salad dressing to moisten. Garnish with sliced hard-cooked eggs. Chill well.

Lettuce and Onion Salad

This was one of my mother's favourite methods of preparing a lettuce salad.

Tear into bite-sized pieces sufficient lettuce required for number of people to be served. Cut up a few green onions in short lengths and add. Make a dressing of equal parts of vinegar and water with a little sugar added or of milk with a little sugar added and pour over the salad. Serve immediately.

Red Cabbage Salad

By the latter half of the 1800s, red cabbage was commonly used in salads. This is a nippy salad for those who like oil and vinegar dressings. It will keep in the refrigerator for several days.

    small red cabbage   ½
    salt   1½ teaspoons (7.5 ml)
    vinegar   1 cup (225 ml)
    oil   2¼ teaspoons (11 ml)
    water   1/3 cup (75 ml)
    sugar   3 tablespoons (45 ml)
    cayenne pepper   dash

Shred the cabbage and mix all the remaining ingredients together. Pour over the cabbage and let stand in the refrigerator for 2 days, stirring once each day.

Yield: 6 servings

Potato Salad

Hot bacon fat adds extra flavour to this salad. I prefer to use an English cucumber, unpared and cut in thin slices.

    unpeeled potatoes   8
    sliced cucumber   1 cup (225 ml)
    chopped celery   1 cup (225 ml)
    small onion, chopped   1
    green pepper, chopped   1/3 cup (75 ml)
    hot bacon fat   1 tablespoon (15 ml)
    salt   ½ teaspoon (2.5 ml)
    salad dressing   ½ cup (110 ml)
    pepper

Boil the unpeeled potatoes. Cool, pare, and dice. Add all the remaining ingredients, tossing together with 2 forks. Serve well chilled on lettuce leaves.

Yield: 8 servings

● SALAD DRESSINGS ●

Aunt Effie's Salad Dressing

This recipe came from my father's sister. A supply of this dressing was always kept on hand in my home.

    milk   2 cups (450 ml)
    sugar   1½ cups (335 ml)
    butter   1 dessertspoon (12 ml)
    pastry flour   6 large tablespoons (135 ml)
    water   2/3 cup (150 ml)
    salt   1 teaspoon (5 ml)
    mustard   1 teaspoon (5 ml)
    egg   1
    vinegar   1 cup (225 ml)

In a flat-bottomed saucepan put the milk, sugar, and butter. Heat to boiling point. Mix the flour, water, salt, and mustard together and beat in the egg. Thicken the milk mixture with the egg mixture. Remove from the stove and add the vinegar, beating well until it is smooth and creamy. Always add the vinegar last to prevent curdling. If dressing is too thick, thin with milk.

Yield: Approximately 4 cups (1 l)

Oil and Vinegar Dressing

A mild-flavoured dressing that is good tossed on a salad with grated Parmesan cheese.

> vinegar   *1/3 cup (75 ml)*
> salad oil   *3 tablespoons (45 ml)*
> salt   *¾ teaspoon (4 ml)*
> sugar   *3 teaspoons (15 ml)*
> instant minced onion   *1½ teaspoons (7.5 ml)*
> celery seed   *1/8 teaspoon (0.5 ml)*
> garlic powder   *dash*

Put all the ingredients in a jar and shake well.

Yield: ½ cup (110 ml)

Tomato Soup Salad Dressing

An excellent creamy French-style dressing. If your family is small, try making it in half quantities.

> sugar   *¼ cup (55 ml)*
> mustard   *1½ teaspoons (7.5 ml)*
> salt   *2 teaspoons (10 ml)*
> black pepper   *¼ teaspoon (1 ml)*
> pinch of paprika
> garlic powder   *¼ teaspoon (1 ml)*
> red wine vinegar   *¾ cup (170 ml)*
> water   *¼ cup (55 ml)*
> salad oil   *1 cup (225 ml)*
> tomato soup   *10-ounce can (280 ml)*

Put all the ingredients in a jar and shake well.

Yield: 3¼ cups (730 ml)

PIES, PASTRIES, & TARTS

EVEN THE ROMANS enjoyed pies! In fact, some of their pies were so exotic that live birds were enclosed in pastry and they were used as showpieces.

By the 14th century, meat and fish pies had become common in England and fruit pies, sometimes called tarts, were made by the 16th century. English settlers brought their pie-making skills to North America and quickly learned to use the native pumpkin and cranberry. Thus pies have always been a part of our Ontario heritage, improving in quality as ovens improved. When a "quick" oven was needed to bake a pie, the early cook tested the oven heat by putting in a piece of white paper. If it turned the paper brown in 5 minutes, it was hot enough to bake the pie.

maple rolling pins 19th Century

Hot Water Pie Crust

This is the only pie crust that I ever make, simply because it is so easy and never fails.

>   boiling water   *½ cup (110 ml)*
>   lard   *1 cup (225 ml)*

Mix together well with mixer or by hand and then add:

>   pastry flour   *3½ cups (785 ml)*
>   salt   *½ teaspoon (2.5 ml)*
>   baking powder   *½ teaspoon (2.5 ml)*

If you are using an electric mixer, the flour mixture can be almost entirely mixed in, leaving a little to stir in by hand. Wrap in waxed paper and chill before rolling. Makes enough for 2 double-crusted 9″ (1 l) pies.

To prevent your pie crust from bubbling up in the middle as it bakes, because of air trapped underneath, prick the undercrust with a sharp, fine-tined fork in a few places before putting in the filling. The filling never seems to cook through the small holes and the crust never bubbles up.

Vanilla Wafer Crust

Chocolate wafers may be substituted for vanilla.

>   crushed vanilla wafers   *1¼ cups (280 ml)*
>   melted butter   *4 tablespoons (60 ml)*
>   sugar   *1/3 cup (75 ml)*

Mix well together and press into a 9″ (1 l) greased pie pan.

Graham Wafer Crust

>   graham wafers   *14*
>   melted butter   *¼ cup (55 ml)*
>   sugar   *3 tablespoons (45 ml)*

With a rolling pin, crush the graham wafers into fine crumbs and mix thoroughly with sugar and butter. Spread over bottom and sides of a 9″ (1 l) pie plate and pat down firmly. Fill with any cream or custard filling.

Meringue Shell

For a glamorous dessert, try using this instead of pastry.

egg whites   4
sugar   *1 cup (225 ml)*
cream of tartar   *¼ teaspoon (1 ml)*

Beat the whites until foamy. Mix the cream of tartar with the sugar and gradually beat in 1 tablespoon (15 ml) at a time into the whites until all the sugar is used and whites are stiff but not dry. Butter a 9″ (1 l) pie plate and spread the meringue, thinner in the centre and thicker up the sides of the pan. Bake at 250°F (121°C) for 1 hour. Turn off heat and allow to sit in the oven until cooled. Fill as desired.

● **MINCE PIES** ●

Mince pie was early associated with the Christmas festival. The Puritans called it "superstitious pie" as a protest against the pagan manner in which this time of holy fasting was celebrated. Traditionally, English mincemeat does not contain meat, but it was an essential ingredient in the Canadian recipe.

I have included in this collection of mince pies the traditional mince, a cranberry mince, a green tomato mince, and a mock mince.

Old-fashioned Mince Pie

ground cooked beef   *9 cups (2.03 l)*
raw, chopped apples   *20 cups (4.5 l)*
suet   *2 cups (450 ml)*
brown sugar   *4 cups (1 l)*
pastry spice   *2 tablespoons (30 ml)*
lemons, grated rind, juice, and pulp   4
molasses   *2 cups (450 ml)*
jellied liquor from cooked beef   *1 cup (225 ml)*
raisins   *2 cups (450 ml)*
currants   *2 cups (450 ml)*
chopped dates (optional)   *2 cups (450 ml)*
mixed peel   *1 cup (225 ml)*
syrup from maraschino cherries (optional)   *½ cup (110 ml)*
vinegar to give tart taste
salt to taste

Stir all together and simmer over low heat for 2 hours, stirring frequently. Freeze in desired quantities or can in sterile jars.

Fill pastry-lined plate with mincemeat. Adjust top crust and cut slits to allow steam to escape. Bake at 425°F (220°C) for 40 to 50 minutes. If edges brown too quickly, cover with foil. Serve warm.

Cranberry Mince

This is equally good for pies or tarts. It makes a delicious pie, although of a slightly different flavour from the traditional mincemeat. Good served warm.

Place in a pot with a heavy bottom to prevent burning:

cranberries   *2 pounds (910 g)*
water   *1 cup (225 ml)*

Cover closely and steam for 15 minutes.

Add:
chopped suet   *½ cup (110 ml)*
finely chopped nuts   *1 cup (225 ml)*
finely chopped citron   *¾ cup (170 ml)*
chopped candied orange peel   *½ cup (110 ml)*
raisins   *2 cups (450 ml)*
peeled, chopped apples   *4 cups (1 l)*
honey or molasses   *1 cup (225 ml)*
vinegar   *¼ cup (55 ml)*
cinnamon   *1 teaspoon (5 ml)*
ginger   *2 teaspoons (10 ml)*
nutmeg   *½ teaspoon (2.5 ml)*
allspice   *1 teaspoon (5 ml)*

Thoroughly mix all the ingredients and simmer for 25 minutes, stirring often to prevent sticking. Cool and freeze in 3-cup quantities for a 9″ (1 l) pie. Immediately after mixing, the mincemeat may also be put into sterilized jars, sealed, and processed in a boiling water bath (with water reaching neck of jar) for 25 minutes.

Yield: 10 cups (2.25 litre)

To Use:

To 3 cups (675 ml) of mince, add ¾ cup (170 ml) brown sugar mixed with 1 tablespoon (15 ml) flour and fill pastry-lined plate. Add top crust and bake at 400°F (205°C) for 50 minutes.

Mock Mincemeat

A nice pie for a cold night!

> apples, peeled and chopped fine   6
> orange, ground   *1*
> raisins   *½ cup (110 ml)*
> brown sugar   *1 cup (225 ml)*
> grated lemon rind   *1 teaspoon (5 ml)*
> flour   *1 tablespoon (15 ml)*
> cinnamon   *1 teaspoon (5 ml)*
> nutmeg   *½ teaspoon (2.5 ml)*
> pastry for a 2-crust pie

Combine the apples, orange, and raisins. Mix the sugar, lemon rind, flour, and spices and combine with the fruit. Set aside while preparing the pastry. Fill pastry-lined plate with fruit mixture and adjust top crust. Bake at 425°F (220°C) for 40 to 45 minutes. Serve warm.

Green Tomato Mincemeat

A nice change from traditional mincemeat.

> ground, green tomatoes, undrained   *8 cups (2 l)*
> ground unpeeled apples   *3 cups (675 ml)*
> orange, ground fine   *1*
> raisins   *1 cup (225 ml)*
> ground cloves   *1¼ teaspoons (6 ml)*
> ground cinnamon   *2 teaspoons (10 ml)*
> ground allspice   *1 teaspoon (5 ml)*
> nutmeg   *1 teaspoon (5 ml)*
> grated lemon peel   *2 teaspoons (10 ml)*
> ground ginger   *¼ teaspoon (1 ml)*
> salt   *1¼ teaspoons (6 ml)*
> brown sugar, firmly packed   *2½ cups (560 ml)*
> cider vinegar   *½ cup (110 ml)*
> butter, a lump the size of a walnut

Wash, core, and grind the tomatoes. Drain and add as much water as drains off. Wash and core apples. Grind and combine with the remaining ingredients in a large saucepan. Simmer until thick, stirring frequently. Taste for seasonings and sweetness. Pack, hot, in sterilized jars and process in a boiling water bath for 25 minutes or freeze in required quantities.

Yield: 10 cups (2.25 l)

To Use:

Fill a 9″ (1 l) pastry-lined plate with 3 cups (675 ml) of mincemeat. Adjust top crust and cut slits to allow steam to escape. Bake at 425°F (220°C) for 40 to 45 minutes or until pastry is golden. Serve warm.

• FRUIT PIES •

Our grandmothers learned early to depend on a variety of fruits and berries for their pies, tarts, and puddings. We are told that as early as 1791 there were orchards being established in the Niagara Peninsula. By 1821 farmers were already producing an abundance of peaches, cherries, apples, pears, plums, and grapes. Many of these fruits were also being grown along the Detroit River at the same time, and a dozen years later orchards were planted in the more remote settlements such as on the Otonabee River.

Apple Pie

The early settlers produced large crops of apples, which soon formed part of their staple diet, being dried in great quantities for year-'round use. Apple pie became one of the most popular desserts and is still a great favourite today.

    medium apples   5 to 6
    sugar   1 cup (225 ml)
    flour   2 rounding tablespoons (45 ml)
    cinnamon   ½ teaspoon (2.5 ml)
    salt   dash
    butter
    pastry for a 2-crust pie

Line a 9″ (1 l) pie pan with pastry. Peel, core, and cut the apples in thin pieces. Mix the sugar, flour, and salt together. Sprinkle a little over the crust. Put in half the apples and sprinkle with one-half the remaining sugar mixture. Add the rest of the apples and sugar mixture and sprinkle with the cinnamon. Dot with butter. Adjust the top crust and cut slits to allow steam to escape. Bake at 400°F (205°C) for 45 to 60 minutes.

Crumb-topped Apple Pie

This is a real favourite with my family.

    medium apples   6
    sugar   1 cup (225 ml)

flour   3 *tablespoons (45 ml)*
cinnamon   ¼ *teaspoon (1 ml)*
pastry to line pie plate

Pare, core, and slice the apples. Mix together the sugar, flour, and cinnamon and stir in the apples with a fork. Pour into a 9″ (1 l) pastry-lined plate. Top with the following:

TOPPING:

flour   1/3 *cup (75 ml)*
cinnamon   1 *teaspoon (5 ml)*
brown sugar   2 *tablespoons (30 ml)*
butter   ¼ *cup (55 ml)*

Mix flour, cinnamon, and sugar together and cut in the butter until the mixture has the texture of fine crumbs.

   Pour topping evenly over the apples. Bake at 400°F (205°C) for 35 to 40 minutes. If the edge of the pastry browns too quickly, cover with a strip of foil. Serve warm or cold.

Dutch Apple Pie

Serve this with whipped cream. It's delicious!

medium apples   5
flour   2 *tablespoons (30 ml)*
sugar   ¾ *cup (170 ml)*
cream   ½ *cup plus 2 tablespoons (140 ml)*
nutmeg
pastry to line an 8″ (1 *l*) pie plate

Pare, core, and quarter the apples, being careful not to break them. Sprinkle ½ tablespoon (7.5 ml) flour over the crust lining the plate. Arrange the apples, cut side down, overlapping slightly, in a pattern around the plate and filling in the centre in a single layer. Mix the sugar and remaining flour and sprinkle over the apples. Pour the cream over all, moistening the sugar as much as possible. Sprinkle with nutmeg. Cut long strips of pastry and braid or twist and arrange around rim of moistened edge of crust. Bake at 425°F (220°C) for 15 minutes and then 350°F (175°C) for 45 minutes.

Blueberry Pie

Nothing tastes better than a fresh blueberry pie.

    fresh blueberries   *3 cups (675 ml)*
    sugar   *2/3 cup (150 ml)*
    flour   *3 tablespoons (45 ml)*
    cinnamon   *¼ teaspoon (1 ml)*
    butter   *1 tablespoon (15 ml)*
    pastry for a 2-crust 9″ (1 *l*) pie

Mix together the sugar, flour, and cinnamon. Stir in the blueberries. Pour into a pastry-lined plate and dot with the butter. Cover with a lattice or full crust. Seal edges. Bake at 400°F (205°C) for 40 to 50 minutes.

• CHERRIES •

Cherries, believed to have originated in Asia Minor, came to North America from Europe, and by the mid 1700s trees were being grown by the French along the Detroit River in Canada. By the 1790s there were cherry orchards in the Niagara area. There are several kinds of wild cherry native to North America, but these are used mainly for jelly or wine.

Cherry Pie

Try this for dessert at your next cook-out.

    pitted fresh cherries   *4 cups (1 l)*
    sugar   *1½ cups (335 ml)*
    flour   *4 tablespoons (60 ml)*
    butter   *1 tablespoon (15 ml)*
    almond extract   *1/8 teaspoon (0.5 ml)*
    cinnamon
    pastry for 2-crust 9″ (1 *l*) pie

Mix together the sugar, flour, and flavouring. Place half the cherries in the pastry-lined plate. Pour on half the sugar mixture. Repeat with remaining cherries and sugar. Dot with butter and sprinkle with cinnamon. Top with either a lattice or full crust. Moisten undercrust edge in order to seal top crust. Bake at 400°F (205°C) for 40 to 50 minutes.

Although this native fruit was mainly used in sauces and jellies, cranberries were also cooked into pies, puddings, breads, and muffins. Indians used them in trade for old clothes, pork, and flour. The berries were found in great numbers at Buckhorn Lake northwest of Peterboro and in a great marsh north of Kingston.

Cranberry or Mock Cherry Pie

A juicy pie that really tastes like cherry.

> cranberries, halved   1 cup (225 ml)
> raisins   ½ cup (110 ml)
> chopped apples   1 cup (225 ml)
> sugar   1 cup (225 ml)
> flour   2 tablespoons (30 ml)
> salt   ¼ teaspoon (1 ml)
> hot water   1 cup (225 ml)
> almond extract   ½ teaspoon (2.5 ml)
> pastry for 2-crust 9″ (1 l) pie

Mix together the sugar, flour, and salt. Toss with fruits. Add water and stir over medium heat until the mixture comes to a boil and thickens. Add flavouring and set aside. Roll out pastry and line pie plate. Fill with partially cooled filling. Adjust top crust. Bake at 425°F (220°C) for 45 minutes. Cool before serving.

Date Custard Pie

Easy to make as well as to eat.

> sliced dates   ½ cup (110 ml)
> milk   2 cups (450 ml)
> sugar   ½ cup (110 ml)
> vanilla   ¾ teaspoon (4 ml)
> salt   ½ teaspoon (2.5 ml)
> eggs   2
> nutmeg
> pastry for single-crust 8″ (1 l) pie

Line pie plate with pastry and pre-bake 5 minutes at 450°F (230°C). Warm the milk and dissolve the sugar and salt in it completely. Beat the eggs slightly and stir in, along with the vanilla. Cover crust with sliced dates and pour custard filling over. Sprinkle top with nutmeg. Bake at 450°F (230°C) for 10 minutes, then at 400°F (205°C) for 20 minutes.

91

Gooseberries belong to the same family as currants — both grew wild in Ontario and were used by the Indians long before settlers arrived. Gradually gooseberries came to be cultivated in gardens, for the fruit could be used in preserves, sauces, and pies. As fresh gooseberries aren't always easily obtainable, I have included a recipe for canned gooseberry pie as well as one using fresh berries.

Gooseberry Pie

We used to have a long row of gooseberry bushes at home, and gooseberry pie was one of our favourites. My aunt, Mrs. Harold Hough of Sillsville, Ontario, with whom we used to exchange Christmases, usually had this old-time favourite for our Christmas dinner. Try it topped off with vanilla ice cream.

> gooseberries in 40% syrup   *14-ounce can (395 ml)*
> sugar   *¾ cup (170 ml)*
> flour   *2 tablespoons (30 ml)*
> pastry for 9″ (1 *l*) lattice topped pie

Mix together the flour and sugar. Add the gooseberries and syrup, mixing thoroughly. Cook, stirring constantly, until thickened. Set aside to cool while you roll pastry and line pie plate. Pour in filling. Top with lattice crust. Bake at 425°F (220°C) for 30 to 40 minutes. Cool before serving.

Fresh Gooseberry Pie

A real old-time taste treat!

> fresh gooseberries   *4 cups (1 l)*
> flour   *5 tablespoons (75 ml)*
> sugar   *1½ cups (335 ml)*
> Pastry for double-crust 9″ (1 *l*) pie

Snip off stem and blossom ends of berries. Wash and drain. Thoroughly mix together flour and sugar, then stir in the berries. Fill pastry-lined pie pan with fruit and cover with full top or lattice crust. Bake at 425°F (220°C) for 35 to 40 minutes. Cool before serving.

Variation:

Frozen gooseberries may be substituted for the fresh berries in the recipe above. Place the frozen berries in a saucepan and, while stirring gently, gradually add the sugar and flour mixture. Cook over medium heat, stirring constantly, until thickened. Fill pastry-lined plate and cook as directed above.

Lemons probably originated in India. Because of their high vitamin content, lemons were early used as a preventive of scurvy. In the early years of Upper Canada, they were expensive and so vinegar often was substituted for one-half the lemon juice called for in a recipe.

Self-frosting Lemon Pie

This pie was also called $15 Lemon Pie in my mother's book. My family always ask for seconds when I bake it.

> juice and grated rind of 1 lemon
> sugar   *1 cup (225 ml)*
> egg, separated   *1*
> flour   *3 tablespoons (45 ml)*
> milk   *1 cup (225 ml)*
> melted butter   *1 tablespoon (15 ml)*
> pastry for 9″ (1 *l*) single-crust pie

Mix the flour and sugar; add lemon juice, rind, egg yolk and butter. Stir in milk. Beat egg white until stiff, then fold into lemon mixture. Pour into unbaked pastry-lined plate. Bake at 350°F (175°C) 35 to 40 minutes.

Lemon Meringue Pie

Brown sugar is the secret to the delicious flavour in this pie.

> 9″ (1 *l*) baked pastry shell   *1*
> cornstarch   *5 tablespoons (75 ml)*
> flour   *5 tablespoons (75 ml)*
> brown sugar   *1¼ cups (280 ml)*
> boiling water   *2 cups (450 ml)*
> eggs, separated   *2*
> butter   *1 tablespoon (15 ml)*
> juice and grated rind of 1 lemon
> yellow food colouring

Mix the cornstarch, flour, and sugar together in the top of a double boiler. Stir in the boiling water and cook over boiling water until the mixture is thickened and the cornstarch cooked, approximately 5 minutes. Beat the yolks and stir into them a little of the hot cornstarch mixture. Add the egg mixture to the cornstarch mixture and stir constantly until thickened. Remove from heat and add the butter, lemon rind, juice, and food colouring. Cool for 5 minutes and then pour into pie shell. Top with meringue and bake at 350°F (175°C) for 15 minutes. Cool well before serving.

MERINGUE:

    egg whites   *2*
    sugar   *4 tablespoons (60 ml)*

Beat whites until foamy. Gradually add sugar and beat until stiff and stands in peaks. Spread over pie filling, making sure to seal edge of pastry with meringue to prevent shrinking from edge when cooking. Bake as directed above.

Maple Meringue Pie

Early settlers used to store away great quantities of both maple syrup and sugar for year-'round use. Here is a rich, creamy pie using maple syrup both as its sweetener and for flavour.

    milk   *1 cup (225 ml)*
    maple syrup   *¾ cup (170 ml)*
    cornstarch   *2½ tablespoons (37.2 ml)*
    salt   *¼ teaspoon (1 ml)*
    eggs, separated   *2*
    butter   *2 teaspoons (10 ml)*
    sugar   *3 tablespoons (45 ml)*
    8″ (1 *l*) baked pie shell

Scald ¾ cup (170 ml) milk and the syrup in the top of a double boiler over boiling water. Mix together the remaining milk, cornstarch, salt, and beaten egg yolks. Stir a little of the hot mixture into the egg mixture and then stir all together and continue to cook over boiling water, stirring constantly until thickened and smooth. Remove from heat and stir in the butter. Allow to cool, stirring twice, while preparing the meringue for the top. Beat the egg whites until foamy. Gradually add the sugar and beat until whites stand in peaks. Pour the filling into the baked shell and top with the meringue, making sure to seal well at the edges so the meringue will not shrink away from the sides of the pastry. Bake at 350°F (175°C) for 10 to 12 minutes. Cool and serve.

• PEACHES •

Peach trees originated in Asia. They were brought to North America by the Spaniards and were naturalized as far north as Pennsylvania by the 17th century.

The first settlers brought them into southern Upper Canada, especially the Niagara Peninsula.

Fresh Peach Pie

    sliced fresh peaches   *4 cups (1 l)*
    sugar   *1 cup (225 ml)*
    flour   *2 rounded tablespoons (45 ml)*
    salt
    cinnamon   *1/3 teaspoon (2 ml)*
    butter   *1 tablespoon (15 ml)*
    pastry for double-crust 9″ (1 *l*) pie

Line pie plate with pastry. Peel, pit, and slice peaches. Mix together sugar, flour, salt, and cinnamon. Place half the peaches in the crust. Sprinkle with half the sugar mixture. Repeat and dot with butter. Adjust top crust. Bake at 425°F (220°C) for 40 to 50 minutes.

Frozen Peach Pie

Partially thaw peaches. Use same ingredients as above except ¾ cup (170 ml) sugar. Place peaches in a saucepan with juice. Pour sugar mixture over and stir gently with a fork over medium heat until juice is thickened, being careful not to break the fruit. Cool before pouring into unbaked pie shell. Bake as above.

Pecan Pie

This recipe came from my husband's late aunt, Mrs. H.P. Green of Harrow, Ontario. It is simple to make and delicious to eat.

    chopped pecans   *1 cup (4 ounces) (225 ml)*
    eggs   *3*
    dark corn syrup   *1 cup (225 ml)*
    sugar   *½ cup (110 ml)*
    cinnamon   *½ teaspoon (2.5 ml)*
    vanilla   *1 teaspoon (5 ml)*
    flour   *1 tablespoon (15 ml)*
    salt   *½ teaspoon (2.5 ml)*
    melted butter   *¼ cup (55 ml)*
    pastry for 9″ (1 *l*) single-crust pie

Chop the pecans finely. Mix the sugar, cinnamon, flour, and salt together. Beat the eggs well. Combine all the ingredients. Pour into unbaked pie shell. Bake at 375°F (190°C) for 1 hour or until undercrust is done. Cool and serve with a little whipped cream.

Yield: 8 servings

Pineapple originated in the American tropics and sub-tropics. As it grows only in warmer regions, it has always been imported to the north.

Pineapple Pie

This recipe came from the family of May Lawson, a first cousin of my grandmother's. It rates as a top favourite in our family. The original recipe called for fresh pineapple and more sugar.

> canned crushed pineapple, drained   ¾ cup (170 ml)
> juice from pineapple plus water to make 1 cup (225 ml)
> sugar   ¾ cup (170 ml)
> cornstarch   3 tablespoons (45 ml)
> butter   1 tablespoon (15 ml)
> salt   1/8 teaspoon (0.5 ml)
> egg yolks   2
> 9'' (1 l) baked pie shell

Mix the sugar, cornstarch, and salt in the top of a double boiler. Add water and pineapple juice to the sugar mixture and stir until smooth. Add the yolks, slightly beaten and the butter. Cook over boiling water, stirring constantly until smooth and thick. Remove from heat and add pineapple. Cool completely. Spoon into a pie shell. Serve with whipped cream, or top with meringue and brown in a 350°F (175°C) oven for 12 to 15 minutes.

Pumpkin was grown by the Indians of North and Central America as well as Peru back in pre-Columbian times. Settlers soon learned the value of the native-grown pumpkin and so incorporated it into their diet. It was always planted with Indian corn and was fed in the fall to cattle and swine, as well as being used in the preparation of a great variety of dishes — soup, bread, muffins, cakes, pies and tarts, cookies, puddings. In the 1800s there was delicious pumpkin bread made with cornmeal baked in long loaves and served hot with plenty of freshly churned butter. Pumpkin could even be used to make a sugar substitute. Because in the early years cane sugar was expensive, maple syrup was used extensively. When the year's supply was exhausted, the settlers make "punkin sass" by boiling pumpkin juice for hours until it acquired the consistency of molasses. Pumpkin was also dried and stored in cotton bags for winter use in the same manner as other fruits and berries.

Pumpkin Pie

My mother-in-law used to tell me that this was the best pumpkin pie she had ever eaten. For a change, try it with either maple syrup or honey spooned on top.

cooked pumpkin   *1 large cup (260 ml)*
sugar   *½ cup (110 ml)*
flour   *2 rounded tablespoons (45 ml)*
salt   *½ teaspoon (2.5 ml)*
cinnamon   *½ teaspoon (2.5 ml)*
ginger   *½ teaspoon (2.5 ml)*
milk   *1 cup (225 ml)*
beaten eggs   *2*
nutmeg
pastry for single-crust 9″ (1 *l*) pie

Mix the spices, except the nutmeg, with the salt, sugar, and flour. Add to the pumpkin. Add the milk and beaten eggs. Pour into pastry-lined plate and sprinkle with nutmeg. Bake at 450°F (230°C) for 10 minutes, then 350°F (175°C) for 40 minutes.

• RAISINS •

Just like so many other fruits, grapes have been dried for year-'round use since ancient times. They were early an important trade item in the Mediterranean. Grapes were grown in Spain, Asia Minor and Greece mainly until the 20th century when Australia and United States began to cultivate them. Late in the 18th century, Spanish missionaries introduced the cultivation of grapes into California but it was not an important industry there until after 1875. Raisins can only be produced from grapes in areas where there is a long, dry growing period because they must be fully ripened on the vines to ensure a high sugar content. They are usually dried in the sun. Raisins are valuable in our diet for their sugar, iron and vitamin A and B content.

Raisin Pie

A favourite of ours to take on a picnic.

> seedless raisins   *1 cup (225 ml)*
> butter   *1 teaspoon (5 ml)*
> boiling water   *1½ cups (335 ml)*
> cloves   *1 teaspoon (5 ml)*
> vinegar or lemon juice   *1 tablespoon (15 ml)*
> sugar   *1 cup (225 ml)*
> flour   *3 tablespoons (45 ml)*
> salt   *½ teaspoon (2.5 ml)*
> pastry for 2-crust 9″ *(1 l)* pie

Mix together the flour, sugar, and salt. Cook the rest of the ingredients together on the stove and thicken with the flour-sugar mixture. Cool slightly before putting into pastry-lined plate. Cover with lattice or full crust. Bake at 400°F (205°C) for 40 minutes.

Osgood Raisin Pie

A cooked filling in a baked shell. This is a delicious change for a raisin pie.

> brown sugar   *¾ cup (170 ml)*
> flour   *2 tablespoons (30 ml)*
> nutmeg, cinnamon   *½ teaspoon (2.5 ml) each*
> eggs, separated   *2*
> vinegar or lemon juice   *2 tablespoons (30 ml)*
> raisins   *1 cup (225 ml)*
> hot water   *1½ cups (335 ml)*
> baked 9″ *(1 l)* pie shell

Mix the sugar, flour, and spice. Add beaten egg yolks, vinegar, raisins, hot water and cook on top of stove, over medium heat, stirring constantly until thickened. Pour into baked shell and frost with egg whites beaten stiff with 3 tablespoons (45 ml) sugar. Brown in a 350°F (175°C) oven for 12 to 15 minutes.

• RHUBARB •

Rhubarb is native to Asia and was brought from Europe to North America, where it grows well in our moderate climate. Used mainly for pie, it is also called pieplant and wine plant, and early cookbooks carry many recipes for Pieplant Pie and Pudding.

Rhubarb Pie

We used to have a great hedge of rhubarb at home, and the first rhubarb pie of the season reinforced the knowledge that spring had really arrived.

fresh rhubarb, cut in 1" (2.54 cm) pieces   *4 cups (1 l)*
packed, brown sugar   *1-1/3 cups (300 ml)*
flour   *5 tablespoons (75 ml)*
butter   *1 tablespoon (15 ml)*
pastry for 9" (1 *l*) double-crust pie

Mix together the sugar and flour, and stir in the rhubarb. Line pie plate with pastry and pour in fruit. Dot with butter. Adjust top crust and seal edges. Bake at 400°F (205°C) for 45 to 50 minutes.

Frozen Rhubarb Pie

Use the above recipe, substituting frozen rhubarb for fresh, and allow to bake 1¼ hours.

Mock Mince Pie

This combination of rhubarb and raisins will have your family fooled.

chopped fresh rhubarb   *3 cups (675 ml)*
raisins   *1 cup (225 ml)*
sugar   *1-1/3 cups (300 ml)*
cracker crumbs   *¾ cup (170 ml)*
juice and grated rind of 1 lemon
egg, well beaten   *1*
melted butter   *2 tablespoons (30 ml)*
salt   *½ teaspoon (2.5 ml)*
pastry for 8" (1 *l*) double-crust pie

Mix all the ingredients and pour into pastry-lined pie plate. Adjust and seal top crust. Bake at 400°F (205°C) for 50 to 60 minutes. Serve warm. If frozen rhubarb is used, bake 60 minutes.

Rhubarb Custard Pie

This recipe was given to me by my sister-in-law, Mrs. J.H. Burt of Weston, Ontario. It is a deliciously moist pie, best eaten the day it is made.

rhubarb   *4 cups (1 l)*
sugar   *1 cup (225 ml)*
cornstarch   *3 tablespoons (45 ml)*
sugar   *½ cup (110 ml)*
egg   *1*
milk   *¾ cup (170 ml)*
salt   *pinch*
vanilla   *1 teaspoon (5 ml)*
pastry for 9″ (1 *l*) double-crust pie

Roll out and line pie plate with pastry. Mix the cornstarch with the 1 cup (225 ml) sugar and mix with the rhubarb. Pour into pastry-lined pan. Roll out top crust. Mix the remaining sugar, egg, milk, salt, and vanilla and pour over rhubarb. Top with upper crust, sealing edges. Bake at 400°F (205°C) for 40 to 50 minutes. If using frozen rhubarb, bake 60 to 70 minutes. Serve warm or cold.

• **REFRIGERATOR PIES** •

Eggnog Pie

This is a nice change of pace for a Christmas dessert. It can also be used as a parfait, layering the pineapple with the eggnog mixture rather than folding in the fruit as in the pie. It will serve 8 in parfait glasses or 6 in a pie.

crushed pineapple, drained   *19-ounce can (560 ml)*
unflavoured gelatin   *1 envelope*
orange juice   *½ cup (110 ml)*
commercial eggnog   *1½ cups (335 ml)*
vanilla   *1½ teaspoons (7.5 ml)*
coconut flavouring   *¼ teaspoon (1 ml)*
whipped topping   *2-ounce package (58 g)*
salt   *1/8 teaspoon (0.5 ml)*

Stir gelatin into the orange juice, set over boiling water, and stir until dissolved. Remove from heat and stir into eggnog. Add salt, flavourings. Chill until partially set. Whip topping as instructed on package and fold into gelatin mixture. Fold in well-drained pineapple. Fill pie shell and refrigerate for several hours until well set. Garnish with pineapple and maraschino cherries.

Strawberry Glaze Pie

Strawberries, native to Chile, were introduced to Europe by New World explorers. Wild strawberries have always grown in eastern North America, but the cultivated variety was introduced from Europe and so made its way to Canada.

fresh strawberries   *1 quart (1.13 l)*
sugar   *1¼ cups (280 ml)*
cornstarch   *3½ tablespoons (52.5 ml)*
9″ (1 *l*) baked pie shell
salt   *pinch*

Crush enough berries to make 1½ cups (335 ml). Stir together with the sugar, cornstarch, and salt. Cook together, stirring constantly, until thickened and clear. Remove from heat and spread ¼ cup (55 ml) over baked pie shell to prevent soaking. Arrange remaining fresh whole berries in shell, leaving a few for garnish on top. Pour remaining glaze over all and allow to cool at least two hours. Garnish with whipped cream and whole berries before serving.

Strawberry Parfait Pie

This recipe was given to me by my sister, Margaret Vannest. It may be made into a pie or doubled and put into a 9″ X 13″ (3 l) shallow pan to serve 12 to 15 people.

crushed, sweetened strawberries   *1 cup (225 ml)*
water   *1 cup (225 ml)*
strawberry gelatin   *3-ounce package (85 g)*
vanilla ice cream   *1 pint (565 ml)*
9″ (1 *l*) vanilla wafer crust

Heat water to boiling, add gelatin, and stir to dissolve. Add ice cream by spoonfuls, stirring until melted. Chill till mixture mounds. Fold in strawberries, and pile mixture into crust. Chill until firm. Garnish with whipped cream and fresh strawberries.

• CREAM PIES •

Butterscotch Pie

This is a rich, creamy pie. Sometimes I use the filling alone for pudding, served with a dab of whipped cream or jam.

white sugar   *3 tablespoons (45 ml)*
butter   *1 tablespoon (15 ml)*
milk   *1½ cups (335 ml)*
brown sugar   *1/3 cup (75 ml)*
flour   *2 tablespoons (30 ml)*
salt   *1/3 teaspoon (2 ml)*
eggs, separated   *2*
9″ (1 *l*) baked pie shell

Caramelize the white sugar by cooking over medium heat until melted and golden brown in color. Add butter. Scald the milk and add very slowly to the caramelized sugar, stirring constantly. Put into top of double boiler and place over boiling water. Mix together the sugar, salt, and flour, and stir into sugar mixture; continue stirring until thickened. Add a little of the hot mixture to beaten yolks, then add egg yolks to sugar mixture, stirring constantly for 3 minutes. Remove from heat and cool slightly. Pour into pie shell. Top with meringue made of egg whites beaten with 4 tablespoons (60 ml) sugar. Brown in a 350°F (175°C) oven for 12 to 15 minutes, or serve topped with whipped cream instead of meringue.

Chocolate Pie

Place in a saucepan:

milk   *1½ cups (335 ml)*
boiling water   *½ cup (110 ml)*

Thicken with the following mixture stirred together:

sugar   *½ cup (110 ml)*
cocoa   *2 tablespoons (30 ml)*
salt   *¼ teaspoon (1 ml)*
flour   *3 tablespoons (45 ml)*

Beat:

egg yolks   *2*

and stir in until cooked, creamy, and smooth. Pour into a baked 9″ (1 l) pie shell and top with a meringue made of the 2 egg whites beaten stiff with 3 tablespoons (45 ml) sugar. Brown in a 350°F (175°C) oven for 12 to 14 minutes. Instead of the meringue, whipped cream may be used as a topping.

Coconut Cream Pie

This pie has a rich, creamy flavour. For a change, place a layer of sweetened, sliced fresh peaches on the bottom, then pour in the filling and top with whipped cream for a real taste treat.

    milk   2¼ cups (505 ml)
    cornstarch   3 tablespoons (45 ml)
    salt   ½ teaspoon (2.5 ml)
    sugar   5 tablespoons (75 ml)
    eggs, separated   2
    coconut flavouring   ½ teaspoon (2.5 ml)
    butter   2 tablespoons (30 ml)
    shredded coconut   2/3 cup (150 ml)
    9″ (1 l) baked pie shell

Scald 2 cups (450 ml) of the milk in the top of the double boiler. Mix remaining milk with the cornstarch, sugar, and salt and add gradually to the hot milk, stirring constantly over simmering water until thick. Cover and allow to cook 15 minutes longer. Beat the egg yolks and mix in several spoonfuls of the hot mixture. Then pour egg mixture into the hot mixture, stirring constantly to prevent lumping. Continue to cook in the double boiler for 5 minutes longer. Remove from heat and mix in butter, flavouring, and coconut. Cool slightly and pour into baked pie shell. Cover with meringue made with egg whites and 4 tablespoons (60 ml) sugar, beaten until stiff. Brown in a 350°F (175°C) oven for 12 to 14 minutes.

Sour Cream Pie

    egg yolks   2
    sour milk   1 cup (225 ml)
    sugar   ½ cup (110 ml)
    raisins   ½ cup (110 ml)
    cinnamon or vanilla   ½ teaspoon (2.5 ml)
    cloves   ¼ teaspoon (1 ml)
    salt   ¼ teaspoon (1 ml)
    pastry for 9″ (1 l) single-crust pie

Mix the sour milk and sugar; add yolks, spices, salt and raisins. Line pie plate with pastry. Fill with the above mixture. Bake in a 400°F (205°C) oven to set pastry for 10 minutes, then 350°F (175°C) oven for 40 minutes. Remove and frost with 2 egg whites beaten with 3 tablespoons (45 ml) sugar until stiff. Brown in 350°F (175°C) oven 12 to 15 minutes.

Pudding Powder Tarts

My first recollection of these tarts is in a lunch my mother packed for a picnic with my cousins on the shores of the Bay of Quinte when I was a very small girl. They were delicious then, and still are today.

caramel or butterscotch pudding powder   *3-ounce package (85 g)*
egg, separated   *1*
medium tart shells, baked   *10*
nuts and bananas

Prepare pudding mix according to directions, using only egg yolk. Cool. Beat egg white with 2 tablespoons (30 ml) sugar. Partly fill a shallow pan with hot water. Place tablespoons of this meringue on hot water and cook in a 350°F (175°C) oven 10 to 12 minutes. Remove to a wire rack and allow to drain. Add chopped nuts and bananas to the cooled pudding and fill tart shells. Top with meringues.

Taffy Tarts

corn syrup   *1 cup (225 ml)*
brown sugar   *2/3 cup (150 ml)*
eggs, slightly beaten   *2*
butter   *¼ cup (55 ml)*
salt   *¼ teaspoon (1 ml)*
chopped walnuts or pecans   *2/3 cup (150 ml)*
vanilla   *½ teaspoon (2.5 ml)*
pastry for 18 medium tart shells

Line tart tins with pastry. Mix syrup and brown sugar in a saucepan and cook gently over direct heat for 5 minutes. Cool slightly and stir into the beaten eggs. Add remaining ingredients and fill the unbaked tart shells 2/3 full. Bake in a 425°F (220°C) oven for 15 to 20 minutes or until set. Half this quantity will make 12 small tarts.

Currant Tarts

currants   *1 cup (225 ml)*
brown sugar   *1 cup (225 ml)*
butter   *1 tablespoon (15 ml)*
egg   *1*

lemon juice   *1 tablespoon (15 ml)*
pastry for 10 medium tart shells

Beat the sugar, butter, egg, and lemon juice together until smooth. Stir in the
currants. Spoon into pastry-lined tart tins. Bake at 375°F (190°C) for 20 minutes.
Cool on a rack.

Yield: 10 medium tarts

Mrs. Runion's Butter Tarts

butter   *3 tablespoons (45 ml)*
corn syrup   *¾ cup (170 ml)*
eggs, well beaten   *2*
salt   *¼ teaspoon (1 ml)*
vanilla   *1 teaspoon (5 ml)*
lemon juice   *2 tablespoons (30 ml)*
lemon rind   *¼ teaspoon (1 ml)*
raisins   *1 cup (225 ml)*
pastry for 16 medium tart shells

Beat all the ingredients together thoroughly, except the raisins. Add the raisins
last. Spoon into pastry-lined tart pans and bake at 375°F (190°C) for 20 to 25
minutes. Cool on a rack.

Yield: 16 medium tarts

Banbury Tarts

These tarts were named after the town of Banbury, England. Cakes, for which the
town has been famous since the 17th century, are still produced there.

raisins, chopped   *1 cup (225 ml)*
cracker crumbs   *1 tablespoon (15 ml)*
brown sugar   *½ cup (110 ml)*
egg, beaten   *1*
juice and grated rind of 1 lemon
pastry for 10 medium tarts or 18 small tartlets

Mix together all the ingredients. Fill pastry-lined tart pans or roll pie pastry thin
and put a layer on a baking sheet, spread with above mixture, and cover with
another thin layer of pastry. Seal edges. Mark off strips 4″ X 2″ (10.16 X 5.08 cm).
Bake at 375°F (190°C), tarts for 20 to 25 minutes, pastries for 15 to 20 minutes.
Cut pastries while still warm. Cool tarts on rack.

Yield: 10 medium tarts or 18 small tartlets

May's Butter Tarts

A choice of spices adds variety to these old-fashioned currant tarts.

eggs   2
white sugar   *½ cup (110 ml)*
brown sugar   *½ cup (110 ml)*
currants   *½ cup (110 ml)*
grated lemon peel   *½ teaspoon (2.5 ml)*
nutmeg or cinnamon   *¼ teaspoon (1 ml)*
piece of butter the size of an egg
pastry for 12 medium tarts

Line tart pans with rolled pastry. Mix all the remaining ingredients together thoroughly. Fill tart shells. Bake at 375°F (190°C) for 20 to 25 minutes.

Yield: 12 medium tarts

Glazed Cherry Tarts

A quick, but delicious, dessert. Try it as well as a filling for an 8″ (1 *l*) pie served with whipped cream.

red cherries in syrup   *14-ounce can (395 ml)*
cornstarch   *2 tablespoons (30 ml)*
sugar   *3 tablespoons (45 ml)*
salt   *1/8 teaspoon (0.5 ml)*
almond extract   *¼ teaspoon (1 ml)*
butter   *1 teaspoon (5 ml)*
baked medium tart shells   *12*

Drain the cherries and add enough water to the juice to make 1 cup (225 ml). Mix in the sugar, cornstarch, and salt. Cook over direct heat, stirring constantly, until thickened. Remove from heat and add the butter and flavouring. Coat bottom of tart shells with a little glaze. Divide cherries evenly among the shells and pour glaze over them. Cool and serve plain or with whipped cream if desired.

VARIATION WITH OTHER CANNED FRUITS:

Follow above recipe as to quantities but vary flavouring to suit fruit. If fruit is very sweet — peaches, for example — use only 2 tablespoons (30 ml) sugar.

DESSERTS
COBBLERS, PUDDINGS, FROZEN AND REFRIGERATOR DESSERTS, SWEET SAUCES

THE FIRST PUDDINGS the settlers made were boiled in a pudding bag or cloth in the kettle as it hung over the fire. Next came puddings in a bowl, covered with a cloth, and steamed. The baked or chilled puddings are a much later innovation and could only be made when ovens had advanced to the point where they were sufficiently reliable for such baking.

Today the term "pudding" covers a broad range of desserts. Included are steamed and baked puddings, custard-type desserts, and even some forms of jellied fruits.

Raisin Brown Betty

> chopped apples   3½ cups (785 ml)
> raisins   1 cup (225 ml)
> brown sugar, packed   ½ cup(110 ml)
> soft bread crumbs   1 cup (225 ml)
> butter   1 teaspoon (5 ml)
> nutmeg   ¼ teaspoon (1 ml)
> cinnamon   ¼ teaspoon (1 ml)

Butter dish, put in layer of apples, then layer of raisins; sprinkle with sugar and spice, dot with butter. Repeat, finishing with crumb topping, dotted with butter and sprinkled with sugar. Cover and bake at 375°F (190°C) for 1 hour. Serve with lemon or butterscotch sauce.

Yield: 4 large servings

Forestry Pudding

This is a delicious raisin dessert with a cake-like texture, smothered in rich butterscotch sauce that bakes along with it.

> sifted flour   1 cup (225 ml)
> white sugar   1/3 cup (75 ml)
> baking powder   2 teaspoons (10 ml)
> salt   ¼ teaspoon (1 ml)
> shortening   2 tablespoons (30 ml)
> raisins   ¾ cup (170 ml)
> milk   ½ cup (110 ml)
> brown sugar   1 cup (225 ml)
> butter   1 tablespoon (15 ml)
> boiling water   2 cups (450 ml)

Sift the flour, baking powder, sugar, and salt into a mixing bowl. Cut in the shortening with a pastry blender or 2 knives. Add the raisins and the milk, stirring lightly with a fork until just moistened. Pour batter into a greased casserole. Mix brown sugar, butter, and boiling water, and pour over the batter. Bake at 375°F (190°C) for 30 to 35 minutes. Serve warm with sauce from the bake dish.

Yield: 6 servings

Cottage Pudding

This is a tasty, simple, and economical pudding with several possible variations.
Raisins, dates, jam, marmalade, or fruit may be put in the bottom of the dish.

butter   *1 tablespoon (15 ml)*
sugar   *½ cup (110 ml)*
egg   *1*
milk   *½ cup (110 ml)*
flour   *1 cup (225 ml)*
baking powder   *3 teaspoons (15 ml)*
salt   *¼ teaspoon (1 ml)*

Sift the dry ingredients. Cream the butter, sugar, and egg. Add flour mixture to
this mixture alternately with the milk. Place in a 9″ (2 l) square cake pan and bake
30 minutes in a 350°F (175°C) oven. Serve warm with sweetened milk and nutmeg
sauce or sauce of your choice.

Yield: 6-9 servings

Cranberry-Apple Pudding

This is another variation of the preceding cottage pudding.

medium apples   *4 or 5*
fresh cranberries   *1 cup (225 ml)*
raisins   *½ cup (110 ml)*
sugar   *1¼ cups (280 ml)*
flour   *1 tablespoon (15 ml)*
cinnamon
Cottage Pudding (preceding)   *1 recipe*

Peel and slice the apples into a greased 9″ square (2 l) cake pan. Cover with the
cranberries and raisins. Mix together sugar and flour and sprinkle over fruit.
Sprinkle lightly with cinnamon. Cover with Cottage Pudding batter. Cook at
375°F (190°C) for 30 minutes. May be served warm with whipped cream or ice
cream.

Yield: 6 large servings

Apple Crumb

This is one of my husband's favourites for he says he always likes "crumby"
desserts.

Fill a buttered shallow baking dish with sliced, peeled tart apples. Add sugar to taste, according to the number of apples used. Sprinkle with cinnamon. Mix together:

brown sugar   1 cup (225 ml)
flour   ¾ cup (170 ml)
Cut in:
butter   3 tablespoons (45 ml)

Crumble finely and spread over the apples. Bake, covered, in a 425°F (220°C) oven for 10 minutes, then uncovered in a 325°F (165°C) oven for 20 minutes. Serve warm with cream or butterscotch or lemon sauce.

Yield: 6 to 8 servings

Bread Pudding

This pudding was an old-time standby for our grandmothers. It was sometimes called Poor Man's Pudding because of the economy of the ingredients called for. Raisins might or might not be added according to the budget, but we much prefer them to be included.

eggs   2
small bread cubes   2 cups (450 ml)
milk   2 cups (450 ml)
sugar   1/3 cup (75 ml)
salt   ¼ teaspoon (1 ml)
nutmeg   ¼ teaspoon (1 ml)
vanilla   1½ teaspoons (7.5 ml)
raisins   ½ cup (110 ml)

Beat the eggs until fluffy. Add the sugar, salt, and vanilla and beat until thick. Stir in the milk, bread, nutmeg, and raisins. Pour into a greased casserole. Set pudding in a pan filled with 1″ (2.5 cm) of hot water. Bake at 350°F (175°C) for 50 to 55 minutes or until a knife blade inserted in the middle of the pudding comes out clean. Serve chilled with whipped cream.

Yield: 5 servings

Peach Cobbler

When peaches come into season, this dessert is a must.

butter   ¼ cup (55 ml)
shortening   2 tablespoons (30 ml)
white sugar   ½ cup (110 ml)
egg   1
flour   1 cup (225 ml)
baking powder   3 teaspoons (15 ml)
salt   pinch
milk   ½ cup (110 ml)
sliced peaches   2 cups (450 ml)
brown sugar   ¾ cup (170 ml)
cinnamon   1 teaspoon (5 ml)

Melt the butter in a 9″ square (2 l) cake pan. Cream together the shortening, sugar, and egg. Sift the dry ingredients and mix into the creamed mixture alternately with the milk. Mix the peaches, brown sugar, and cinnamon thoroughly until juice is blended with sugar. Spread evenly over butter in bottom of pan. Spread the batter over the fruit. Bake at 350°F (175°C) for 1 hour. Serve warm with whipped cream.

Yield: 6 to 8 servings

Applesauce Gingerbread

This is especially good served with liquid honey or Lemon Sauce (page 129).

shortening   1/3 cup (75 ml)
egg   1
brown sugar   1/3 cup (75 ml)
molasses   ½ cup (110 ml)
flour   1¾ cups (395 ml)
baking soda   ¾ teaspoon (4 ml)
baking powder   1 teaspoon (5 ml)
salt   ½ teaspoon (2.5 ml)
cinnamon   1 teaspoon (5 ml)
ginger   1 teaspoon (5 ml)
nutmeg   ½ teaspoon (2.5 ml)
sweetened applesauce   ¾ cup (170 ml)

Cream the shortening; add the sugar and the molasses, beating until fluffy. Add the egg and beat well. Sift the dry ingredients and add alternately with the applesauce. Bake in an 8″ square (2 l) well-greased cake pan in a 350°F (175°C) oven for 50 minutes. Serve hot and buttered with sauce of your choice.

Yield: 9 servings

Fruit Shortcake

This light and tasty shortcake may be used with any desired sweetened fruit.

    flour   2 cups (450 ml)
    baking powder   4 teaspoons (20 ml)
    salt   ¾ teaspoon (4 ml)
    sugar   1/3 cup (75 ml)
    butter   4 tablespoons (60 ml)
    milk   2/3 cup (150 ml)
    egg   1

Sift the dry ingredients. With a pastry blender or 2 knives cut in butter until particles resemble coarse meal. Mix together the egg and milk and stir into the dry ingredients with a fork, just until moistened. Turn out on a slightly floured board and knead just until smooth. Roll out ¾″ (1.90 cm) thick and cut into individual shortcakes with a floured cutter. Brush over the tops with melted butter or milk. Bake at 425°F (220°C) for 12 to 15 minutes. Split and serve warm with butter and desired fruit. Garnish with whipped cream.

Yield: 12 shortcakes

Apple Tapioca

Apples were one of the fruits our pioneer forebears had plenty of, so they devised countless ways of cooking them. This recipe dates back to the mid-1800s.

    tapioca   ½ cup (110 ml)
    medium cooking apples   6
    salt   pinch
    sugar   ¾ cup (170 ml)
    lemon juice   2 teaspoons (10 ml)
    cinnamon

Soak the tapioca overnight. Early in the day, butter thickly a 1½-quart (2 l) baking dish. Peel, core, and quarter the apples and lay in the dish. Pour the drained tapioca over, mixing it gently through the fruit. Sprinkle with salt and add enough water until the tapioca is covered. Place in a 375°F (190°C) oven and cook for ½ hour. Add ½ cup (110 ml) sugar and stir gently to prevent the tapioca from caking. Allow to cook another ½ hour and add ¼ cup (55 ml) sugar and the lemon juice and sprinkle with cinnamon. Stir gently, being careful not to break the apples. Allow to cook for another 15 minutes or until the tapioca is clear and tender. Chill before serving with or without cream.

Yield: 8 servings

Johnny Cake

An old time favourite! Serve it hot with butter and lots of fresh maple syrup.

```
flour     1 cup (225 ml)
sugar     1/3 cup (75 ml)
baking soda     1 teaspoon (5 ml)
baking powder     2 teaspoons (10 ml)
salt     ½ teaspoon (2.5 ml)
yellow cornmeal     1 cup (225 ml)
egg, beaten     1
sour milk     1 cup (225 ml)
cooking oil     ¼ cup (55 ml)
```

Sift the dry ingredients, except the corn meal. Mix in the corn meal. Stir together the beaten egg, milk, and oil, then mix them with the dry ingredients only until moistened. Pour into a greased 8″ square (2 l) square cake pan. Bake at 375°F (190°C) for 25 to 30 minutes. Serve hot.

Yield: 9 servings

Lemon Squares

An excellent lemon dessert that bakes to a golden brown.

```
baking soda     ½ teaspoon (2.5 ml)
sifted flour     1 cup (225 ml)
butter, melted     ½ cup (110 ml)
brown sugar     ¾ cup (170 ml)
soda crackers, rolled fine     1 cup (225 ml)
coconut     1 cup (225 ml)
lemon pie filling     1 package
```

Mix the soda with the flour and stir in the sugar, cracker crumbs, coconut, and melted butter. Blend thoroughly. Put ¾ of the crumb mixture in a greased 9″ square (2 l) cake pan. Make a lemon pie filling and allow to cool for 5 minutes. Pour over crumbs and spread evenly. Cover with remaining crumbs. Bake at 350°F (175°C) for 20 minutes. Chill before serving in squares.

Yield: 8 servings

Date Pudding

This pudding bakes to a crunchy, golden top.

        eggs   2
        brown sugar   ¼ cup (55 ml)
        white sugar   ¼ cup (55 ml)
        chopped dates   2/3 cup (150 ml)
        chopped nuts   ¼ cup (55 ml)
        milk   1 cup (225 ml)
        fine bread crumbs   1 cup (225 ml)
        salt   ¼ teaspoon (1 ml)
        nutmeg   ¼ teaspoon (1 ml)
        baking powder   1 teaspoon (5 ml)
        vanilla   1 teaspoon (5 ml)
        whipped cream

Beat the eggs and gradually add the sugars. Stir in the dates and nuts. Combine the crumbs, salt, nutmeg, and baking powder. Add alternately with the milk to the creamed mixture. Stir in the vanilla. Pour into a greased casserole dish and bake at 350°F (175°C) for 45 minutes. Cool and serve topped with whipped cream.

Yield: 5 servings

• MILK DESSERTS •

Floating Island

        milk   2 cups (450 ml)
        eggs, separated   4
        sugar   4 tablespoons (60 ml)
        salt   ¼ teaspoon (1 ml)
        vanilla   1 teaspoon (5 ml)
        sugar for meringue   4 tablespoons (60 ml)
        fresh strawberries   2 cups (450 ml)

Heat the milk in the top of a double boiler over boiling water. Mix together the egg yolks, sugar, and salt and stir in a little hot milk. Then add egg mixture to remaining hot milk, stirring constantly over boiling water until mixture thickens enough to coat the spoon. Add vanilla and chill. Pour the cooled custard into serving dishes. Drop 2 cups (450 ml) fresh strawberries, halved, into custard around sides of dish. Top with cooled meringues for floating islands.

MERINGUES:

Beat the egg whites until foamy; slowly add sugar. Continue to beat until very stiff. Lower heaping tablespoons (30 ml) of beaten whites into a saucepan of hot water. Cover pan and simmer over a low heat for 1 minute or until meringue doubles in size. Remove with slotted spoon and place on a cake rack to drain for 15 minutes. Arrange on chilled custard.

Yield: 8 servings

Orange Custard

Make a soft custard as directed in Floating Island, preceding, but flavour with coconut extract instead of vanilla. Peel and cut up two oranges into bite-sized pieces in a bowl. Sprinkle with coconut and pour chilled custard over all. Arrange meringues on top as in Floating Island.

Trifle

      stale cake
      fruit juice   ½ cup (110 ml)
      jam or jelly   ½ cup (110 ml)
      peach halves or other fresh or canned fruit   8
      soft custard as in Floating Island   2 cups (450 ml)

Divide cake into 8 individual serving dishes or sherbets. Sprinkle with fruit juice and dot with jam or jelly. Add fruit cut in large pieces. Pour cooled custard over all. Top with meringues as in Floating Island or serve with whipped cream.

Yield: 8 servings

Self-frosting Lemon Pudding

      grated rind and juice of 1 lemon
      sugar   1 cup (225 ml)
      eggs, separated   3
      butter, melted   1 tablespoon (15 ml)
      flour   2 tablespoons (30 ml)
      milk   1 cup (225 ml)

Mix the flour, sugar, grated rind, juice, butter, and egg yolks. Add milk. Fold in beaten egg whites. Bake in a pudding dish set in hot water at 350°F (175°C) for 45 minutes.

Yield: 6 servings

Caramel Pudding

Use your imagination to dress this up with fruit or whipped cream and make it into a fancy sherbet.

    brown sugar   ¾ cup (170 ml)
    boiling water   ½ cup (110 ml)
    white sugar   ¼ cup (55 ml)
    cornstarch   3 tablespoons (45 ml)
    salt   ¼ teaspoon (1 ml)
    hot milk   1¼ cups (280 ml)
    hot water   1¼ cups (280 ml)
    vanilla   ½ teaspoon (2.5 ml)

Cook the brown sugar over medium heat until it has thoroughly melted, being careful not to let it scorch. Slowly add the boiling water and stir until dissolved. Mix together the white sugar, cornstarch, and salt and stir it into the milk in the top of a double boiler. Add the hot water and stir over hot water until thickened. Stir in the caramel syrup. Cover and cook, stirring occasionally, for 20 minutes. Remove from heat and add vanilla. Serve chilled.

Yield: 6 servings

Snow Pudding

This is quick to make and nice to serve with a variety of fruit placed on top of the pudding with the sauce poured over.

    milk   2 cups (450 ml)
    cornstarch   3 tablespoons (45 ml)
    sugar   ½ cup (110 ml)
    egg whites, beaten stiff   2
    salt   ¼ teaspoon (1 ml)

Heat the milk and add the sugar and salt. Thicken with the cornstarch mixed with a little cold milk. Remove from heat and fold in the beaten egg whites. Set aside while you make the sauce.

SAUCE:

    milk   1½ cups (335 ml)
    salt   1/8 teaspoon (0.5 ml)
    vanilla   ½ teaspoon (2.5 ml)
    cornstarch   1½ tablespoons (22.5 ml)
    sugar   1/3 cup (75 ml)
    egg yolks, beaten   2

Heat the milk with the sugar. Add the salt. Mix the yolks with cornstarch and a little cold milk. Add a little of the hot mixture to the yolk mixture and then turn into the milk mixture to thicken. Stir until thickened but do not boil. Remove from heat and add the vanilla. Chill both the sauce and the pudding. Serve in individual dessert dishes, pouring the sauce over the pudding.

Yield: 6 servings

Butterscotch Pudding

My family rates this pudding "excellent". It is full-bodied and rich.

>white sugar   *3 tablespoons (45 ml)*
>butter   *1 tablespoon (15 ml)*
>milk   *1½ cups (335 ml)*
>brown sugar   *1/3 cup (75 ml)*
>flour   *2 tablespoons (30 ml)*
>salt   *1/3 teaspoon (2 ml)*
>egg yolks or 1 whole egg   *2*

Heat the white sugar slowly until melted and golden brown, then add the butter. Scald the milk by heating slowly to just below the boil. Mix the brown sugar, flour, salt, and egg together. Add scalded milk to caramelized sugar very slowly, stirring constantly. Thicken with egg mixture. Chill and serve with whipped cream.

Yield: 4 servings

• TAPIOCA PUDDINGS •

Tapioca Cream

>eggs, well beaten   *2*
>instant tapioca   *3 tablespoons (45 ml)*
>sugar   *2/3 cup (150 ml)*
>milk   *4 cups (1 l)*
>salt   *1/8 teaspoon (0.5 ml)*
>vanilla   *¾ teaspoon (4 ml)*

Combine all the ingredients but the vanilla in a saucepan or double boiler and cook 12 to 14 minutes, stirring constantly until thickened. Remove from heat. Stir in vanilla. Chill before serving.

CHOCOLATE MARBLE PARFAIT:

Mix 3 tablespoons (45 ml) cocoa, 1 tablespoon (15 ml) butter, and enough boiling water just to dissolve. Divide Tapioca Cream in half and stir chocolate mixture into one half. In parfait glasses, alternate layers of chocolate and vanilla cream. Top with whipped cream.

Tapioca Soufflé

instant tapioca   3 tablespoons (45 ml)
sugar   1/3 cup (75 ml)
salt   pinch
egg, separated   1
milk   2 cups (450 ml)
butterscotch flavouring   ½ teaspoon (2.5 ml)

Combine all the ingredients except the egg white and flavouring in the top of a double boiler. Cook for 15 minutes, stirring often. Beat egg white until stiff and fold into tapioca mixture. Add flavouring and chill. Serve garnished with whipped cream, if desired.

Yield: 5 servings

Chocolate Tapioca

This recipe came from the recipe book of the late Mrs. Duncan Hough of Sillsville, Ontario. When I make it, my son says, "Ummmmmm, I may just eat the whole dish!"
Soak overnight:

whole tapioca   ½ cup (110 ml)
water   2 cups (450 ml)
(or use 1/3 cup (75 ml) instant tapioca and do not soak).

In the morning, drain off the water and add 2 cups (450 ml) of hot milk and cook in the top of a double boiler over boiling water for 1 hour or until tapioca is clear. Then add and stir well:

sugar   1/3 cup (75 ml)
vanilla   1 teaspoon (5 ml)
cocoa   3 tablespoons (45 ml)
salt   ¼ teaspoon (1 ml)

Remove from heat and fold in:
2 egg whites, beaten stiff with 1 tablespoon (15 ml) sugar. Chill and serve with cream, jelly, or whipped cream.

Yield: 6 servings

Creamy Rice Pudding

If your family likes rice pudding, then this is an easy one to make. Try serving it with a little maple syrup poured over it.

> rice   *3 tablespoons (45 ml)*
> sugar   *4 tablespoons (60 ml)*
> milk   *4 cups (1 l)*
> salt   *½ teaspoon (2.5 ml)*
> nutmeg   *½ teaspoon (2.5 ml)*
> raisins   *2/3 cup (150 ml)*
> butter   *1 tablespoon (15 ml)*
> vanilla   *½ teaspoon (2.5 ml)*

Stir all the ingredients together and pour into a greased baking dish. Bake at 325°F (165°C) for 2 hours, stirring several times.

Yield: 6 servings

• STEAMED PUDDINGS •

Christmas Pudding (Vegetable Pudding)

This was called Vegetable Pudding in my mother's book, but to me it is the very essence of Christmas, for that was the only time it was ever made in our house. Serve it warm, with a butterscotch sauce.

```
sugar      1 cup (225 ml)
eggs      2
raisins      1 cup (225 ml)
currants      1 cup (225 ml)
mixed minced peel      1 cup (225 ml)
bread crumbs      1 cup (225 ml)
molasses      ½ cup (110 ml)
salt      1 ¼ teaspoons (6 ml)
sifted pastry flour      4 cups (1 l)
pastry spice      1 tablespoon (15 ml)
soda      2 teaspoons (10 ml)
ground suet      2 cups (450 ml)
finely ground potatoes      1 cup (225 ml)
finely ground apples      1 cup (225 ml)
finely ground carrots      1 cup (225 ml)
```

Sift the flour, soda, salt, and spices. Dust the raisins, currants, and mixed peel with a little of the flour. Mix together all the recipe ingredients except the dusted fruits, which should be gently stirred in last. Grease a 2-quart (2.5 l) pudding dish and line it with greased wax paper. Pour in the pudding mixture and steam 4 hours. Serve warm in slices with sauce. This may be stored, well-wrapped, in your refrigerator for 6 weeks or frozen indefinitely.

Suet Pudding

This pudding is easy to make and will keep in your refrigerator for a week or indefinitely in your freezer. Serve it with a butterscotch or lemon sauce.

```
eggs      2
molasses      ½ cup (110 ml)
ground suet      1 cup (large) (275 ml)
flour      3 cups (675 ml)
baking powder      2 teaspoons (10 ml)
pastry spice      1 dessertspoon (12 ml)
salt      1 teaspoon (5 ml)
milk to make a stiff batter
raisins (optional)
```

Beat the eggs and molasses together. Beat in the suet. Sift the dry ingredients and add alternately with the milk. Lastly add floured raisins, if desired. Place in greased pudding dish, cover tightly with waxed paper and steam 2 hours. Cut in slices and serve warm with sauce.

Yield: 8 to 10 servings

Raisin Roly Poly

This pudding is equally good served with either a lemon sauce or the special raisin sauce that follows the recipe.

flour   2 cups (450 ml)
sugar   2 tablespoons (30 ml)
baking powder   4 teaspoons (20 ml)
salt   1 teaspoon (5 ml)
shortening   ¼ cup (55 ml)
milk   ¾ cup (170 ml)
raisins   1 cup (225 ml)
brown sugar   3 tablespoons (45 ml)
cinnamon

Sift the first four ingredients into a mixing bowl. Cut in the shortening until crumbly. Add the milk and stir in lightly with a fork, only until dry ingredients are moistened. Turn out on a lightly floured board and knead a few times. Roll out into a 9 X 8" (22.86 X 20.32 cm) rectangle. Spread with soft butter, scatter the raisins, evenly over dough. Sprinkle cinnamon and sugar over all. Roll as a jelly roll. Pinch ends together well. Place seam side down on a pie plate and steam 40 minutes. Slice and serve hot with Butterscotch Raisin Sauce.

BUTTERSCOTCH RAISIN SAUCE:

water   1½ cups (335 ml)
lightly packed brown sugar   ¾ cup (170 ml)
raisins   ½ cup (110 ml)
cloves   ¼ teaspoon (1 ml)
cornstarch   1½ tablespoons (22.5 ml)
lemon juice   1½ teaspoons (7.5 ml)

Boil the water, sugar, raisins, and cloves together for 2 to 3 minutes. Thicken with the cornstarch mixed with a little water to dissolve. Remove from heat and add lemon juice.

Yield: 8 servings

St. James' Pudding

This dessert is feathery in texture and spicy in flavour.

flour   1-2/3 cups (375 ml)
salt   ¼ teaspoon (1 ml)
cloves   ¼ teaspoon (1 ml)
allspice, nutmeg   ½ teaspoon (2.5 ml) each
baking soda   ½ teaspoon (2.5 ml)
raisins   1 cup (225 ml)
melted butter   3 tablespoons (45 ml)
molasses   ½ cup (110 ml)
milk   ½ cup (110 ml)

Sift the dry ingredients together. Stir in the raisins. Mix the molasses, milk, and butter together and add to the dry ingredients, stirring until blended. Pour into a greased mould, cover with waxed paper, and steam 2½ hours. Serve hot with sweet sauce of choice.

Yield: 8 servings

Golden Pudding

This dessert is light in texture, and marmalade gives it its flavour.

butter   ¼ cup (55 ml)
sugar   ½ cup (110 ml)
eggs   2
flour   1 cup (225 ml)
baking soda   ½ teaspoon (2.5 ml)
salt   ¼ teaspoon (1 ml)
milk   ¼ cup (55 ml)
marmalade   2 tablespoons (30 ml)

Cream the butter, eggs, and sugar. Sift the dry ingredients and add to the egg mixture alternately with the milk. Beat in the marmalade. Steam in a covered and greased mould for 1½ hours. Serve warm with any tangy sauce.

Yield: 6 to 8 servings

Ginger Pudding

Light and tender with the tang of ginger.

shortening   ¼ cup (55 ml)
sugar   ½ cup (110 ml)
egg   1
milk   1 cup (225 ml)
sifted pastry flour   2½ cups (560 ml)

baking powder   *3 teaspoons (15 ml)*
salt   *¾ teaspoon (4 ml)*
ginger   *2 teaspoons (10 ml)*

Cream the shortening, sugar, and egg together. Sift the dry ingredients and mix into the creamed mixture alternately with the milk. Pour into a greased mould, cover with waxed paper or foil, and steam for 1½ hours. Serve warm with Lemon Sauce (page 129).

Yield: 8 servings

Six-cup Pudding

This recipe came from my stepmother, Mrs. Helen Vannest of Mississauga, Ontario. It is a light and spicy pudding that may be varied with different fruits.

bread crumbs   *1 cup (225 ml)*
brown sugar   *1 cup (225 ml)*
chopped suet   *1 cup (225 ml)*
flour   *1 cup (225 ml)*
fruit (apples, raisins, etc.)   *1 cup (225 ml)*
buttermilk or sour milk   *1 cup (225 ml)*
baking soda   *1 teaspoon (5 ml)*
salt   *½ teaspoon (2.5 ml)*
cloves, ginger, and nutmeg   *½ teaspoon (2.5 ml), each*

Mix the sugar, suet, and crumbs together. Sift the dry ingredients and mix into first mixture alternately with the milk. Stir in chopped fruit of choice (I like to use apples). Pour into a greased pudding dish and steam for 2 hours. Serve warm with lemon, custard, or caramel sauce.

Yield: 6 to 8 servings

• **REFRIGERATOR DESSERTS** •

Lime Jelly Cake

A delightfully fresh-tasting, light dessert.

lime gelatin   *3-ounce package (85 g)*
sugar   *½ cup (110 ml)*
boiling water   *1 cup (225 ml)*
evaporated milk, well chilled   *¾ cup (170 ml)*
lemon or lime juice   *2 tablespoons (30 ml)*

Mix the gelatin with the sugar and boiling water until thoroughly dissolved. Allow to partially set. Whip the evaporated milk with the fruit juice, fold into the gelatin mixture, and whip together. Add green colouring if necessary. Pour into graham crust.

CRUST:

graham crackers   *25*
sugar   *½ cup (110 ml)*
melted butter   *½ cup (110 ml)*

Roll the crackers into fine crumbs and mix with the sugar and butter. Press into bottom of a 9″ square (2 l) greased cake pan, saving some for the top. Pour in gelatin mixture and top with remaining crumbs. Chill several hours before serving. Cut in squares.

Yield: 6 large or 8 small servings

Fruit Torte

I make this in a 10″ (25.40 cm) round shallow pan that has a raised section in the middle, but any large shallow pan would do. It's a luscious-looking dessert and may be cut into pie-shaped wedges.

golden or vanilla single layer cake mix   *1*

Make up cake as directed. Make 6 medium muffins of part of the batter and pour the rest into a well-greased and floured pan. Bake at 350°F (175°C) for 20 minutes. Set aside the muffins for another use. Turn out torte cake and allow to cool thoroughly. Make the following glaze:

fruit juice   *1 cup (225 ml)*
sugar   *¼ cup (55 ml)*
cornstarch   *1 tablespoon (15 ml)*
fresh or canned fruit

Mix together the juice and sugar and bring to a boil, then thicken with cornstarch dissolved in a small amount of water. Allow the glaze to cool for 10 to 15 minutes. Spread a thin layer over the cake, then cover the top with any fresh or well-drained canned fruits arranged in a pattern. I usually use peach halves, pineapple chunks, bananas, strawberries, and seeded grapes. Pour the rest of the glaze over the fruit, covering it well. Instead of fresh fruit, any fruit pie filling may be used. Garnish with whipped cream before serving.

Yield: 8 servings

Maple Bisque

I usually make this dessert with whipped topping instead of whipped cream to save on calories. It looks very festive if set in a fancy mould, garnished with nuts and a few maraschino cherries and served at the table.

    unflavoured gelatin   *2½ teaspoons (12.5 ml)*
    maple syrup or maple-flavoured syrup   *5 fluid ounces (150 ml)*
    egg, well beaten   *1*
    whipped topping   *2-ounce package (58 g)*
    or
    whipping cream, whipped   *1 cup (225 ml)*
    chopped walnuts   *½ cup (110 ml)*

Mix the gelatin with just enough cold water to dissolve it. Stir it into the maple syrup along with the beaten egg. Cook on the stove just until the mixture comes to a boil. Cool until syrupy. Prepare whipped topping or cream. Fold in syrup mixture and walnuts. Pour into individual sherbets or a mould and garnish as desired.

Yield: 4 servings

Orange Velvet Jelly Cream

This creamy dessert, with a hint of pineapple, looks particularly nice served in sherbet glasses, although it may be made in a mould and served at the table.

    orange gelatin   *3-ounce package (85 g)*
    pineapple juice   *1 cup (225 ml)*
    sugar   *1/3 cup (75 ml)*
    milk   *1 cup (225 ml)*
    cream, whipped   *2/3 cup (150 ml)*
    coconut   *¾ cup (170 ml)*
    drained crushed pineapple
    red and green maraschino cherries
    finely chopped nuts

Dissolve the gelatin and sugar in hot pineapple juice. Chill until slightly thickened. Add milk and chill again until slightly set. Whip cream, add coconut, and fold into gelatin mixture. Chill until firm in a 5 cup (1.13 l) mould. If desired, put drained pineapple in the bottom of a sherbet. Sprinkle with nuts and cut red and green cherries. Pour above mixture on top.

Yield: 6 large servings

Judge Peters' Pudding

This recipe came from the recipe book of the late Mrs. E.H. Wright of Conway, Ontario. It can be made in a mould, garnished with whipped cream, and served at the table, but I like to layer it with the whipped cream in parfait glasses. The original recipe called for unflavoured gelatin, 2 cups of sugar and 2 lemons, chopped. I find using lemon gelatin is a good substitute.

> lemon gelatin   *3-ounce package (85 g)*
> sugar   *1/3 cup (75 ml)*
> water   *2 cups (450 ml)*
> bananas   *2*
> chopped fruit and grated rind of 1 orange
> chopped walnuts   *1/3 cup (75 ml)*
> figs   *5*
> dates   *10*
> dessert topping   *2-ounce package (58 g)*
> *or*
> whipping cream,   *¾ cup (170 ml)*

Dissolve the gelatin and sugar in 1 cup (225 ml) boiling water. Add the remaining cold water and allow to set until mixture is beginning to thicken. Chop the figs and dates a little and add with nuts to the gelatin. At this point either pour into a mould or layer with the whipped topping or cream in parfait glasses. Chill well before serving.

Yield: 6 servings

• FROZEN DESSERTS •

Lemon Sherbet

This recipe came from the cookbook of the late Mrs. E.H. Wright of Conway, Ontario. Until the days of refrigerator freezers, these desserts could only be made in the winter months.

milk   *4 cups (1 l)*
sugar   *1½ cups (335 ml)*
lemon juice   *8 tablespoons (120 ml)*
yellow food colouring

Mix the juice and the sugar, then slowly add the milk and food colouring, stirring constantly to prevent the mixture from curdling. Freeze in ice-cube trays until just firm. Turn into bowl and beat until slushy but not thawed. Pour into freezer container and return quickly to freezer. Freeze until hard.

Yield: 1 quart (1.13 l)

From the above recipe, I have made several variations using the same method of preparation.

Lime Sherbet

lime juice   *¼ cup (55 ml)*
sugar   *¾ cup (170 ml)*
milk   *2 cups (450 ml)*
green food colouring

Prepare as for Lemon Sherbet.

Yield: 1 pint (565 ml)

Pineapple Sherbet

pineapple juice   *1 cup (225 ml)*
sugar   *2/3 cup (150 ml)*
lemon juice   *½ tablespoon (7.5 ml)*
milk   *2 cups (450 ml)*
yellow food colouring

Prepare as for Lemon Sherbet.

Yield: 1½ pints (848 ml)

Vanilla Ice Cream

My sister and I used to freeze this ice cream, in an ice freezer, almost every weekend in the winter months. It is the best ice cream I have ever eaten and the three quarts it made disappeared in the same number of days. My mother made it with half heavy cream so it was very rich and it used to coat your spoon as you ate it. Sometimes we used to top it with corn syrup but more often with maple syrup. I have discovered you can make it in smaller quantities in your refrigerator freezer with excellent results, although nothing will ever touch the flavour and texture of the rich ice cream made in the ice freezer of my childhood.

cornstarch   *2/3 tablespoon (10 ml)*
milk   *1-2/3 cups (375 ml)*
cream   *1-2/3 cups (375 ml)*
egg   *1*
sugar   *1 cup (225 ml)*
salt   *1 teaspoon (5 ml)*
vanilla   *1 teaspoon (5 ml)*

Place the milk, cream, sugar, and salt in the top of a double boiler. Beat the egg well and add the cornstarch and a little cold milk to mix smoothly. Add a little of the hot milk and stir into the egg mixture. Add egg mixture to hot milk, stirring constantly. Continue to cook until thickened, stirring constantly. Remove from heat and mix in the vanilla. Cool and pour into ice-cube trays to freeze. When just frozen but not hard, turn into a bowl and beat with mixer at highest speed until smooth but not melted. Pour into freezer container and return quickly to freezer, freezing until hard.

Yield: 1 quart (1.13 l)

VARIATIONS:

Nuts and fruits or various flavourings may be added to the custard after it cools and before it is frozen. Chocolate may be added for chocolate ice cream.

FOR A 3-QUART (3.39l) FREEZER:

cornstarch   *2 tablespoons (30 ml)*
milk   *¾ quart (848 ml)*
cream   *¾ quart (848 ml)*
eggs   *3*
sugar   *3 cups (675 ml)*
salt   *3 teaspoons (15 ml)*
vanilla or desired flavouring   *3 teaspoons (15 ml)*

Follow directions for cooking as above and freeze in an ice freezer.

Maple Mousse

This recipe came from the book of the late Mrs. E.H. Wright, Conway, Ontario. It is a delicious hot-weather dessert.

    unflavoured gelatin   *2 teaspoons (10 ml)*
    cold water   *2 tablespoons (30 ml)*
    maple syrup   *1 cup (225 ml)*
    whipped cream   *2 cups (450 ml)*
    chopped walnuts   *1 cup (225 ml)*

Dissolve the gelatin in the cold water. Heat over boiling water until gelatin dissolves. Stir into the maple syrup. Fold the syrup and nuts into the whipped cream and pour into a mould. Freeze hard before serving.

Yield: 6 servings

● **SWEET SAUCES** ●

Well-chosen sweet sauces can enhance the flavour of any dessert. Our grandmothers were experts at dressing up everyday dishes, specially steamed puddings, with sauces or "dressings", as they sometimes called them.

Lemon Sauce

    sugar   *½ cup (110 ml)*
    boiling water   *1 cup (225 ml)*
    cornstarch   *1 tablespoon (15 ml)*
    salt   *pinch*
    butter   *1 tablespoon (15 ml)*
    lemon juice   *2 tablespoons (30 ml)*

Caramelize the sugar slightly if desired. Add the water slowly. Thicken with cornstarch dissolved in a little water. Remove from heat. Add the salt, butter, and lemon juice. Stir until butter is melted. Serve warm.

Yield: 1¼ cups (280 ml)

Butterscotch Sauce

    brown sugar   *¾ cup (170 ml)*
    water   *1 cup (225 ml)*
    cornstarch   *1 tablespoon (15 ml)*
    salt   *pinch*
    butter   *1 tablespoon (15 ml)*
    vanilla   *1 teaspoon (5 ml)*

Mix together the sugar and water and bring to a boil. Dissolve the cornstarch in a little cold water and stir into the first mixture to thicken. Remove from heat, add the remaining ingredients and stir well. Serve warm.

Yield: 1½ cups (335 ml)

Milk Sauce

In our family, this became known as "crumby milk" because of the nutmeg. It is nice served on apple puddings and Cottage Pudding.

milk   *1 cup (225 ml)*
brown sugar   *1/3 cup (75 ml)*
vanilla   *¾ teaspoon (4 ml)*
nutmeg   *dash*

Mix until the sugar is dissolved and serve chilled.

Yield: 1¼ cups (280 ml)

Blueberry Sauce (Frozen)

Early settlers called them whortleberries and hurtleberries. Around Napanee, we always called them huckleberries. Try serving this sauce with waffles, pancakes, ice cream, or puddings.

frozen sweetened blueberries   *3 cups (675 ml)*
cornstarch   *3 tablespoons (45 ml)*
sugar   *7/8 cup (210 ml)*
water   *½ cup (110 ml)*
lemon juice   *3 tablespoons (45 ml)*
nutmeg (optional)   *½ teaspoon (2.5 ml)*

Mix sugar with the cornstarch. Stir into frozen berries in a saucepan and add the water. Bring to a boil, breaking up the berries with a fork. Stir gently until sauce thickens, being careful not to break the berries. Remove from heat and add the lemon juice and optional nutmeg.

Yield: 3 cups (675 ml)

Cherry Sauce

There are endless ways to use this sauce, but try it over Cottage Pudding. It's an easy way to dress up an everyday dessert.

canned tart pie cherries, drained   *1 cup (225 ml)*
juice from cherries plus water to make 1½ cups (335 ml)
sugar   *½ cup (110 ml)*
cornstarch   *2 tablespoons (30 ml)*
almond flavouring   *½ teaspoon (2.5 ml)*
red food colouring

Combine the sugar and cornstarch in a saucepan. Stir cherry juice into the
cornstarch mixture. Cook until thick. Stir in the cherries, flavouring, and food
colouring. Bring just to a boil, then cool.

Yield: 2 cups (450 ml)

Vanilla Sauce

sugar   *½ cup (110 ml)*
water   *1 cup (225 ml)*
cornstarch   *1 tablespoon (15 ml)*
salt   *pinch*
butter   *1 tablespoon (15 ml)*
vanilla   *¾ teaspoon (4 ml)*

Mix the sugar, cornstarch, and salt with the water. Bring to a boil, stirring
constantly until smooth and thick. Remove from heat and add vanilla and butter.
Cool.

Yield: 1¼ cups (280 ml)

teapot c. 1880 –1900

CAKES,
FROSTINGS, AND FILLINGS

"CANADA IS THE land of cakes. A tea-table is generally furnished with several varieties of cakes and preserves." So observes Mrs. Catharine Parr Traill in her *Female Emigrants Guide* of 1854.

The earliest cakes consisted of bread dough to which fruit or other ingredients were added, the forerunners of today's fancy breads. Later recipes called for wine or brandy and for many eggs, which supplied the leavening for fruitcakes or poundcakes. Cream of tartar and baking soda were used as they became available to the settlers, and around the turn of the 20th century, baking powder was introduced. Because butter and eggs were in plentiful supply in the farm kitchen, cake recipes became very rich, calling for large quantities of both. A lemon cake recipe of the 1850s called for 6 eggs, 3 cups sugar, and 1 cup butter. Sometimes lard was used as part of the shortening. All the fat that could be removed from the slaughtered pig was "tried" out, made into lard, and kept in stone jars.

Since most of the old recipes called for butter, which was salted, salt was either not called for or used in very small quantities.

Sugar, particularly white sugar, was expensive in the early days of

Upper Canada, and so brown sugar was used very often. The first sugar refinery in Canada was established in Montreal in 1854. Before that, refined sugar was imported from Britain. It came in the form of a conical "sugar loaf" weighing at least 14 pounds. For use, it had to be cut with sugar cutters, then crushed and rolled. Settlers relied on making great supplies of maple sugar, some farmers making as much as 400 to 500 pounds in one year. Sometimes honey, even wild honey, and molasses were used as sweetening.

The manufacture of maple syrup was bequeathed to us by the native people of North America. First, the tree was gashed, then a chip of wood inserted which carried the sap into a birch-bark bucket. Some tribes used earthenware pots to boil the sap, others dropped red-hot stones into the sap trough until the sap had reached syrup stage. They also made a small amount of sugar this way.

The settlers carried on in a similar fashion. Some used spiles in the trees and made their sap troughs out of pine, ash, cherry, or butternut logs, each holding three or four gallons of sap. The sap from the trees ran directly into these. They then boiled the sap down to either the syrup or sugar stage.

We are luckier than our grandmothers, who had to rely on elbow power to cream together the butter, sugar, and eggs for their cakes. Making a cake with an electric beater is quite a different story. It is important to have a thick and creamy mixture as a basis for your cake; in fact, I have discovered that you cannot really beat your shortening, sugar, and eggs too long. I let mine beat while I gather the other ingredients together, sift the dry ingredients, and grease the cake pans — probably at least 10 minutes or more. Always start mixing the dry ingredients in first, alternating with the liquid, but always ending with the dry ingredients. Don't overbeat at this stage; just mix well. If your recipe calls for fruit, save a little of the flour mixture to dust it with, then fold in the fruit at the end.

Before thermometers became standard equipment on ovens, housewives used to test the temperature of their oven by placing a piece of white paper in it. The oven was at the proper temperature to bake cake when the piece of paper turned yellow in five minutes.

Chiffon cakes contain both butter and beaten egg whites.

Cornstarch Cake

Cornstarch is corn flour in its starchy, rather than its granular form. It is the cornstarch that gives this cake its unique flavour.

> shortening   1/3 cup (75 ml)
> sugar   ¾ cup (170 ml)
> eggs, separated   2
> cornstarch   ½ cup (110 ml)
> sifted pastry flour   1 cup (225 ml)
> baking powder   3 teaspoons (15 ml)
> salt   ½ teaspoon (2.5 ml)
> milk   ½ cup (110 ml)
> vanilla   1 teaspoon (5 ml)

Beat the egg whites stiff and set aside. Cream the shortening and sugar, add the egg yolks, and beat until mixture is very creamy. Sift the dry ingredients and add alternately with the milk. Stir in the vanilla. Fold in the beaten egg whites. Bake in a 9″ (2 l) square greased cake pan at 350°F (175°C) for 45 to 50 minutes. Cool on a rack. Ice with a lemon butter icing.

Yield: 12 servings

Plain Chiffon Cake

This is a small cake. I like to use a strawberry whipped cream filling both to fill it and ice the top and sides.

> butter   ¼ cup (55 ml)
> sugar   ½ cup (110 ml)
> egg, separated   1
> sifted pastry flour   1-1/8 cups (253 ml)
> baking powder   2 teaspoons (10 ml)
> salt   ½ teaspoon (2.5 ml)
> milk   ½ cup (110 ml)
> vanilla   ¼ teaspoon (1 ml)

Beat the egg white stiff and set aside. Cream the butter, sugar, and egg yolk. Sift the dry ingredients and add alternately with the milk. Mix in the flavouring.

134

Fold in the stiffly beaten egg white. Bake in a waxed-paper lined 8″ (2 l) square cake pan at 350°F (175°C) for 25 minutes. Remove from pan and cool on a rack. Ice with a beaten icing or cut into two 4″ X 8″ (10 cm X 20 cm) rectangles and fill and ice with whatever desired. Cut in slices to serve.

Yield: 8 servings

Cocoa Layer Cake

Tastes like old-fashioned country chocolate cake!

> shortening   *½ cup (110 ml)*
> brown sugar   *1 cup (225 ml)*
> eggs, separated   *2*
> vanilla   *1 teaspoon (5 ml)*
> sour milk   *1 cup (225 ml)*
> sifted pastry flour   *2 cups (450 ml)*
> salt   *1 teaspoon (5 ml)*
> baking soda   *½ teaspoon (2.5 ml)*
> baking powder   *1½ teaspoons (7.5 ml)*
> cinnamon   *1 teaspoon (5 ml)*
> cocoa   *3 tablespoons (45 ml)*

Beat the egg whites until stiff but not dry. Cream the shortening, sugar, and egg yolks together. Add the vanilla. Sift together all the dry ingredients and add alternately with the sour milk. Fold in the beaten egg whites. Bake in greased layer pans at 350°F (175°C) for 30 to 35 minutes. Cool on racks. Fill with chocolate cream filling and frost with chocolate butter icing.

Jersey Lily Cake

I like to bake this in a long loaf pan and cut it in slices to serve.

> shortening   *½ cup (110 ml)*
> sugar   *1 cup (225 ml)*
> sifted pastry flour   *1¾ cups (395 ml)*
> baking powder   *2 teaspoons (10 ml)*
> salt   *¾ teaspoon (4 ml)*
> egg whites, beaten stiff   *2*
> milk   *1 cup (225 ml)*
> raisins   *½ cup (110 ml)*
> nuts   *½ cup (110 ml)*

Cream the shortening and sugar until light. Sift the dry ingredients and add alternately with the milk, mixing well. Fold in the beaten egg whites last. Grease and line the bottom of a loaf pan with waxed paper or an 8" square (2 l) cake pan. Put half the batter in pan, cover with raisins and nuts, then add rest of batter. Bake at 350°F (175°C) for 60 minutes in loaf pan or 40 minutes in square pan. Cool and ice.

● FAT CAKES ●

An old-fashioned name for ordinary cake that takes both shortening and whole eggs. Never grease the sides of a cake pan, only the bottom. The cake needs the ungreased sides of the pan to climb on.

King Edward Cake

This is a favourite of my daughter's and is especially good when teamed up with Maple Cream Icing.

    shortening   1/3 cup (75 ml)
    yellow sugar   1 cup (225 ml)
    egg yolks   2
    sifted pastry flour   2 cups (450 ml)
    baking soda   1 teaspoon (5 ml)
    baking powder   2 teaspoons (10 ml)
    salt   1 teaspoon (5 ml)
    cinnamon   1 teaspoon (5 ml)
    nutmeg   1 teaspoon (5 ml)
    floured raisins   ½ cup (110 ml)
    sour milk   1 cup (225 ml)

Cream the shortening and add the sugar, beating until fluffy. Add the yolks and mix well. Sift together the dry ingredients, using a little to flour the raisins. Add the dry ingredients alternately with the milk to the first mixture. Fold in the fruit. Bake in 8" (1.2 l) greased and floured layer cake pans at 350°F (175°C) for 30 to 35 minutes. Cool on racks. Fill and ice with Maple Cream or Sea Foam Beaten Icing.

Coffee Cake

Spices enhance the subtle flavour of coffee. The original recipe called for "strong" coffee. I like to add instant coffee for a better flavour.

    shortening   ½ cup (110 ml)
    sugar   1 cup (225 ml)

```
eggs    2
sifted pastry flour    2 cups (450 ml)
salt    1 teaspoon (5 ml)
cinnamon    1 teaspoon (5 ml)
nutmeg    ½ teaspoon (2.5 ml)
baking powder    3 teaspoons (15 ml)
milk    ¾ cup (170 ml)
coffee    ¼ cup (55 ml)
instant coffee    ½ teaspoon (2.5 ml)
```

Cream the shortening and beat in the sugar until fluffy. Add the eggs, beating well, until mixture is creamy. Sift the dry ingredients. Mix the liquid coffee with the milk and add alternately with the dry ingredients. Bake in a greased 8″ (2 l) square cake pan at 350°F (175°C) for 50 minutes. Cool on a rack. Ice with Mocha Icing.

Gold Cake

A really delicious golden yellow cake.

```
shortening    ¼ cup (55 ml)
sugar    ¾ cup (170 ml)
egg yolks    3
sifted pastry flour    1½ cups (335 ml)
baking powder    3 teaspoons (15 ml)
salt    ½ teaspoon (2.5 ml)
milk    ½ cup (110 ml)
vanilla    1 teaspoon (5 ml)
```

Cream shortening and sugar together. Add yolks and beat until very creamy. Sift the dry ingredients and add alternately with the milk. Add the flavouring. Bake in a greased 8″ (2 l) square cake pan at 350°F (175°C) for 35 to 40 minutes. Cool on a rack.

VARIATION:

MARGUERITES

These lemon-filled cupcakes are delicious at any time of day. Freeze them for ready use.

Prepare Gold Cake batter and fill 18 paper-lined muffin cups. Bake at 350°F (175°C) for 15 to 20 minutes. Cool. Prepare Lemon Filling. Cool. Cut a wedge from the top of each cupcake and fill with Lemon Filling. Replace wedge on top of cake and dust with icing sugar.

Yield: 1½ dozen 2″ (5 cm) cupcakes

Grandma Lawson's White Cake

This recipe of my great grandmother's turns out snowy white and light. Use the yolks to make Gold Cake.

shortening   ½ cup (110 ml)
sugar   1 cup (225 ml)
egg whites   3
sifted pastry flour   2 cups (450 ml)
baking powder   4 teaspoons (20 ml)
salt   1 teaspoon (5 ml)
milk   1 cup (225 ml)
lemon extract   1 teaspoon (5 ml)

Cream the shortening and sugar and add the egg whites. Beat until creamy. Sift the dry ingredients and add alternately with the milk. Stir in the flavouring. Bake in 8″ (1.2 l) greased layer cake pans in 350°F (175°C) oven for 30 minutes. Cool on racks. Fill with Lemon Filling and sprinkle icing sugar over the top.

Banana Cake

Have you ever tried freezing mashed bananas for use in later baking? Just mash as usual and freeze in quantities recipes call for. Thaw before using.

shortening   1/3 cup (75 ml)
sugar   1 cup (225 ml)
eggs   2
sifted pastry flour   2 cups (450 ml)
salt   1 teaspoon (5 ml)
baking powder   1½ teaspoons (7.5 ml)
baking soda   1 teaspoon (5 ml)
sour milk   ½ cup (110 ml)
mashed bananas   1 cup (225 ml)

Cream the shortening and the sugar until light. Beat in the eggs until mixture is very creamy. Sift the dry ingredients and add alternately with the mashed bananas and milk, blending well. Bake in two greased and floured 8″ (1.2 l) layer cake pans at 350°F (175°C) for 30 to 35 minutes. Cool on racks.

138

Spanish Bun

Cinnamon and molasses give this cake a spicy flavour. I like to bake it in a tube pan.

shortening   *1/3 cup (75 ml)*
egg yolks   *2*
brown sugar   *1 cup (225 ml)*
molasses   *2 tablespoons (30 ml)*
sifted pastry flour   *2 cups (450 ml)*
salt   *1 teaspoon (5 ml)*
cinnamon   *2 teaspoons (10 ml)*
baking powder   *4 teaspoons (20 ml)*
milk   *1 cup (225 ml)*

Cream the shortening; add the sugar and the eggs, beating until creamy. Add the molasses. Sift the dry ingredients and add alternately with the milk. Bake in a greased and floured 8″ (2 l) tube pan at 350°F (175°C) for 40 to 45 minutes. Cool on a rack. Ice with a beaten Mocha Icing, allowing it to dribble down the sides.

Orange Cake

This rich and delicious layer cake, with a moist and tender texture, is one of my father's favourites. Fill it with Orange Filling and frost with Orange Butter Icing.

shortening   *½ cup (110 ml)*
sugar   *1 cup (225 ml)*
eggs   *2*
sifted pastry flour   *2¼ cups (500 ml)*
baking soda   *½ teaspoon (2.5 ml)*
baking powder   *2 teaspoons (10 ml)*
salt   *1 teaspoon (5 ml)*
raisins   *1 cup (225 ml)*
orange, unpeeled   *1*
sour milk   *1 cup (225 ml)*

Cream the shortening and sugar and add eggs, beating until very light. Put the orange through the fine blade of the food chopper, or chop in a blender. Sift the dry ingredients and, using 2 tablespoons (30 ml) of flour, dredge the raisins. Stir the ground orange into the creamed mixture. Then add the dry ingredients to the creamed mixture alternately with milk. Fold in the raisins. Bake in two 9″ (2 l) round greased and floured layer cake pans at 350°F (175°C) for 35 to 40 minutes.

Prince of Wales Cake

A marble-like cake that looks inviting when cut in slices.

shortening   ½ cup (110 ml)
sugar   1 cup (225 ml)
eggs   2
sifted pastry flour   2 cups (450 ml)
baking powder   3 teaspoons (15 ml)
salt   1 teaspoon (5 ml)
milk   1 cup (225 ml)
raisins   ½ cup (110 ml)
molasses   1 tablespoon (15 ml)

Cream the shortening and beat in the sugar until light. Beat in eggs until very creamy. Sift the dry ingredients together and add to creamed mixture alternately with milk. Grease and line the bottom of a loaf pan with waxed paper. Place in one half of the batter. Mix into the other half the raisins and molasses and pour this mixture on top of the first batter. Bake at 350°F (175°C) for 50 minutes. Cool on rack. This cake may also be baked in layer pans.

Mrs. Robertson's Tomato Soup Cake

An excellent, moist, and fruit-filled cake.

eggs   2
sugar   1 cup (225 ml)
cooking oil   ½ cup (110 ml)
condensed tomato soup   10-ounce can (280 ml)
baking soda   1 teaspoon (5 ml)
sifted pastry flour   2 cups (450 ml)
baking powder   2 teaspoons (10 ml)
salt   1 teaspoon (5 ml)
nutmeg   1 teaspoon (5 ml)
cinnamon   1 teaspoon (5 ml)
vanilla   ½ teaspoon (2.5 ml)
raisins   ½ cup (110 ml)
dates, chopped   ½ cup (110 ml)
walnuts, chopped   1 cup (225 ml)

Stir the soda into the tomato soup. Cream the oil, sugar, and eggs together until light. Sift together the dry ingredients, saving a little to dust the fruit. Add the vanilla to the egg mixture. Mix in the dry ingredients alternately with the soup. Fold in the fruit and nuts. Pour into 2 9" (1.2 l) greased layer pans. Bake at 350°F (175°C) for 30 minutes. Cool on a rack. Ice with the following:

Sufficient to fill and ice a layer cake.

butter   *2 tablespoons (30 ml)*
milk   *2 tablespoons (30 ml)*
icing sugar   *1½ cups (335 ml)*
almond flavouring   *½ teaspoon (2.5 ml)*

Mix thoroughly.

Gumdrop Cake

This recipe came from the book of the late Mrs. Charles Burt, Smith's Falls,
Ontario. It has the texture of fruit cake and is nicer the second day after baking.

eggs   *2*
sugar   *1 cup (225 ml)*
butter   *½ cup (110 ml)*
salt   *½ teaspoon (2.5 ml)*
cinnamon   *1 teaspoon (5 ml)*
nutmeg   *1 teaspoon (5 ml)*
baking powder   *2 teaspoons (10 ml)*
sifted pastry flour   *2 cups (450 ml)*
unsweetened applesauce   *1 cup (225 ml)*
gumdrops, cut fine   *2 cups (450 ml)*
raisins   *1 cup (225 ml)*

Cream the butter, sugar, and eggs well. Sift the dry ingredients using a little to
flour the raisins and gumdrops. Mix the dry ingredients into the creamed mixture
alternately with the applesauce. Fold in the fruits. Turn into a greased 9″ X 13″
(3 l) cake pan. Bake at 350°F (175°C) for 45 minutes. Cool before icing. Orange
Butter Icing is nice on this cake.

Wilhelmina Cake

A moist, light cake flavoured with molasses. Fill it with Butterscotch Raisin Filling
and top it off with a maple-flavoured butter icing.

141

shortening   ½ cup (110 ml)
sugar   ¾ cup (170 ml)
eggs   2
molasses   ½ cup (110 ml)
sifted pastry flour   2 cups (450 ml)
cream of tartar   2 teaspoons (10 ml)
baking soda   1 teaspoon (5 ml)
salt   1 teaspoon (5 ml)
milk   1 cup (225 ml)

Cream the shortening, sugar, and eggs together well. Sift the dry ingredients and mix into egg mixture alternately with the molasses and milk. Bake in two 9″ (1.2 l) greased layer pans or a 9″ X 13″ (3 l) cake pan for 30 minutes for the layers, or 40 to 45 minutes for the larger cake, at 350°F (175°C). Cool on racks.

Date Cake

An old-fashioned spice cake filled with dates.

shortening   ½ cup (110 ml)
brown sugar   1 cup (225 ml)
eggs   2
milk   1 cup (225 ml)
sifted pastry flour   2 cups (450 ml)
baking powder   2 teaspoons (10 ml)
salt   1 teaspoon (5 ml)
cinnamon, nutmeg, cloves   ½ teaspoon (2.5 ml) each
finely chopped dates   1 cup (225 ml)

Beat the shortening, sugar, and eggs until creamy. Sift the dry ingredients and mix into creamed mixture alternately with the milk. Fold in the floured dates at the last. Pour into two 9″ (1.2 l) greased layer pans and bake for 30 to 35 minutes at 350°F (175°C) or pour into one 9″ (2 l) square pan and bake at the same temperature for 45 to 50 minutes. Cool on rack. Ice and fill with Maple Cream Frosting.

CHOCOLATE AND COCOA CAKES

Cocoa beans are the seeds inside a pod on the cacao tree, native to South America, where it was first domesticated and prized by the Aztecs. Like so many other food items, it was carried by the Spanish to Europe and eventually imported to North America. The seeds are removed from the pod after fermenting and are cured and roasted. Chocolate does not have the fat of the bean removed, whereas cocoa is the powder resulting from grinding the residue after the fat has been removed for other uses.

Mahogany Cake

A dark, moist cake spiced with cinnamon.

shortening   ½ cup (110 ml)
sugar   1 cup (225 ml)
eggs   2
sifted pastry flour   2 cups (450 ml)
cocoa   1/3 cup (75 ml)
baking powder   2 teaspoons (10 ml)
baking soda   ½ teaspoon (2.5 ml)
cinnamon   1 teaspoon (5 ml)
salt   1 teaspoon (5 ml)
sour milk   1 cup (225 ml)

Cream the shortening and sugar and add the eggs and beat until very smooth and creamy. Sift the dry ingredients and add to the creamed mixture alternately with the sour milk. Bake in greased layer pans at 350°F (175°C) for 30 minutes. Cool on racks.

Devil's Food Cake

In my mother's book it says that this cake is "meant for inhabitants of lower regions". This recipe originally called for part butter and part cream.

shortening   ½ cup (110 ml)
sugar   1 cup (225 ml)
eggs   2
sifted pastry flour   2 cups (450 ml)
baking powder   2 teaspoons (10 ml)
baking soda   1 teaspoon (5 ml)
salt   1 teaspoon (5 ml)
cocoa   ½ cup (110 ml)
sour milk   ½ cup (110 ml)
coffee   ½ cup (110 ml)
vanilla   1 teaspoon (5 ml)

Beat the shortening, sugar, and eggs until creamy and light. Sift the dry ingredients and add to the creamed mixture alternately with the milk and coffee. Stir in the vanilla. Bake in 9″ (1.2 l) greased layer pans at 350°F (175°C) for 35 to 40 minutes. Cool on racks.

Moon Cake

This recipe was originally given to one of my great grandmothers by a Mrs. Moon. The recipe originally called for one half a 10¢ cake of unsweetened chocolate. It

143

is an extra large cake and deliciously moist. Try making it in three layers, filled with chocolate cream filling and frosted with chocolate icing, for your next big party. The cake is made in two parts, a custard that is later mixed into a cake batter.

CUSTARD:

> unsweetened chocolate   *2 1-ounce squares (58 g)*
> milk   *4 tablespoons (60 ml)*
> sugar   *1 cup (225 ml)*
> milk   *1 cup (225 ml)*
> egg, well beaten   *1*

CAKE:

> sugar   *1 cup (225 ml)*
> shortening   *2/3 cup (150 ml)*
> sour milk   *½ cup (110 ml)*
> egg   *1*
> vanilla   *1 teaspoon (5 ml)*
> sifted pastry flour   *3 cups (675 ml)*
> baking soda   *2 teaspoons (10 ml)*
> salt   *1¼ teaspoons (6 ml)*

Make the custard first. In the top of a double boiler, over boiling water, dissolve the chocolate. Remove from heat and stir in the 4 tablespoons of milk until smooth. Add the sugar and remaining milk. Return to double boiler and heat to scalding. Add a little of the hot mixture to the beaten egg, then add the egg to the hot mixture, stirring over hot water until thickened and smooth. Allow to cool in refrigerator while making cake.

Cake: Cream the shortening, sugar and egg well. Add the vanilla. Sift together the flour, salt, and soda. Add to the creamed mixture alternately first with the milk, then with the chocolate custard. Beat well. Bake in a greased 9″ X 13″ (3 l) cake pan or in three 9″ (1.2 l) layer cake pans. Bake the large cake for 50 minutes or the layers for 30 to 35 minutes at 350°F (175°C). Cool on racks and ice with Chocolate Icing.

EGGLESS CAKES

In the early days of Upper Canada, eggs were scarce, for no poultry could be kept until shelters were built to protect the birds from marauding foxes. Consequently, pioneer housewives were forced to do much of their baking without benefit of eggs. The following three recipes are for eggless cakes.

Clove Cake

This recipe originally called for "dark" sugar, butter, and no salt. It has a moist and tender texture and rises well.

brown sugar   *1 cup (225 ml)*
shortening   *½ cup (110 ml)*
sifted pastry flour   *2½ cups (560 ml)*
salt   *1 teaspoon (5 ml)*
cinnamon, cloves, nutmeg   *1 teaspoon (5 ml) each*
baking soda   *1 large teaspoon (6 ml)*
sour milk   *1 cup (225 ml)*
stoned raisins   *½ cup (110 ml)*

Cream together the sugar and shortening. Sift the dry ingredients and mix alternately with the sour milk into the creamed mixture. Dust the raisins with a little flour mixture and fold in. Bake in 2 9″ (1.2 l) greased layer pans 25 to 30 minutes at 350°F (175°C). Cool on rack. Frost with a beaten vanilla or sea-foam icing (double boiler).

Crumb Cake

This is a tender and light cake that has the topping included in the baking.

brown sugar   *1 cup (225 ml)*
shortening   *½ cup (110 ml)*
sifted pastry flour   *2 cups (450 ml)*
cinnamon   *1 teaspoon (5 ml)*
allspice   *1 teaspoon (5 ml)*
cloves   *½ teaspoon (2.5(ml)*
baking soda   *1 teaspoon (5 ml)*
baking powder   *2 teaspoons (10 ml)*
sour milk   *1 cup (225 ml)*
raisins   *1 cup (225 ml)*

Beat together the sugar and shortening. Sift the dry ingredients and add to the shortening mixture, beating with mixer or cutting with a pastry cutter until mixture resembles fine crumbs. Remove ½ cup (110 ml) and set aside for topping. To the remainder, add sour milk and beat vigorously until smooth and creamy. Fold in the raisins, dusted with a teaspoon of the flour mixture. Pour into a 9″ (2 l) greased square cake pan and sprinkle reserved crumb mixture over the top. Bake at 350°F (175°C) for 40 minutes. Cool on a rack.

145

Eggless Applesauce Cake

This is one of the best cakes I have ever eaten and a favourite in our house. It is eggless, but light, moist, and full of flavour.

> shortening   1/3 cup (75 ml)
> brown sugar   1 cup (225 ml)
> thick, unsweetened applesauce   1-1/3 cups (300 ml)
> baking powder   1½ teaspoons (7.5 ml)
> baking soda   1 teaspoon (5 ml)
> salt   1 teaspoon (5 ml)
> sifted pastry flour   2 cups (450 ml)
> cinnamon   1 teaspoon (5 ml)
> cloves   ½ teaspoon (2.5 ml)
> raisins   1 cup (225 ml)

Beat the shortening and sugar until light. Sift the dry ingredients and use a little to dust the raisins. Mix the dry ingredients into the sugar mixture alternately with the applesauce. Gently stir in the raisins last. Pour into an 8″ (2 l) greased square pan. Bake at 350°F (175°C) for 45 to 50 minutes.

● **FRUIT CAKES** ●

Dark Fruitcake

My mother always made two fruitcakes at Christmas, a dark one and a "pork" or light cake. To me, the only true shape for a Christmas cake is round, for I still bake this cake in the 9½″ round spring-form pan used by my mother and my grandmother before her. My grandmother used to put a bank of wood ashes under the pan in the oven to prevent the cake from burning on the bottom. The pan is now dark and old, patented, it says on the bottom, on May 30, 1876, but it still bakes this moist, fruity cake beautifully.

> shortening   1 cup (225 ml)
> brown sugar   2 cups (450 ml)
> eggs   3
> sifted flour   4 cups (1 l)
> baking powder   4 teaspoons (20 ml)
> salt   1 teaspoon (5 ml)
> pastry spice   1½ teaspoons (7.5 ml)
> milk, scalded   1 cup (225 ml)
> molasses   ½ cup (110 ml)
> raisins   2 cups (450 ml)

currants   *2 cups (450 ml)*
mixed glacé fruits   *1 cup (225 ml)*
red maraschino cherries   *1 cup (225 ml)*
green maraschino cherries   *1 cup (225 ml)*

Cream together the shortening and sugar. Add the eggs and beat until creamy. Sift 3 cups (675 ml) of flour together with the baking powder, salt, and pastry spice. Beat the molasses into the egg mixture. Add the dry ingredients alternately with the milk. Dredge the fruit with the remaining flour and fold into the batter. Pour into a 9″ (3 l) tube pan, greased and lined with greased waxed paper. Bake at 300°F (150°C) for 2 to 2½ hours. Place a pan of hot water in the bottom of the oven while baking. Put on a rack to cool. Wrap in foil and store in refrigerator or freeze indefinitely.

White Holiday Fruitcake

I like to bake this fruitcake in tiny cupcake pans in 1½″ (3.8 cm) paper liners. These resemble large bonbons with their red and green candied fruit peeking out through the golden batter. I freeze them; then I can take out as many as desired at one time.

shortening   *1 cup (225 ml)*
sugar   *1 cup (225 ml)*
eggs   *4*
flour   *4 cups (1 l)*
baking powder   *4 teaspoons (20 ml)*
salt   *1-1/3 teaspoons (300 ml)*
red maraschino cherries and juice   *6 ounces (170 ml)*
green maraschino cherries and juice   *6 ounces (170 ml)*
white raisins   *2 pounds (1 kg)*
mixed candied peel   *1 cup (225 ml)*
mixed candied fruit   *1 cup (225 ml)*
candied pineapple   *½ cup (110 ml)*
warm water   *½ cup (110 ml)*

Cream shortening with the sugar. Add the eggs and beat until light and creamy. Sift together 3 cups (675 ml) of flour, baking powder, and salt. Drain the juice from the cherries and add enough water to make 2/3 cup (150 ml). Cut the cherries in quarters and dredge all the fruit in the remaining flour. Mix the sifted ingredients into the egg batter alternately with the cherry juice and the water. Fold in the fruit. Line 1½″ (3.8 cm) muffin pan cups with paper liners. Place one rounded tablespoon (20 ml) of batter in each. Bake at 350°F (175°C) for 20 minutes or until golden. Cool on racks. Remove paper liners before storing in a cool place or freezing.

Yield: 8 dozen fruitcake bonbons

Sponge cakes are cakes that contain no shortening.

Hot Water Sponge Cake

If you are a weight watcher, you'll especially appreciate this cake, but it's equally good for the whole family.

    eggs, separated   4
    sugar   1½ cups (335 ml)
    boiling water   ½ cup (110 ml)
    lemon extract or vanilla   1 teaspoon (5 ml)
    sifted pastry flour   1½ cups (335 ml)
    baking powder   1 teaspoon (5 ml)
    salt   ¼ teaspoon (1 ml)

Beat the egg whites until stiff and set aside. Beat the yolks until thick, add the sugar, and combine well. Beat in water and add the flavouring. Sift the dry ingredients and stir in. Fold in the beaten whites. Place in a 10″ (3 l) angel cake pan, ungreased, and bake at 375°F (190°C) for 35 to 40 minutes. Invert pan and cool upside down. This cake doesn't need icing, but you might like to put a light dusting of icing sugar over the top.

Jelly Roll

A special treat in our house, these were extra-good when filled with home-made jam.

    sugar   ¾ cup (170 ml)
    eggs, separated   3
    lemon extract   ½ teaspoon (2.5 ml)
    cold water   2 tablespoons (30 ml)
    sifted pastry flour   1 cup (225 ml)
    baking powder   1 teaspoon (5 ml)
    salt   1/8 teaspoon (0.5 ml)

Line a 10″ X 15″ (1 l) jelly-roll pan with waxed paper. Sift the dry ingredients. Beat egg whites with sugar until stiff and set aside. Beat yolks until thick; add lemon extract and water and beat again until thick and creamy. Fold yolks into whites. Fold the flour mixture into egg mixture. Spread batter evenly over pan. Bake at 400°F (205°C) for 10 to 12 minutes. Remove from oven and turn out on a damp towel sprinkled with icing sugar. Remove waxed paper and trim hard edges.

148

Roll up until cool. Unroll and spread with jam, lemon filling, or chocolate filling. Re-roll.

Yield: 12 slices

Mock Angel Cake

My husband prefers this cake to true angel cake. It rises well and has the tender texture of angel cake.

flour   *1 cup (225 ml)*
sugar   *1 cup (225 ml)*
baking powder   *3 teaspoons (15 ml)*
salt   *¼ teaspoon (1 ml)*
milk   *1 cup (225 ml)*
egg whites   *2*

Beat the egg whites stiff and set aisde. Sift the dry ingredients four times. Scald the milk, then beat together alternately with the dry ingredients until smooth. Fold in the beaten egg whites. Spoon into an ungreased 8″ (2 l) tube pan. Bake at 350°F (175°C) for 25 to 30 minutes. Turn pan upside down on a rack until cake is completely cool.

Sour Cream Sponge Cake

A light and tender cake that is good just sprinkled with icing sugar, or try topping it with fresh fruit and whipped cream.

egg   *1*
sugar   *¾ cup (170 ml)*
sour cream   *1 cup (225 ml)*
nutmeg   *½ teaspoon (2.5 ml)*
salt   *¼ teaspoon (1 ml)*
baking soda   *1 teaspoon (5 ml)*
sifted pastry flour   *2 cups (450 ml)*

Beat the egg and sugar until very light and creamy. Sift the dry ingredients and beat in alternately with the sour cream. Turn into a greased 8″ (2 l) square pan and bake at 375°F (190°C) for 30 minutes. Cool on a rack.

Mocha Icing

This quantity will ice an 8″ (20 cm) square cake. The icing is rich and creamy in texture.

> butter   *1 tablespoon (15 ml)*
> icing sugar   *1 cup (225 ml)*
> cocoa   *2 teaspoons (10 ml)*
> cold coffee   *2 tablespoons (30 ml)*

Cream the butter. Mix the cocoa with the icing sugar and add to butter alternately with enough coffee to make the icing of spreading consistency. Beat well.

Maple Cream Icing

This icing tastes like candy and is particularly good on applesauce or spice cakes.

> brown sugar   *1 cup (225 ml)*
> milk   *3 tablespoons (45 ml)*
> butter   *1 tablespoon (15 ml)*
> cream of tartar   *pinch*
> vanilla   *1 teaspoon (5 ml)*
> icing sugar

Put first three ingredients in a saucepan and bring just to a boil, stirring. Remove from heat and add vanilla, cream of tartar, and just enough icing sugar to make frosting of spreading consistency. If it becomes too hard, add a little milk. This quantity will fill and ice a layer cake.

Maple Syrup Frosting

> pure maple syrup   *1/3 cup (70 ml)*
> salt   *pinch*
> brown sugar   *2/3 cup (150 ml)*
> egg white   *1*
> vanilla   *½ teaspoon (2.5 ml)*

Place all ingredients except vanilla in top of double boiler. Place over boiling water and beat constantly with electric mixer until stiff enough to stand in peaks, 5 to 7 minutes. Remove from stove and beat in vanilla.

Yield: Icing to cover and fill a layer cake

Vanilla Beaten Icing

    egg white   1
    sugar   2/3 cup (150 ml)
    water   3 tablespoons (45 ml)
    salt   pinch
    cream of tartar   ¼ teaspoon (1 ml)
    vanilla   ½ teaspoon (2.5 ml)

Put all ingredients but vanilla in top of the double boiler and place over boiling water. Beat until mixture stands in peaks. Remove from heat and beat in vanilla.

Yield: Icing to frost and fill a layer cake

VARIATIONS:

SEA-FOAM ICING

Use brown sugar and omit vanilla.

CHOCOLATE

Add 3 tablespoons (45 ml) cocoa.

MOCHA

Use 2½ tablespoons (37.5 ml) cold strong coffee instead of water.

COCONUT

Sprinkle vanilla icing before it hardens with coconut.

Crumb Topping

This is a quick way to top a cake, as it bakes along with the cake. The recipe originally called for lard.

    brown sugar   1/3 cup (70 ml)
    cinnamon   ½ teaspoon (2.5 ml)
    flour   ½ cup (110 ml)
    butter   4 tablespoons (60 ml)

Combine the dry ingredients. Cut in the butter until fine and crumbly. Sprinkle over uncooked cake batter. Bake as usual.

Coconut Broiler Frosting

    brown sugar   6 tablespoons (90 ml)
    butter   2 tablespoons (30 ml)
    cream   2 tablespoons (30 ml)
    coconut   1 cup (225 ml)

Cream together the butter and sugar. Add the cream and mix in the coconut.
Spread over baked cake and broil about 5″ (13 cm) from heat for approximately 4
minutes or until golden brown. Nice served warm but may also be served cold.

Maple Icing

To equal quantities of butter and maple syrup add enough icing sugar to make
mixture of spreading consistency. Cream may be used instead of butter.

Baked Icing

    egg white   1
    brown sugar   ½ cup (110 ml)
    baking powder   ½ teaspoon (2.5 ml)

Beat the egg white until stiff, add the baking powder and sugar, and beat well.
Spread on unbaked cake batter, sprinkle with chopped nuts, and bake cake as
directed.

Orange Butter Icing

Use an orange filling with this icing for a change.

    icing sugar   2 cups (450 ml)
    butter   4 tablespoons (60 ml)
    juice and grated rind of 1 orange

Blend together the sugar and butter. Add the orange rind plus enough orange
juice to make icing of spreading consistency.

Yield: Icing to frost and fill a layer cake

Chocolate Butter Icing

    icing sugar   2 cups (450 ml)
    butter   4 tablespoons (60 ml)
    cocoa   4 tablespoons (60 ml)
    boiling water   3 tablespoons (45 ml)

milk   *2 tablespoons (30 ml)*
salt   *pinch*

Mix the boiling water with the cocoa. Add to the butter and mix well. Add the sugar and milk, beating until smooth and creamy. Mix in the salt.

Yield: Icing to fill and frost a layer cake

V ARIATIONS:

C HOCOLATE P EPPERMINT I CING. Add ¼ teaspoon (1 ml) peppermint flavouring.

F RENCH C HOCOLATE I CING. Add ½ teaspoon (2.5 ml) maple flavouring.

• CAKE FILLINGS •

Lemon Filling

brown sugar   *¾ cup (170 ml)*
salt   *1/8 teaspoon (0.5 ml)*
cornstarch   *2 tablespoons (30 ml)*
juice and grated rind of 1 lemon
water   *½ cup (110 ml)*
egg, well beaten   *1*
butter   *2 teaspoons (10 ml)*
yellow food colouring

Blend together in the top of a double boiler the sugar, salt, and the cornstarch. Add the water and cook over boiling water, stirring constantly until thickened. Pour gradually over the well-beaten egg, stirring continuously. Return to top of double boiler and continue to cook over boiling water for 3 minutes more. Remove from heat and stir in butter, lemon juice, rind, and food colouring. Allow to cool completely before using.

Yield: Filling for a layer cake

Lemon Fruit Filling

Apples are the surprise in this filling.

sugar   *½ cup (110 ml)*
finely grated apple   *1 cup (225 ml)*
lemon juice   *2 tablespoons (30 ml)*
lemon rind   *1 teaspoon (5 ml)*

153

butter   *½ tablespoon (7.5 ml)*
salt   *1/8 teaspoon (0.5 ml)*
beaten egg   *2 tablespoons (30 ml)*

Peel, core, and grate the apple. Mix together all the ingredients except the egg, in the top of the double boiler. Cook over boiling water, stirring occasionally, for 15 minutes. Pour part of the mixture over the beaten egg, stirring constantly. Pour egg mixture into double boiler contents, stirring and cooking for 2 minutes. Cool thoroughly.

Yield: Filling for a layer cake

ORANGES

Oranges are native to China and Indo-China. Columbus brought them to the West Indies from where they spread to Florida and California. By the beginning of the 1900s, citrus fruits were beginning to be imported in good supply in Ontario, especially in the cities.

Orange Filling

sugar   *½ cup (110 ml)*
flour   *1 tablespoon (15 ml)*
orange juice   *¼ cup (55 ml)*
lemon juice   *½ tablespoon (7.5 ml)*
egg, slightly beaten   *1*
butter   *1 teaspoon (5 ml)*

Mix the ingredients. Cook for 10 minutes in the top of a double boiler over boiling water, stirring constantly. Cool before spreading.

Yield: 2/3 cup (150 ml)

Fruit Filling

Use this for the filling when you make a Vanilla Beaten Icing.

Vanilla Beaten Icing   *1 recipe*
chopped dates, chopped pecans, raisins   *¼ cup each (55 ml)*

To 1/3 of the icing add the dates, pecans, and raisins. Use between the layers. Use plain icing for the top.

Maple Cream Cake Filling

This filling is much like the Maple Cream Icing, but with chopped raisins. It originally called for "brown or maple" sugar and butter "the size of a hickory nut".

brown sugar   *1 cup (225 ml)*
butter   *1 teaspoon (5 ml)*
milk   *½ cup (110 ml)*
cream of tartar   *½ teaspoon (2.5 ml)*
chopped raisins   *1 cup (225 ml)*

Boil all but the raisins to the soft ball stage (236°F, 114°C). Add raisins. Beat until cool, adding more milk until of right consistency to spread. This quantity is sufficient to fill a layer cake.

Vanilla Cream Filling

sugar   *3 tablespoons (45 ml)*
salt   *1/8 teaspoon (0.5 ml)*
milk   *¾ cup (170 ml)*
egg yolk   *1*
flour   *2½ tablespoons (37.5 ml)*
vanilla   *½ teaspoon (2.5 ml)*
butter   *1 tablespoon (15 ml)*

Mix the sugar, salt, and ½ cup (110 ml) of the milk in the top of a double boiler over boiling water. Stir until dissolved and hot. Mix the egg yolk, flour, and remaining milk well. Stir a little hot mixture into egg mixture, then stir quickly into hot mixture and beat well until thickened and smooth. Remove from heat and add butter and vanilla.

Yield: 1 cup (225 ml)

VARIATION: CHOCOLATE CREAM FILLING

Make recipe as for Vanilla Cream Filling but mix 1½ tablespoons (22.5 ml) cocoa with the sugar before mixing with the salt and milk in the double boiler.

Strawberry Filling

whipping cream   *1 cup (225 ml)*
icing sugar   *¼ cup (55 ml)*
mashed strawberries   *¾ cup (170 ml)*
vanilla   *½ teaspoon (2.5 ml)*

Beat the cream until foamy, add the sugar and vanilla, and continue beating until stiff. Fold in the strawberries.

Yield: 2½ cups (560 ml)

COOKIES & SQUARES

Spices and seasonings have been in demand since ancient times. They were brought by caravan from the east to the ports of the Mediterranean or the Persian Gulf and sold at very high prices. Certain spices were used as payment in matters of trade. In Western Europe, spices were in demand, partly because of poor facilities for preservation of food, especially of meat and also for medicinal purposes.

Spices were an important part of pioneer baking of cookies and cakes. Generally, only whole spices were obtainable until the 1900s, when they became available already ground. Recipes called for 1 nutmeg, grated, cinnamon to be pounded and sifted, cloves to be crushed, etc.

In many of these recipes, cream of tartar and soda are used for rising power. Baking powder or "rising mix" did not come into general use until the turn of the 20th century. Just as today's cake mix is convenient, so this rising mix was more convenient to use; all brands contained baking soda, and some included cream of tartar mixed with starch and other ingredients. Cream of tartar tends to destroy vitamins in cooking, but in cookies and cakes, where it is mainly used, the vitamins that it would attack are not important to our daily total intake.

Most of the old cake and cookie recipes in our family book call for butter and no salt; because butter was made at home, there was always a plentiful supply on hand. I have substituted shortening in most recipes, although I sometimes use a good grade of vegetable margarine. If you use butter or margarine instead of shortening, be sure to adjust the amount of salt called for in the recipe; since butter and margarine are already salted, you may need little or no salt at all.

To save having to grease baking sheets each time you use them, wipe off cookie tins with a paper towel as soon as you take the cookies from them. This removes any particles adhering to the sheet but not the oil, so your tin is ready for the next baking.

Drop Cookies

Because oatmeal was in plentiful supply, it was one of the most commonly used ingredients in early kitchens, from oatmeal porridge right through oatmeal breads and rolls, puddings, cakes, and cookies. Oatmeal was very coarse and porridge had to be cooked for hours. Many of the early recipes called for putting it through the food chopper before using.

Crinkles

I like to add chocolate chips to this recipe. It originally called for "a little corn flakes or a few nuts and raisins". Try them all for variation.

shortening	½ cup (110 ml)
brown sugar	1/3 cup (75 ml)
white sugar	1/3 cup (75 ml)
egg	1
flour	1 cup (225 ml)
salt	¾ teaspoon (4 ml)
baking soda	½ teaspoon (2.5 ml)
rolled oats	1-1/3 cups (300 ml)
warm water	¼ cup (55 ml)
vanilla	½ teaspoon (2.5 ml)
chocolate chips	¾ cup (170 ml)

Cream together the shortening, sugar, and egg. Sift together the flour, salt, and soda. Add the water and vanilla to the egg mixture, then mix in the dry ingredients and rolled oats. Add the chocolate chips and mix thoroughly. Drop by spoonfuls 2″ (5 cm) apart onto a greased cookie sheet. Bake at 350°F (175°C) for 12 minutes.

Yield: 2½ dozen

Oatmeal Cookies

Corn syrup added to any cookie recipe produces a delicious flavour, quite different from that of all sugar.

        shortening (part margarine if desired)   *1 cup (225 ml)*
        sugar   *2/3 cup (150 ml)*
        corn syrup   *1/3 cup (75 ml)*
        egg   *1*
        flour   *2½ cups (560 ml)*
        baking soda   *½ teaspoon (2.5 ml)*
        baking powder   *2 teaspoons (10 ml)*
        salt   *½ teaspoon (2.5 ml)*
        oatmeal   *1 cup (225 ml)*
        sour milk   *1/3 to ½ cup (75 - 110 ml)*

Cream the shortening and sugar until fluffy. Add corn syrup and egg. Sift together the flour, soda, baking powder, and salt, and add the flour mixture and the oatmeal to the creamed mixture alternately with the milk. Drop by spoonfuls 2″ (5 cm) apart on a greased tin. Bake at 375°F (190°C) for 10 minutes.

Yield: 5 dozen cookies

Leafa's Fruit Drops

A tasty combination — raisins and cinnamon!

        raisins   *1 cup (225 ml)*
        shortening   *½ cup (110 ml)*
        sugar   *1 cup (225 ml)*
        eggs   *2*
        milk   *¼ cup (55 ml)*
        oatmeal   *1-2/3 cups (375 ml)*
        flour   *1½ cups (335 ml)*
        baking soda   *1 teaspoon (5 ml)*
        salt   *½ teaspoon (2.5 ml)*
        cinnamon   *1 teaspoon (5 ml)*
        chopped nuts (optional)   *¾ cup (170 ml)*

Cream the shortening and sugar until light. Add the eggs and milk and beat well. Combine the oatmeal with the raisins and add to the mixture, mixing well. Sift the remaining ingredients and beat in thoroughly. Add nuts if desired. Drop by spoonfuls onto a greased cookie sheet, about 2″ (5 cm) apart. Bake in a 350°F (175°C) oven for 12 minutes.

Yield: 3 dozen cookies

Oatmeal Drop Cookies

Chewy and full of brown sugar goodness.

> margarine   *1 cup (225 ml)*
> brown sugar   *1 cup (225 ml)*
> vanilla   *1 teaspoon (5 ml)*
> milk   *¼ cup (55 ml)*
> oatmeal   *1 cup (225 ml)*
> flour   *2 cups (450 ml)*
> salt   *½ teaspoon (2.5 ml)*
> baking soda   *½ teaspoon (2.5 ml)*
> raisins   *1 cup (225 ml)*

Cream the margarine and beat in the sugar until fluffy. Add the vanilla. Sift the soda and salt with the flour and mix with the oatmeal. Add to the creamed mixture alternately with the milk. Add the raisins. Drop by spoonfuls onto a well-greased cookie sheet about 2″ (5 cm) apart, as they spread while baking. Bake at 375°F (190°C) for 8 to 10 minutes.

Yield: 2½ dozen cookies

Inda's Oatmeal Macaroons

A favourite in our house, with their slightly chewy texture.

> butter   *¼ cup (55 ml)*
> brown sugar   *1 cup (225 ml)*
> eggs   *2*
> milk   *1 tablespoon (15 ml)*
> vanilla   *1 teaspoon (5 ml)*
> flour   *1 cup (225 ml)*
> baking powder   *1 teaspoon (5 ml)*
> salt   *¾ teaspoon (4 ml)*
> oatmeal   *2 cups (450 ml)*
> raisins, nuts, coconut   *½ cup (110 ml) each*

Cream the sugar, butter, and eggs well. Sift together the flour, baking powder, and salt, and stir into the butter mixture. Add the oatmeal, raisins, nuts, and coconut, mixing thoroughly. Drop by spoonfuls on a waxed-paper lined cookie sheet, about 2″ (5 cm) apart. Bake at 375°F (190°C) for 8 to 10 minutes.

Yield: 3 dozen cookies

Chocolate Chews

These are made on top of the stove. They taste like candy and are so simple to make your children will love to bake them.

    sugar   2 cups (450 ml)
    milk   ½ cup (110 ml)
    butter or margarine   ½ cup (110 ml)

Place in a saucepan and bring to a full rolling boil. Remove from stove and add:

    salt   pinch
    vanilla   1 teaspoon (5 ml)
    quick oatmeal   3 cups (675 ml)
    cocoa   4 tablespoons (60 ml)
    or
    melted chocolate   2 1-ounce squares (58 g)
    coconut   ½ cup (110 ml)

Mix quickly while mixture is hot. Let cool slightly and then drop by spoonfuls on waxed paper or plates. Cool and store. You may use peppermint instead of vanilla.

Yield: 3 dozen cookies

Chocolate Cookies

There are not many recipes for chocolate cookies, but this is a good one.

    margarine   ½ cup (110 ml)
    brown sugar   1 cup (225 ml)
    egg   1
    maple flavouring   1 teaspoon (5 ml)
    flour   1¾ cups (395 ml)
    cocoa   3 tablespoons (45 ml)
    baking powder   3 teaspoons (15 ml)
    salt   1/8 teaspoon (0.5 ml)
    milk   1/3 cup (75 ml)
    chopped nuts   ½ cup (110 ml)

Cream the margarine and sugar. Add the egg, beating well, then add the flavouring. Sift the dry ingredients and mix into the creamed mixture alternately with the milk. Stir in the nuts. Drop by spoonfuls onto a greased cookie sheet, about 2'' (5 cm) apart. Bake at 375°F (190°C) for 10 minutes.

Yield: 3 dozen cookies

Date Cookies

A moist cookie that keeps well.

       flour   2 cups (450 ml)
       baking powder   2 teaspoons (10 ml)
       salt   ¾ teaspoon (4 ml)
       dates, sliced   1 cup (225 ml)
       shortening   ¾ cup (170 ml)
       sugar   2/3 cup (150 ml)
       egg   1
       milk or water   2 to 4 teaspoons (10 - 20 ml)
       vanilla   ½ teaspoon (2.5 ml)

Sift together the dry ingredients. Cream shortening, add sugar gradually, then unbeaten eggs and sliced dates. Mix well, then add milk and flavouring. Stir in dry ingredients. Drop by spoonfuls on greased cookie sheet, about 2'' (5 cm) apart and bake at 375°F (190°C) for 15 to 20 minutes.

Yield: 3 dozen cookies

Boston Cookies

Nutmeg is the flavouring in these.

       butter or margarine   1 cup (225 ml)
       sugar   1 cup (225 ml)
       eggs   2
       flour   3 cups (675 ml)
       salt   ½ teaspoon (2.5 ml)
       baking soda dissolved
       in 1 tablespoon (15 ml) warm water   ½ teaspoon (2.5 ml)
       nutmeg   1 teaspoon (5 ml)
       raisins   1½ cups (335 ml)

Cream the butter and sugar and add the eggs, beating until creamy. Add the salt, soda solution, and nutmeg. Mix well. Stir in the flour and raisins. Drop by spoonfuls onto a greased cookie sheet, about 2'' (5 cm) apart. Bake at 350°F (190°C) for 12 minutes.

Yield: 3 dozen cookies

Curly Peters

A good combination of spice and fruits.

> butter   1 cup (225 ml)
> white sugar   1 cup (225 ml)
> or
> brown sugar   1½ cups (335 ml)
> egg   1
> corn syrup   1 tablespoon (15 ml)
> flour   3 cups (675 ml)
> salt   ½ teaspoon (2.5 ml)
> baking soda   1 teaspoon (5 ml)
> cinnamon   1 teaspoon (5 ml)
> chopped raisins   1 cup (225 ml)
> chopped nuts   1 cup (225 ml)

Cream the butter and sugar, then beat in the eggs and syrup. Sift together the flour, soda, salt, and cinnamon and stir into creamed mixture. Add the fruit and nuts and stir well, adding a little milk if necessary. Drop by spoonfuls onto a greased cookie sheet 2″ (5 cm) apart. Bake at 325°F (165°C) for 15 to 20 minutes.

Yield: 4 dozen cookies

Mrs. McMurrin's Tea Cookies

A handy recipe to have, for it may be varied by changing the flavourings. The original recipe called for 1 cup melted butter or "use ½ of it drippings".

> shortening   1 cup (225 ml)
> sugar   1 cup (225 ml)
> eggs   2
> sweet milk   2 large tablespoons (35 ml)
> orange extract   1½ teaspoons (7.5 ml)
> orange rind or bits   2 teaspoons (10 ml)
> (You may substitute any flavouring for the orange.)
> flour   3 cups (675 ml)
> cream of tartar   2 teaspoons (10 ml)
> baking soda   1 teaspoon (5 ml)
> salt   1 teaspoon (5 ml)

Cream the first three ingredients and add flavouring and milk. Sift dry ingredients and beat into creamed mixture. Drop by large spoonfuls 2″ (5 cm) apart onto a greased tin and bake at 350°F (175°C) for 12 to 15 minutes. This dough may also be chilled, rolled out, and cut.

Yield: 4 dozen cookies

Cousin Rebecca's Ginger Cookies

A light and moist cookie.

shortening   1 cup (225 ml)
molasses   2/3 cup (150 ml)
sugar   ½ cup (110 ml)
eggs   2
water   1/3 cup (75 ml)
flour   3 cups (675 ml)
ginger   3 teaspoons (15 ml)
cinnamon   3 teaspoons (15 ml)
baking soda   2 teaspoons (10 ml)
salt   1¼ teaspoons (6 ml)

Cream the shortening, add the sugar, molasses, eggs and water, and beat well. Sift dry ingredients and beat into shortening mixture. Drop by spoonfuls 2'' (5 cm) apart on greased tins and bake at 375°F (190°C) for 10 to 12 minutes.

Yield: 5 dozen cookies

Hermits

A spicy fruit cookie — they don't last long with my family.

butter   ½ cup (110 ml)
eggs, beaten well   2
sugar   1½ cups (335 ml)
flour   3 cups (675 ml)
baking soda   1 teaspoon (5 ml)
salt   1 teaspoon (5 ml)
cinnamon   1 teaspoon (5 ml)
cloves   ½ teaspoon (2.5 ml)
nutmeg   ½ teaspoon (2.5 ml)
sour milk   ½ cup (110 ml)
chopped nuts and raisins   1 cup (225 ml)

Cream butter, add sugar, and beat until fluffy. Add eggs and beat thoroughly. Sift the dry ingredients and add to the creamed mixture alternately with the milk. Stir in fruit and nuts. Drop by spoonfuls 2'' (5 cm) apart on greased baking sheets. Bake at 375°F (190°C) for 10 minutes.

Yield: 4 to 5 dozen cookies

Fruit Jumbles

Rich and fruity, these cookies bake to a golden brown.

> butter or margarine   *1 cup (225 ml)*
> sugar   *1 cup (225 ml)*
> eggs   *2*
> baking soda   *¾ teaspoon (4 ml)*
> hot water   *1 tablespoon (15 ml)*
> salt   *½ teaspoon (2.5 ml)*
> vanilla   *1 teaspoon (5 ml)*
> flour   *2½ cups (560 ml)*
> chopped nuts   *½ cup (110 ml)*
> chopped dates   *1 cup (225 ml)*

Cream the butter and sugar and beat in the eggs. Dissolve the soda in the hot water and add to the creamed mixture along with the salt and vanilla. Stir in the flour and mix well, then add the nuts and dates. Drop by spoonfuls 2" (5 cm) apart on a greased cookie sheet, and sprinkle the tops with a little sugar. Bake at 375°F (190°C) for 10 to 12 minutes.

Yield: 5 dozen cookies

Sour cream Cookies

These have a cake-like texture, and sour cream gives an extra tang.

> shortening   *½ cup (110 ml)*
> brown sugar   *1½ cups (335 ml)*
> eggs   *2*
> sifted flour   *2½ cups (560 ml)*
> baking powder   *1 teaspoon (5 ml)*
> baking soda   *½ teaspoon (2.5 ml)*
> salt   *½ teaspoon (2.5 ml)*
> sour cream   *1 cup (225 ml)*
> *or*
> sour milk   *2/3 cup (150 ml)*
> vanilla   *1 teaspoon (5 ml)*
> chopped nuts, fruit, or peel   *½ cup (110 ml)*

Cream the shortening and the sugar. Beat in the eggs. Sift together the dry ingredients and add to the creamed mixture alternately with the sour cream. Add the vanilla and the fruit or nuts. Drop in small spoonfuls, about 2" (5 cm) apart, on a greased cookie sheet. Bake at 375°F (190°C) for 12 to 15 minutes.

Yield: 5 dozen cookies

Corn-flake Cookies

Flaked cereals were not manufactured until after 1890.

> shortening   ¾ *cup (170 ml)*
> sugar   *1 cup (225 ml)*
> eggs   2
> flour   *1½ cups (335 ml)*
> baking powder   *2 teaspoons (10 ml)*
> salt   *¼ teaspoon (1 ml)*
> vanilla   *1 teaspoon (5 ml)*
> corn flakes   *2 cups (450 ml)*

Cream together the shortening, sugar, and eggs. Sift together the dry ingredients and stir into the creamed mixture. Add the vanilla and fold in the corn flakes. Drop by spoonfuls about 1″ (2.5 cm) apart, on greased tins. Bake at 350°F (175°C) for 12 to 15 minutes.

Yield: 3 dozen cookies

Peanut Macaroons

> melted butter   *4 tablespoons (60 ml)*
> sugar   *¾ cup (170 ml)*
> eggs, separated   2
> vanilla   *1 teaspoon (5 ml)*
> salt   *1/8 teaspoon (0.5 ml)*
> rolled oats   *1 cup (225 ml)*
> rolled peanuts   *1 cup (225 ml)*
> flour   *½ cup (110 ml)*
> baking powder   *2 teaspoons (10 ml)*

Sift the baking powder with the flour. Beat the egg whites until stiff and set aside. Mix the butter and sugar together and add the egg yolks. Mix thoroughly with the flour mixture, then add the rest of the ingredients in the order given. Fold in the beaten egg whites last. Drop by spoonfuls on well-greased pans about 2″ (5 cm) apart to allow room for spreading. Bake at 375°F (190°C) for 8 to 10 minutes.

Yield: 3 dozen macaroons

paddle spoons
c. 1830

Applesauce Cookies

Moist and tangy with spices.

  sugar   ¾ cup (170 ml)
  shortening   1 cup (225 ml)
  egg   1
  flour   2½ cups (560 ml)
  cloves   ½ teaspoon (2.5 ml)
  allspice   ½ teaspoon (2.5 ml)
  cinnamon   1 teaspoon (5 ml)
  baking soda   1 teaspoon (5 ml)
  baking powder   1 teaspoon (5 ml)
  salt   ½ teaspoon (2.5 ml)
  sweetened applesauce   1 cup (225 ml)
  vanilla   1 teaspoon (5 ml)
  raisins   1 cup (225 ml)
  chopped nut meats   1 cup (225 ml)

Cream together the shortening, sugar, and egg. Sift the dry ingredients together and add alternately to the creamed mixture with the applesauce. Stir in the vanilla, raisins, and nuts. Drop by spoonfuls 2″ (5 cm) apart onto a greased baking sheet and bake at 350°F (175°C) for 10 to 12 minutes.

Yield: 6 dozen cookies

Date Rocks

Spicy, moist, and chewy!

  butter or margarine   1 cup (225 ml)
  brown sugar   1½ cups (335 ml)
  eggs   2
  flour   2½ cups (560 ml)
  cinnamon   1 teaspoon (5 ml)
  cloves   ½ teaspoon (2.5 ml)
  baking soda   1 teaspoon (5 ml)
  salt   ¾ teaspoon (4 ml)
  sour milk   2 tablespoons (30 ml)
  chopped dates   1 cup (225 ml)
  chopped walnuts   ½ cup (110 ml)

Cream the shortening, sugar, and eggs well. Sift together the dry ingredients. Add the milk to the creamed mixture and stir in the sifted flour, adding the dates and nuts last. Drop by spoonfuls 2″ (5 cm) apart on a greased cookie sheet. Bake at 375°F (190°C) for 10 minutes.

Yield: 5 dozen cookies

Ball Cakes

Citron and orange peel give flavour to these crisp cookies.

    shortening   *1 cup (225 ml)*
    sugar   *1 cup (225 ml)*
    eggs   *2*
    sifted pastry flour   *2 cups (450 ml)*
    baking powder   *1 teaspoon (5 ml)*
    cinnamon   *2 teaspoons (10 ml)*
    cloves   *¼ teaspoon (1 ml)*
    nutmeg   *¼ teaspoon (1 ml)*
    salt   *½ teaspoon (2.5 ml)*
    grated orange rind   *1 teaspoon (5 ml)*
    chopped citron   *¼ cup (55 ml)*

Cream the shortening, sugar, and eggs. Sift together the dry ingredients and combine with first mixture. Add the orange peel and stir in the citron. Drop by spoonfuls 2″ (5 cm) apart, on a greased sheet. Bake at 375°F (190°C) for 12 to 15 minutes.

Yield: 3½ dozen cookies.

Lace Cookies

Crisp, macaroon texture — specially good with ice cream on a hot day. We like them with coconut flavouring.

    butter   *1 tablespoon (15 ml)*
    eggs   *2*
    sugar   *1 cup (225 ml)*
    flour   *¾ cup (170 ml)*
    salt   *¼ teaspoon (1 ml)*
    baking powder   *2 teaspoons (10 ml)*
    desired flavouring   *1 teaspoon (5 ml)*
    rolled oats   *1 cup (225 ml)*
    corn flakes   *1 cup (225 ml)*

Cream the butter, eggs, and sugar. Sift together the flour, salt, and baking powder. Add the flavouring to the creamed mixture, then add the dry ingredients. Stir in the oats and corn flakes. Drop 2″ (5 cm) apart, by spoonfuls, on tins covered with brown paper. Bake at 375°F (190°C) for 10 to 12 minutes. Remove immediately from paper and cool on racks.

Yield: 2 dozen cookies

Blanche's Drop Cakes

I like to use ginger and currants in this recipe, but it may be varied with other spices and fruits.

brown sugar   *2 cups (450 ml)*
shortening   *1 cup (225 ml)*
molasses   *1 cup (225 ml)*
boiling water   *1 cup (225 ml)*
flour   *6 cups (1.35 l)*
baking soda   *1 teaspoon (5 ml)*
cream tartar   *1 teaspoon (5 ml)*
salt   *1½ teaspoons (7.5 ml)*
spices or currants if desired

Cream the shortening and sugar until light and fluffy. Add the molasses and beat well. Mix in the boiling water. Sift together the dry ingredients and stir into creamed mixture along with fruit if desired. Drop 2″ (5 cm) apart on greased or floured tins. Bake at 375°F (190°C) for 10 to 12 minutes.

Yield: 7½ dozen cookies

Miss Gibson's Coconut Kisses

These mounds of delicately golden meringue taste just as good as they look. Miss Gibson was a school teacher.

egg whites   *2*
sugar   *6 tablespoons (90 ml)*
coconut   *½ pound (227 g)*

Beat the egg whites until frothy, then slowly beat in sugar, continuing to beat until whites are very stiff but not dry. Fold in coconut. Heat a cookie sheet and rub it with paraffin or line it with brown paper. Drop batter by tablespoonfuls (15 ml) 2″ (5 cm) apart and bake in a 325°F (165°C) oven for 20 minutes. Remove immediately to racks to cool.

Yield: 1½ dozen kisses

Corn-flake Fancies

Fancy enough to dress up any cookie plate.

    egg whites   2
    sugar   ½ cup (110 ml)
    crisp corn flakes   2 cups (450 ml)
    coconut   ½ cup (110 ml)
    salt   pinch

Beat the egg whites until dry. Slowly add the sugar, beating constantly. Fold in the corn flakes, coconut, and salt. Drop from a spoon onto a sheet lined with brown paper, 1″ (2.54 cm) apart. Bake at 350°F (175°C) for 15 minutes. Remove at once from paper onto racks to cool.

Yield: 2 dozen cookies

Coconut Macaroons

A truly crisp macaroon.

    egg white   1
    powdered sugar   1 cup (225 ml)
    coconut   1 cup (225 ml)
    cornstarch   1 tablespoon (15 ml)
    rolled biscuit crumbs   1½ tablespoons (7.5 ml)
    salt   ¼ teaspoon (1 ml)
    vanilla   ½ teaspoon (2.5 ml)

Beat the egg white stiff, then slowly add the sugar, beating constantly. Heat over steam until well heated. Add the remaining ingredients. Drop in small spoonfuls 2″ (5 cm) apart onto a brown-paper lined cookie sheet. Bake at 350°F (175°C) for 15 minutes. Remove at once to cool on racks.

Yield: 1½ dozen macaroons

● MOULDED COOKIES ●

Walnut Rolls

These little sugar-covered rolls add interest to any cookie plate. The recipe came from my sister, Margaret Vannest.

butter or margarine   ¾ cup (170 ml)
icing sugar   6 tablespoons (90 ml)
flour   2 cups (450 ml)
salt   1/8 teaspoon (0.5 ml)
chopped walnuts   ¾ cup (170 ml)
maple extract   1 teaspoon (5 ml)
milk   1 teaspoon (5 ml)

Cream margarine and 4 tablespoons (60 ml) icing sugar. Sift together flour and salt and blend into creamed mixture. Beat in nuts, maple flavouring and milk. Chill and form into date-sized rolls. Place 1″ (2.5 cm) apart on a greased cookie sheet. Bake at 400°F (205°C) for 10 to 12 minutes. Roll in remaining icing sugar while still warm.

Yield: 5 dozen rolls

Butter Cookies

These cookies would not taste right to me if they were not criss-crossed with the tines of a fork and a large raisin pressed into the top.

butter or margarine   ¾ cup (170 ml)
brown sugar   1 cup (225 ml)
egg   1
ginger   1 teaspoon (5 ml)
cream tartar   1 small teaspoon (5 ml)
baking soda   1 small teaspoon (5 ml)
flour   2 cups (450 ml)

Cream butter and sugar. Beat in the egg. Sift together the dry ingredients and stir well into the creamed mixture. Take a small quantity in the hand and make a 1″ (2.5 cm) ball. Place 2″ (5 cm) apart on a greased cookie sheet. Press down both ways with a fork and top with a raisin. Bake at 350°F (175°C) for 5 to 6 minutes.

Yield: 2 dozen cookies

Swedish Pastry Balls

This recipe was given to me by my sister, Margaret Vannest. These decorative little cakes will melt in your mouth.

butter or margarine   ½ cup (110 ml)
sugar   1/3 cup (75 ml)
egg, separated   1
sifted flour   1 cup (225 ml)

salt   *pinch*
chopped peanuts   *2/3 cup (150 ml)*
maraschino cherries, halved   *15*

Cream the butter and sugar and beat in egg yolk. Add the flour and pinch of salt. Form in small balls with wet hands. Roll each ball in egg white that has been slightly beaten. Then roll in chopped peanuts. Place 2″ (5 cm) apart on a greased cookie sheet. Flatten by placing ½ cherry on top of each ball. Bake at 350°F (175°C) for 10 to 12 minutes.

Yield: 2½ dozen cookies

Butterscotch Cookies

This cookie flattens out and is deliciously chewy in the middle.

molasses   *1 cup (225 ml)*
butter   *1 cup (225 ml)*
brown sugar   *1 cup (225 ml)*
baking soda   *1 teaspoon (5 ml)*
flour   *3 cups (675 ml)*

Boil together for 3 minutes the molasses, butter, and sugar. Cool to lukewarm and beat in the soda. Add the flour to make a soft dough. It will resemble maple cream candy at this stage. Shape into balls and place 2″ (5 cm) apart on a greased cookie sheet. Press down with a fork. Nuts and raisins may be pressed on top of each cookie. Bake at 350°F (175°C) for 8 to 10 minutes.

Yield: 4 dozen cookies

Spongies

Golden meringue with a dab of jam make these extra festive.

shortening   *1/3 cup (75 ml)*
brown sugar   *1/3 cup (75 ml)*
egg, separated   *1*
pastry flour   *1 cup (225 ml)*
baking powder   *1 teaspoon (5 ml)*
salt   *¼ teaspoon (1 ml)*
icing sugar   *4 tablespoons (60 ml)*
jam

Thoroughly cream together the shortening, sugar, and egg yolk. Sift together the dry ingredients except for icing sugar and blend into creamed mixture. Make small balls from spoonfuls of dough. Place 2″ (5 cm) apart on a greased cookie sheet. Flatten into small cakes and bake at 325°F (165°C) till barely golden, about 7 to 8 minutes. Beat the white of the egg stiff and add icing sugar, mixing well. Top each cookie with this meringue and a dab of jam and bake at 350°F (175°C) until nicely browned, about 8 to 10 minutes.

Yield: 2 dozen cookies

• REFRIGERATOR COOKIES •

Ice-box Cookies

My mother always used to have a supply of these on hand. Before the days of refrigerators, she used to keep the dough, in the winter, inside the roasting pan out in our laundry room, which was unheated.

> shortening   *1 cup (225 ml)*
> vanilla   *½ teaspoon (2.5 ml)*
> brown sugar   *1 cup (225 ml)*
> eggs   2
> cream of tartar   *½ teaspoon (2.5 ml)*
> baking soda   *1 teaspoon (5 ml)*
> sifted flour   *3½ cups (785 ml)*
> salt   *pinch*

Cream shortening. Add vanilla and brown sugar and beat well. Mix in the egg and beat until light and creamy. Sift together the dry ingredients and mix in to form dough. Form into two rolls and refrigerate overnight. Bake in thin slices 1″ (2.5 cm) apart on a greased cookie sheet at 375°F (190°C) for 8 to 10 minutes. When cool, put together with jam or date filling.

Yield: 2½ dozen sandwiches

VARIATIONS:

Divide dough into three. Leave one portion plain. Mix ½ cup (110 ml) chopped red and green cherries into the second part. Add ½ cup (110 ml) chopped nuts to the third. Form into rolls and bake as above. Make sandwiches of the plain roll only.

May's Overnight Cookies

These spicy cookies used to be left overnight in a cool place for easier slicing. Try adding raisins and nuts for variation.

brown sugar   *1 cup (225 ml)*
white sugar   *1 cup (225 ml)*
shortening   *1½ cups (335 ml)*
eggs   *2*
soda, cinnamon, cloves, and salt   *1 teaspoon each (5 ml each)*
flour   *2-2/3 cups (600 ml)*

Cream together the shortening, sugar, and eggs. Sift the dry ingredients and mix in. Roll into a long bar 2" (5 cm) in diameter. Chill for several hours or overnight. Slice and bake 2" (5 cm) apart on a greased cookie sheet at 350°F (175°C) for 8 to 10 minutes.

Yield: 6 dozen cookies.

Raisin Nut Cookies

Refrigerate or freeze them — handy to have on hand to bake freshly when needed.

shortening   *¾ cup (170 ml)*
sugar   *¾ cup (170 ml)*
egg   *1*
grated orange rind   *2 teaspoons (10 ml)*
orange juice   *3 tablespoons (45 ml)*
flour   *2½ cups (560 ml)*
salt   *½ teaspoon (2.5 ml)*
cream of tartar   *¼ teaspoon (1 ml)*
baking soda   *1 teaspoon (5 ml)*
nutmeg   *¼ teaspoon (1 ml)*
chopped nuts   *1/3 cup (75 ml)*
raisins or dates   *½ cup (110 ml)*

Cream shortening, sugar, and egg. Add the juice and rind. Sift together the dry ingredients and add, mixing well. Stir in the raisins and nuts. Form into two rolls and chill for several hours or overnight. Bake when ready to use, in thin slices, 2" (5 cm) apart on a greased cookie sheet at 350°F (175°C) for 8 to 10 minutes.

Yield: 3 dozen cookies

Oatmeal Cookies

I can remember when I was a small child visiting my grandparents, my aunt, Miss Hattie Magee, used to give me these delicious biscuit-like cookies to eat. Since they do not have the richness of so many cookies, they make excellent snacks with milk for children, or with coffee, for adults.

> shortening   *1 cup (225 ml)*
> sugar   *¾ cup (170 ml)*
> corn syrup   *1 tablespoon (15 ml)*
> flour   *3 cups (675 ml)*
> salt   *1½ teaspoons (7.5 ml)*
> baking soda   *1 teaspoon (5 ml)*
> sour milk   *1 cup (225 ml)*
> oatmeal   *2 cups (450 ml)*

Cream the shortening, sugar, and corn syrup. Sift together the flour, salt, and soda. Stir the dry ingredients into the creamed mixture alternately with sour milk. Stir in the oatmeal last. Roll thin and place 1″ (2.5 cm) apart on a greased cookie sheet. Bake at 375°F (190°C) for 7 to 8 minutes.

Yield: 5 dozen cookies

Trilbys

These oatmeal turnovers may be filled with dates, raisins, or jam.

> shortening or butter   *1 cup (225 ml)*
> brown sugar   *2/3 cup (150 ml)*
> egg   *1*
> flour   *3 cups (675 ml)*
> baking soda   *½ teaspoon (2.5 ml)*
> salt   *1 teaspoon (5 ml)*
> rolled oats   *2½ cups (560 ml)*
> sour milk   *1 cup (225 ml)*

FILLING:

> finely cut dates   *1¼ cups (280 ml)*
> cold water   *1 cup (225 ml)*
> sugar   *¼ cup (55 ml)*

Cut the dates into the cold water and stir in the sugar. Cook over medium heat until syrupy and thickened. Remove from heat and set aside while making cookies. Sift together the flour, soda and salt. Cream the sugar, butter, and egg. Add the rolled oats to the creamed mixture, stir in the milk, and add the flour mixture. Chill. Roll out on a lightly floured board and cut with a 2¾″ (7 cm) cookie cutter. Put a teaspoon of date filling in the centre of each cookie and fold over, pressing the edges together with a fork to prevent filling from leaking out. Place 2″ (5 cm) apart on a greased cookie sheet. Bake at 375°F (190°C) for 10 to 12 minutes.

Yield: 6½ dozen turnovers

Oatmeal Snaps

A crisp, sweet cookie full of oatmeal flavour.

> oatmeal   *6 cups (1.35 l)*
> flour   *4 cups (1 l)*
> sugar   *2 cups (450 ml)*
> melted butter or margarine   *1-1/3 cups (300 ml)*
> baking soda   *2 teaspoons (10 ml)*
> warm water   *1 cup (225 ml)*

Thoroughly blend the oatmeal, flour, and sugar. Add the melted butter and stir with a fork until crumbly and well mixed. Dissolve the soda in the water and add, mixing to obtain a dough that can be rolled. Roll thinly on a lightly floured board and cut into 2″ (5 cm) rounds. Place 1″ (2.5 cm) apart on a greased cookie sheet. Bake at 400°F (205°C) for 8 to 10 minutes.

Yield: 8 dozen cookies

Valentine Cookies

The orange in these gives them a delicious flavour.

> shortening   *2/3 cup (150 ml)*
> sugar   *1½ cups (335 ml)*
> eggs   2
> pastry flour   *3 cups (675 ml)*
> salt   *1½ teaspoons (7.5 ml)*
> baking powder   *2 teaspoons (10 ml)*
> orange juice   *1 tablespoon (15 ml)*
> grated rind of 1 orange

Cream the shortening and beat in the sugar. Add the eggs and mix until creamy. Sift the dry ingredients and add gradually with the orange rind and juice. Chill. Roll and cut with a heart-shaped cutter. Place 2″ (5 cm) apart on a greased cookie sheet. Bake at 350°F (175°C) for 12 to 15 minutes. Decorate as desired.

Yield: 3½ dozen cookies

Bachelor's Buttons

These small round "buttons" are filled with jam.

> shortening   *1 cup (225 ml)*
> brown sugar   *¾ cup (170 ml)*
> egg   *1*
> flour   *2¼ cups (505 ml)*
> baking powder   *2 teaspoons (10 ml)*
> salt   *¾ teaspoon (4 ml)*
> vanilla   *1 teaspoon (5 ml)*
> jam or jelly

Cream the shortening and sugar, add the egg, and beat well. Stir in the vanilla. Sift together the dry ingredients and mix well into the creamed mixture. Chill thoroughly. Roll out on a well-floured board about 1/8″ (0.3 cm) thick. Cut into 2″ (5 cm) rounds; spread half the rounds with jelly or jam and cover each with another round. Place 2″ (5 cm) apart on a greased cookie sheet. Bake at 375°F (190°C) for 8 to 10 minutes.

Yield: 5 dozen cookies

New Hampshire Cookies

Raisins are the filling in these cookies. Prepare the filling first and cool before using.

Filling:

> flour   *2 tablespoons (30 ml)*
> sugar   *½ cup (110 ml)*
> chopped raisins   *1 cup (225 ml)*
> salt   *pinch*
> boiling water   *¼ cup (55 ml)*
> lemon juice   *2 tablespoons (30 ml)*

Mix together the flour and sugar. Add the salt and raisins. Stir in the boiling water and cook over a medium heat until thickened. Stir in the lemon juice and set aside while you make the cookie dough.

    butter   *½ cup (110 ml)*
    sugar   *1 cup (225 ml)*
    egg   *1*
    lemon extract   *1 teaspoon (5 ml)*
    pastry flour   *6 cups (1.35 l)*
    baking powder   *2 teaspoons (10 ml)*
    salt   *1 teaspoon (5 ml)*
    baking soda   *½ teaspoon (2.5 ml)*
    sour milk   *1 cup (225 ml)*

Cream the butter and sugar. Add the egg and beat until creamy. Add the lemon extract. Sift together the dry ingredients and add with the milk to the creamed mixture. Chill for ½ hour before rolling. Roll 1/8″ (0.3 cm) thick on a floured board. Cut with a 2″ (5 cm) cookie cutter. Place 1 teaspoon (5 ml) filling on half the cookies and cover with remaining cookies. Press together slightly, sprinkle with sugar, place 1″ (2.5 cm) apart on a greased cookie sheet and bake at 375°F (190°C) for 12 minutes.

Yield: 4½ dozen cookies

Sugar Cookies

Orange juice and a raisin filling add zest to these cookies.

Filling:

    raisins   *1 cup (225 ml)*
    sugar   *1 tablespoon (15 ml)*
    orange juice   *2 tablespoons (30 ml)*
    fine cracker crumbs   *2 tablespoons (30 ml)*
    grated rind of ½ orange

Mix all together and set aside while rolling cookies.

    butter   *¼ cup (55 ml)*
    shortening   *¼ cup (55 ml)*
    sugar   *1 cup (225 ml)*
    eggs   *2*
    orange juice   *1 tablespoon (15 ml)*
    orange rind   *3 teaspoons (15 ml)*
    flour   *2 cups (450 ml)*
    baking powder   *2 teaspoons (10 ml)*
    salt   *½ teaspoon (2.5 ml)*

Cream the butter, shortening, sugar and eggs. Add the juice and rind of the orange. Sift together the dry ingredients and mix in. Chill well before rolling thinly on a lightly floured board. Cut with a 2″ (5 cm) round cookie cutter. Top half the cookies with filling, then cover with remaining halves. Pinch edges of cookies together and prick tops. Place 2″ (5 cm) apart on a greased cookie sheet. Bake at 375°F (190°C) for 10 to 12 minutes.

Yield: 2½ dozen cookies

Orange-Apple Filling for Any Plain Rolled Cookie

```
grated, peeled apples    2 cups (450 ml)
corn syrup    ¾ cup (170 ml)
brown sugar    2 tablespoons (30 ml)
orange juice    ¼ cup (55 ml)
salt    pinch
grated rind of 1 orange
```

Combine all ingredients and bring to a boil. Simmer, stirring occasionally, until thick. Cool before using.

Yield: Approximately 2 cups (450 ml)

• SQUARES AND BARS •

Oatmeal Shortcakes with Dates

These are sometimes called Date Squares or Matrimonial Cake. Dates, raisins, or jam may be used as filling.

```
oatmeal    3 cups (675 ml)
brown sugar    1 cup (225 ml)
flour    2 cups (450 ml)
baking soda    1 teaspoon (5 ml)
salt    1 teaspoon (5 ml)
shortening    1 cup (225 ml)
sour milk or cream    1/3 cup (or more) (75 ml or more)
```

Mix together the oatmeal, sugar, flour, soda, and salt. Cut in the shortening until mixture is crumbly. Divide the mixture into 2/3 and 1/3 and add the sour milk to the 2/3 part. Pat into the bottom of a greased 9″ X 13″ (3 l) cake pan. Make the filling.

178

FILLING:

> chopped dates   *1 cup (225 ml)*
> water   *1 cup (225 ml)*
> brown sugar   *½ cup (110 ml)*

Combine all ingredients and cook until syrupy. Spread over the oatmeal mixture and scatter remaining oatmeal mixture on top. Sprinkle with milk. Bake at 350°F (175°C) for 15 to 20 minutes or till golden on top. Cool and cut into squares.

Yield: 3 dozen squares

Coconut Slices

These two layered butterscotch slices will melt in your mouth.

> butter or margarine   *½ cup (110 ml)*
> brown sugar   *3 tablespoons (45 ml)*
> sifted flour   *1 cup (225 ml)*
> salt   *¼ teaspoon (1 ml)*

Cream butter or margarine and sugar. Add flour and salt. Press dough into a greased 8″ (2 l) square cake pan. Bake in 350°F (175°C) oven for 15 minutes or until light brown. Spread with topping, below. Continue baking at 300°F (150°C) for about 30 minutes.

TOPPING:

> eggs   *3*
> brown sugar   *1 cup (225 ml)*
> flour   *2 tablespoons (30 ml)*
> baking powder   *½ teaspoon (2.5 ml)*
> chopped walnuts   *2/3 cup (150 ml)*
> shredded coconut   *1¼ cups (280 ml)*
> vanilla   *1 teaspoon (5 ml)*

Beat eggs until fluffy. Add brown sugar and beat until dissolved. Add flour and baking powder sifted together. Mix until smooth. Fold in chopped nuts, coconut, vanilla. Spread over baked layer and continue baking.

Chocolate Marshmallow Brownies

These brownies won't stay around the kitchen long with their layer of melted marshmallows peeking out.

    butter   ½ cup (110 ml)
    sugar   1 cup (225 ml)
    eggs   2
    pastry flour   ¾ cup (170 ml)
    baking powder   1 teaspoon (5 ml)
    cocoa   5 tablespoons (75 ml)
    salt   ¼ teaspoon (1 ml)
    vanilla   ¾ teaspoon (4 ml)
    walnut meats, chopped   ¾ cup (170 ml)
    large marshmallows   20

Melt butter and cool to just warm. Beat in sugar and eggs until creamy. Sift together dry ingredients and add to first mixture. Stir in vanilla and nuts. Bake in a greased 9″ (2 l) square cake pan at 350°F (175°C) for 18 to 20 minutes. Meanwhile, cut each marshmallow in three pieces. Remove brownies from oven and cover with marshmallows, cut side up. Return to oven for 5 minutes. Cool. Ice with chocolate butter frosting, below.

FROSTING:

    butter   3 tablespoons (45 ml)
    unsweetened chocolate   2 2-ounce squares (113 g)
    thin cream or milk   ¼ cup (55 ml)
    vanilla   ½ teaspoon (2.5 ml)
    salt   pinch
    icing sugar   2 cups (450 ml)

Melt together the chocolate and the butter. Add the cream, vanilla, and salt. Stir in the sugar and beat until smooth and creamy.

Yield: 2 dozen squares

Gumdrop Squares

These are simple to make but delectable and chewy.

    eggs   2
    brown sugar   ¾ cup (170 ml)
    orange flavouring   ½ teaspoon (2.5 ml)
    flour   1 cup (225 ml)
    salt   ½ teaspoon (2.5 ml)
    baking soda   ¼ teaspoon (1 ml)
    baking powder   ¾ teaspoon (4 ml)
    cut-up gumdrops   1 cup (225 ml)

Beat the eggs until very light. Add the sugar and flavouring, beating well. Sift together the dry ingredients and add the gumdrops to them. Blend well with egg mixture. Spread in a greased 9″ (2 l) square cake pan. Bake at 350°F (175°C) for 20 to 25 minutes. Cut into squares when cool.

Yield: 2 dozen squares

Oatmeal Jams

A choice of fillings adds variety to these squares. The original instructions for these jams said to "turn a large dripping pan upside down and roll out on the bottom, covering the whole pan".

butter or shortening   *¾ cup (170 ml)*
sugar   *1 cup (225 ml)*
egg   *1*
flour   *1¾ cups (395 ml)*
baking soda   *½ teaspoon (2.5 ml)*
salt   *1 teaspoon (5 ml)*
rolled oats   *3½ cups (785 ml)*
milk   *½ cup (110 ml)*
jam, raisins or dates

Cream the shortening and sugar. Add the egg and beat until smooth. Sift together the flour, soda, and salt, and stir into first mixture along with the rolled oats and milk. Place half of the dough in each of two waxed-paper lined 9″ X 13″ (3 l) cake pans. Roll or press out evenly, to cover bottoms. Bake at 375°F (190°C) for 10 to 12 minutes or until lightly browned. Cool partially on racks, being careful not to break. Before they are completely cool, spread one rectangle generously with jam or a raisin or date filling. Place second rectangle on top and cut in squares.

Yield: Approximately 3 dozen squares

Indian Date Bars

The "Indian" in the name probably came from the use of cornmeal. Try these with your morning coffee.

milk   *1 cup (225 ml)*
cornmeal   *1 cup (225 ml)*
sugar   *½ cup (110 ml)*
shortening   *½ cup (110 ml)*
flour   *1 cup (225 ml)*
baking powder   *2 teaspoons (10 ml)*
salt   *¾ teaspoon (4 ml)*
dates, chopped   *12*

Scald the milk and stir in the cornmeal. Allow to almost cool. Cream the shortening and the sugar. Blend in the cornmeal mixture. Sift together the dry ingredients and add to first mixture, stirring well. Mix the dates in last. Spread evenly over a greased 10″ X 12″ (1 l) jelly roll pan. Bake at 350°F (175°C) for 25 minutes. Cut when cool.

Yield: 30 1″ X 3″ (2.5 X 7.5 cm) bars

Butterscotch Squares

A delicious chewy cake, tastes like candy.

> butter or margarine   *¾ cup (170 ml)*
> brown sugar   *2 cups (450 ml)*
> eggs   2
> butterscotch flavouring   *½ teaspoon (2.5 ml)*
> flour   *1½ cups (335 ml)*
> baking powder   *2 teaspoons (10 ml)*
> salt   *1/8 teaspoon (0.5 ml)*
> walnuts, chopped   *2/3 cup (150 ml)*

Melt the butter and allow to cool until only warm. Beat in the sugar, eggs, and flavouring. Sift together the dry ingredients and stir into first mixture until smooth and creamy. Add the nuts. Spread in a buttered cake pan about 6″ X 10″ (1.5 l). Bake at 350°F (175°C) about 40 minutes. Cool and cut into squares.

Yield: 24 squares

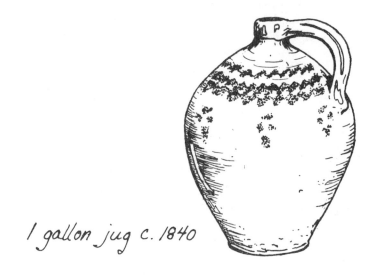

1 gallon jug c. 1840

BREADS, ROLLS, BISCUITS, COFFEE CAKES

"THE MAKING AND baking of good, nourishing, palatable bread, is perhaps one of the most important duties of the practical housewife." Thus wrote Mrs. Catharine Parr Traill in 1854, an early settler on the Otonabee River.

Today many women and men still enjoy turning out a good loaf of home-made bread. Indeed, psychiatrists suggest making bread, giving the dough a good pounding, is a tonic for frustration. Not only will it relieve feelings, but a superior loaf of bread will result. Whatever your reason for bread making, there is nothing your family will enjoy more than a good loaf of bread, fresh from the oven.

The various kinds of grain that the settlers raised enabled them to enjoy a great many kinds of bread. Excellent cakes and breads could be made from wheat, buckwheat, Indian corn, and rye flours. Oatmeal was a staple food in early pioneer days, specially among the Scots. From our Scottish ancestors come our quick breads, biscuits, scones, and muffins or gems. Cornmeal denotes North American cooking; in Canada yellow cornmeal is preferred to white, which has a stronger flavour.

Today many varieties of flour are readily available in supermarkets. Not so for the early settlers! Lucky was the settler who lived within walking distance of a grist mill! On their arrival in Upper Canada the British government gave some Loyalists hand grain grinders, which resembled a coffee grinder and were difficult to operate. They produced a coarse flour called samp. Some ground the grain between two stones, as did the Indians, or pounded out corn in the hollowed-out stump of a tree. Others sometimes boiled the grain in lye and then dried it near the fire until the kernels of grain burst. It was then eaten as "mush". The first settlers in the Peterborough area in 1818 resorted to chewing kernels of dried corn until soft, and then giving them to their children.

Stone-ground flour has been known since people first began to cultivate grain and learned to crush the kernels by hand between two stones. By the 3rd century B.C. a revolving mill had been developed in Italy in which the lower stone remained stationary while the upper stone revolved. The Romans first used water power for milling and introduced it to Britain, and the process of stone grinding remained basically the same until the late 19th century. In Upper Canada the mills were usually operated by water wheels or driven by oxen or horses where water power was not available. In 1783 the first Loyalist settlers built a grist mill near Kingston. Another one was built at Four-Mile Creek in the Niagara area. In 1787 a third mill was built on the Napanee River and this later resulted in the Napanee Settlement. By 1840 Upper Canada had about 400 grist mills.

"Stone flour", or the flour that was ground at a mill, was very precious to settlers. The flour that resulted from stone grinding, with only the larger particles of bran removed, was suitable for making brown bread but not for porous white loaves. Much sieving was required to make a refined white flour from stone-ground flour, thus making it an expensive luxury. Because of this, white flour was often mixed with other flours in baking. It was not until roller milling was introduced in the late 19th century that a refined white flour became readily available.

Our cake and dry yeasts of today are a far cry from the "barm" or "rising" that was used by our ancestors. Several types were made in those early days. One, known as hop-rising, was made by boiling the ripe cones from hops and thickening the liquid with flour. Salt was added and then it was stored in a jar in a cool cellar. If it soured, a little baking soda was added when it was used.

Potatoes were sometimes boiled in water with a little salt, until mushy, and then mixed with flour. Sugar and "rising" were added before it was stored in a jar.

Sugar and salt yeasts were made when no old yeasts were available, as they would ferment by themselves. Sugar yeast was made from a mixture of soft sugar and flour, while salt yeast was a mixture of salt, flour, and warm water or milk. The latter sometimes produced an undesirable flavour in baking.

Some yeast cakes were made because they would last many months. Hop liquor and rye-meal were heated together and allowed to cool before the yeast or "rising" was added. This mixture was made into a stiff dough by the addition of corn meal. The dough was pressed out to about 1-inch thickness, cut into cakes, put in the sun to dry for several days, and stored in bags.

Many settlers made bread with no leavening. In Peterborough County, early settlers made their mixing bowls from basswood logs, hollowing them out to act as a vessel for mixing and kneading. The dough consisted of flour mixed with water. Flat loaves were formed and then baked in a long-handled pan before the fire with coals beneath and behind it. In wet weather the dough was covered in ashes and placed directly in the coals. The ashes prevented it from burning.

Bake-kettles were commonly used as the settlers' first ovens. Iron kettles with iron lids were set on hot coals and more coals were placed on the lid. These "ovens" didn't bake very uniformly and often the bread, although brown on the outside, was doughy on the inside. Later, ovens were built with sides of clay and a top of bark or slabs and placed on top of a large stump. Sometimes buttonwood trees were hollowed out and used as ovens. When fireplaces were built in the settler's cabin, a bake-oven was built at one side with a door on the front. This was a great improvement. By the 1830s advertisements for iron cooking stoves were becoming common in Upper Canada newspapers. Before the days of built-in oven thermometers, a piece of white paper was placed in the oven to gage its temperature. If it turned brown in 3 minutes, it was hot enough to bake the bread.

There are a few simple but basic rules for the use of yeast to ensure a good product.

The water in which the yeast is dissolved must only be lukewarm, as too high a temperature will kill the yeast. Always be sure that the yeast is well dissolved in the sugar and water liquid before putting it into your bread mixture. If you wish to cut your rising time in half, just use double quantities of the dissolved yeast, unless the recipe already calls for 2 tablespoons (30 ml) of yeast.

Before adding the flour, make sure you have beaten the other ingredients together until smooth. Add only enough flour to make a slightly sticky dough. Amounts of flour vary with humidity, so you may find the same recipe requiring differing quantities from baking to baking. You will soon learn the right "feel". Don't skimp on the kneading. It pays off in good texture.

In order to ensure proper rising, the bread must be placed in a warm place, about 88°F (31°C). Be sure it isn't too hot or the yeast may be killed. A gas oven with a pilot light is fine. (Grandmother had no such problem with her big iron cook stove and warming oven or upper shelf.) Lacking the proper place, fill a large bowl with the hottest water from your tap, set the bowl of dough on a rack over it and cover all closely with a cloth. Refill with hot water after one hour. This is the right temperature to ensure good rising.

When baking the loaves, after 15 to 20 minutes check to see how brown the tops are. If they appear to be browning too quickly, make "caps" of aluminum foil and place one loosely over each loaf.

Follow these few rules and there will be nothing left to do but to enjoy a slice of beautiful hot bread when it comes from the oven.

Old-fashioned White Bread

The recipe in my mother's book suggests that this bread be started by mid-afternoon; the old cake yeasts were slow acting. As a small child, I can remember my mother mixing the final flour into the sponge in the evening, placing two hot-water bottles on the lid of the pan, and covering it all with one of my great-grandmother's heavy quilts. By morning the dough had risen high and ready for baking.

    lukewarm water   *1 cup (225 ml)*
    dry yeast   *1 tablespoon (15 ml)*
    sugar   *1 teaspoon (5 ml)*
    potato water   *2 cups (450 ml)*
    milk   *1 cup (225 ml)*
    sugar   *4 tablespoons (60 ml)*
    salt   *5 teaspoons (25 ml)*
    melted shortening   *4 tablespoons (60 ml)*
    flour   *9½ cups (2.14 l)*

Dissolve the 1 teaspoon (5 ml) sugar in the lukewarm water and sprinkle the yeast over. Let stand 10 minutes. Add potato water and milk, sugar and salt. Stir well. Add 4 cups of flour and beat thoroughly. Stir in shortening and beat well. Add enough more flour to make the dough easily handled. Knead until smooth and elastic. Cover and let rise in a warm place about 1½ hours or until doubled. Punch down and let rise 15 minutes. Turn out onto a lightly floured board and divide into 3 equal portions. Shape into loaves and place in greased 9" X 5" (1.5 l) loaf pans. Cover and let rise until doubled — about 1 hour. Bake at 400°F (205°C) for 45 minutes.

Yield: 3 loaves

Pioneer Potato Bread

Potato bread was originally made with a sourdough starter based on the action of wild yeasts on mashed potatoes, but it is now prepared with bakers' yeast.

> sugar   *1 teaspoon (5 ml)*
> lukewarm water   *½ cup (110 ml)*
> dry yeast   *1 tablespoon (15 ml)*
> mashed potatoes   *1 cup (225 ml)*
> warm water   *1 cup (225 ml)*
> salt   *2 teaspoons (10 ml)*
> sugar   *3 tablespoons (45 ml)*
> cooking oil   *3 tablespoons (45 ml)*
> flour   *5 cups, approx. (1.13 l)*

Dissolve the 1 teaspoon (5 ml) sugar in the ½ cup (110 ml) lukewarm water. Scatter the yeast over the water and set aside for 10 minutes to dissolve. Gradually beat the remaining water into the mashed potatoes until smooth. Add the salt, sugar, and oil. Beat in 2 cups (450 ml) flour. Add the yeast, stir well, and work in remaining flour. Turn out on a floured board and knead until smooth and elastic. Put in a warm place and allow to rise until doubled, about 1½ hours. Punch down and form into two loaves. Put in greased loaf pans. Allow to rise in a warm place 1 hour or until tops have rounded above the sides of the pan. Bake at 425°F (220°C) for 10 minutes and then at 350°F (175°C) for 30 minutes or until done. Cap loosely with foil after the first 20 minutes to prevent too much browning.

Yield: 2 loaves

Here are two versions of oatmeal bread that are both used in our family.

Oatmeal Bread with Molasses

When I was a small child visiting my grandparents, there was always a plentiful supply of home-made bread on hand. I used to ask my aunt, Miss Margaret Magee, for snacks of bread because she used to put the butter on so generously. This is one of the home-made breads that we still enjoy. It is not a sweet bread but has a beautiful moist texture and rises high. It is one of my family's favourites.

oatmeal   1½ cups (335 ml)
boiling water   3 cups (675 ml)
molasses   2 tablespoons (30 ml)
sugar   2 tablespoons (30 ml)
salt   1 tablespoon (15 ml)
dry yeast   1 tablespoon (15 ml)
lukewarm water   1 cup (225 ml)
sugar   1 teaspoon (5 ml)
flour   7 cups (1.58 l)

Scald oatmeal with boiling water in mixing bowl. Stir in the molasses, sugar, and salt. Allow to cool to lukewarm. Stir 1 teaspoon (5 ml) sugar into lukewarm water and add yeast. Allow to stand for 10 minutes. Stir into lukewarm oatmeal mixture. Mix in flour until dough is still somewhat sticky. Knead until smooth and elastic. Place in a greased bowl and allow to rise, covered, in a warm place until double, about 1½ hours. Punch down, let rise 15 minutes. With greased hands, shape into 3 loaves on a well-floured board, 2 large and 1 small loaf. Thoroughly grease 3 loaf pans. Place loaves in pans and allow to rise until doubled in size or until tops are well past the edges of the pans, about 1 hour. Bake in a 400°F (205°C) oven for 15 minutes, then 375°F (190°C) for 30 minutes. When baked, brush tops with melted butter if a soft crust is desired.

Yield: 2 medium loaves and 1 small loaf

The original recipe for oatmeal bread suggests beginning to make the bread at 3:00 in the afternoon, mixing in the remaining flour after the sponge has risen, later in the evening. Then the dough was kept warm overnight, worked down in the morning, and formed into loaves. Thanks to our instant yeasts of today, it is a much shorter process.

Rolled Oat Bread

This is a moist bread, sweeter than the preceding one. It has a flavour all its own. The recipe came from my aunt, Mrs. W.R. Henwood, of Napanee, Ontario.

rolled oats   1 cup (225 ml)
salt   2 teaspoons (10 ml)

shortening   *1½ tablespoons (22.5 ml)*
boiling water   *1¾ cups (395 ml)*
lukewarm water   *½ cup (110 ml)*
sugar   *2 teaspoons (10 ml)*
dry yeast   *2 tablespoons (30 ml)*
lightly packed brown sugar   *¾ cup (170 ml)*
molasses   *2 tablespoons (30 ml)*
flour   *4½ cups (900 ml)*

Measure the oats, salt, and shortening into a bowl. Stir in boiling water and let stand until lukewarm. Into a large mixing bowl, measure lukewarm water and the white sugar. Stir to dissolve. Sprinkle yeast on top and let stand for 10 minutes. Stir well. Stir in rolled oat mixture, brown sugar, molasses, and 2 cups (450 ml) flour. Beat until smooth. Work in another 2½ cups (560 ml) flour. Knead until smooth and elastic. Place in greased bowl and let rise 1 hour. Punch down and let rise 15 minutes. Form into 2 loaves. Thoroughly grease 2 loaf pans, place bread in pans, and brush with melted butter. Let rise about 45 minutes or until doubled. Bake at 375°F (190°C) for 50 minutes.

Yield: 2 medium loaves

Wheat originated as a grass in the fertile valleys of ancient Mesopotamia and was domesticated by the people of that land sometime before 5000 B.C. Bread wheat was growing in the Nile valley by 5000 B.C. and it is to the Egyptians that we must give credit for the discovery of leaven and the first bake ovens. From here, the growing of wheat spread through Europe and by 2500 B.C., wheat was being cultivated in England. English colonists introduced this grain into Virginia in the 17th century. Seed was supplied by the British government to the early settlers in Ontario for their first three years after arrival.

Whole-wheat Bread

Recipes for brown bread vary widely, but my family particularly enjoys this version.

white sugar   *1 teaspoon (5 ml)*
lukewarm water   *½ cup (110 ml)*
dry yeast   *1 tablespoon (15 ml)*
shortening   *3 tablespoons (45 ml)*
brown sugar   *3 tablespoons (45 ml)*
salt   *2 teaspoons (10 ml)*
molasses   *¼ cup (55 ml)*
milk   *1 cup (225 ml)*
water   *½ cup (110 ml)*
whole-wheat flour   *3 cups (675 ml)*
all-purpose flour   *2½ cups (560 ml)*

Dissolve the one teaspoon (5 ml) of sugar in the lukewarm water and sprinkle with yeast. Set aside for 10 minutes. Cream the shortening, sugar, and salt. Beat in the molasses. Add the milk and water and beat in 2 cups (450 ml) of whole-wheat flour. Stir the yeast to completely dissolve and stir into flour mixture. Gradually work in remaining whole-wheat flour and the all-purpose flour. Turn out on lightly floured board and knead until smooth and elastic. It will be a little sticky. Put in warm place and allow to rise for 1½ to 2 hours or until doubled in bulk. Punch down and divide in half, forming each into a loaf. Place in greased pans and let rise until doubled, about ¾ of an hour. Bake at 400°F (205°C) for 15 minutes and then 375°F (190°C) for 35 minutes. Cool on racks.

Yield: 2 medium loaves

100% Whole-wheat Bread

Breads using only whole-wheat flour must be handled a little differently from breads made with all-purpose flour. The dough forms a crust easily, so it is necessary to cover it with a damp towel while it is rising. Whole-wheat bread tends to have a heavier and coarser texture than white bread. For this reason it requires longer kneading to help lighten it. Some shortening in the dough makes it easier to handle. Stone-ground, hard whole-wheat flour may be used equally well in this recipe for a bread that yields top nutritional value.

brown sugar	*2 teaspoons (10 ml)*
warm water	*½ cup (110 ml)*
dry yeast	*2 tablespoons (30 ml)*
molasses	*¼ cup (55 ml)*
salt	*2½ teaspoons (12.5 ml)*
cooking oil	*¼ cup (55 ml)*
warm water	*2½ cups (560 ml)*
whole-wheat flour	*6 to 7 cups (1.4 to 1.5 l)*

Dissolve the sugar in the ½ cup (110 ml) warm water and stir in the yeast. Allow to stand for 10 minutes. In the meantime mix together the molasses, salt, and oil. Stir in remaining warm water and 3 cups (675 ml) of flour. Mix in dissolved yeast. Gradually mix in 3 cups (675 ml) more flour. Turn out on a board and knead in as much more flour as is necessary to prevent sticking to bread board. Knead for 15 minutes. Let rise 1½ hours or until doubled. Punch down and shape into 2 loaves. Place in greased loaf pans and let rise 50 to 60 minutes or until well above rim of pan. Bake at 375°F (190°C) for 35 to 40 minutes. Cool on racks.

Yield: 2 loaves

Light Rye Bread

This bread rises high and light.

  lukewarm water ½ *cup (110 ml)*
  sugar *1 teaspoon (5 ml)*
  dry yeast *1 tablespoon (15 ml)*
  shortening ¼ *cup (55 ml)*
  salt *2 teaspoons (10 ml)*
  molasses *1/3 cup (75 ml)*
  warm water *1 cup (225 ml)*
  whole-wheat flour *1 cup (225 ml)*
  sour milk *1¼ cups (280 ml)*
  rye flour *2 cups (450 ml)*
  all-purpose flour *3 cups (675 ml)*

Dissolve the sugar in the lukewarm water and sprinkle with the yeast. Set aside for 10 minutes. Beat together the shortening, salt, and molasses. Add the 1 cup (225 ml) of warm water. Stir in whole-wheat flour. Add the milk and yeast and mix well. Beat in the rye flour. Work in the all-purpose flour. Turn out on a floured board and knead until smooth and elastic, about 8 to 10 minutes. Put in a large bowl, cover, and place in a warm place to rise until doubled, about 1¾ to 2 hours. Punch down and form into two loaves. Place in greased loaf pans. Cover and allow to rise in a warm place until doubled in bulk, about 45 minutes to 1 hour. Bake at 375°F (190°C) for 35 minutes or until done. Cap loosely with foil if crust browns too quickly. Cool on racks.

Yield: 2 loaves

Dark Rye Bread

A nutritious and tasty bread.

  sugar *2 teaspoons (10 ml)*
  lukewarm water *1 cup (225 ml)*
  dry yeast *2 tablespoons (30 ml)*
  shortening ¼ *cup (55 ml)*
  salt *2 teaspoons (10 ml)*
  molasses *1/3 cup (75 ml)*
  warmed sour milk *2 cups (450 ml)*
  wheat germ ½ *cup (110 ml)*
  rye flour *2 cups (450 ml)*
  cornmeal ½ *cup (110 ml)*
  all-purpose flour *3¾ cups (840 ml)*

Dissolve the sugar in the water and sprinkle the yeast over it. Set aside for 10 minutes. Beat together the shortening, salt, and molasses. Add the milk and wheat germ. Beat well and add the rye flour. Stir in the yeast and then add the cornmeal. Work in the white flour. Turn out on a floured board and knead for 8 to 10 minutes. The dough will be of a granular and heavy texture. Place in a greased bowl and cover with towels. Allow to rise for 1¼ to 1½ hours, until doubled. Punch down, divide in half, and form into loaves. Place in greased loaf pans. Allow to rise, covered, 1 hour in a warm place. Bake at 375°F (190°C) for 45 minutes.

Yield: 2 loaves

• ROLLS •

Cold Water Buns

This recipe came from Mrs. R.J. Magee of Sandhurst, Ontario. These buns must stand for 1 day before baking and so are handy to make ahead of time for company. The rolls are light and fine-textured.

> dry yeast *1 tablespoon (15 ml)*
> sugar *1 teaspoon (5 ml)*
> warm water *1 cup (225 ml)*
> flour *1½ cups (335 ml)*
> melted shortening, slightly cooled *1 cup (225 ml)*
> sugar *½ cup (110 ml)*
> salt *2 teaspoons (10 ml)*
> cold water *3 cups (675 ml)*
> flour *7 to 7½ cups (1.69 l)*

Dissolve the sugar in warm water, then dissolve the yeast. Stir in the 1½ cups (335 ml) flour, beat well, and let rise in a warm place for 1½ hours. Add remaining ingredients, using as much flour as necessary to make a slightly sticky dough. Knead well on a lightly floured board, then transfer to a bowl, cover with a damp cloth and waxed paper, placing the waxed paper next to the dough. Refrigerate for 24 hours. The dough will have to be punched down in refrigerator if it rises above top of bowl. After standing, the dough can be used as needed, either all at once or in batches over a period of 3 days. Take out desired quantity, make into buns about the size of an egg and let rise until doubled, about 1½ to 2 hours over hot water before baking. Bake at 375°F (190°C) for 15 to 20 minutes.

Yield: 4½ dozen

Dinner Rolls

In my mother's cookbook, these are called "Muriel's Buns". I began to bake these when I was 12 and, ever after, that was my job on a Saturday morning.

dry yeast *1 tablespoon (15 ml)*
sugar *1 teaspoon (5 ml)*
lukewarm water *1 cup (225 ml)*
shortening *1/3 cup (75 ml)*
sugar *1/3 cup (75 ml)*
egg *1*
salt *1½ teaspoons (7.5 ml)*
lukewarm milk *1 cup (225 ml)*
flour *5½ cups (1.24 l)*

Dissolve the 1 teaspoon (5 ml) sugar in the lukewarm water and sprinkle the yeast over it. Let stand for 10 minutes. Cream together the shortening and sugar and beat in the egg thoroughly. Add the salt. Stir the yeast mixture and add to the creamed mixture, along with the warm milk. Stir well. Beat in 2 cups (450 ml) flour. Gradually work in the remaining flour until dough is still somewhat sticky. Turn out on lightly floured board and knead for 8 to 10 minutes, until smooth and elastic. Place in a greased bowl and turn once to grease the top. Cover and set in a warm place to rise until doubled, about 1½ hours. Punch down and form into small balls the size of an egg. Place on greased baking sheets, about 2" (5 cm) apart as they rise well. Cover and let rise in a warm place until double, about ½ hour. Bake in a 375°F (190°C) oven for 15 to 20 minutes, until nicely browned on top.

Yield: 3 dozen rolls

VARIATION: BUTTERSCOTCH DESSERT ROLLS

Make up 1 recipe of Dinner Rolls as directed above. After the first rising, make up 30 dinner rolls and follow instructions to complete and bake these. Roll remaining dough into a 9" (23 cm) square. Melt ¼ cup butter in an 8" (2 l) square pan. Brush part of butter over the dough. Sprinkle the dough with cinnamon and ¼ cup (55 ml) raisins. Roll up as a jelly roll. Mix with remaining butter in pan 2 tablespoons (30 ml) brown sugar and 2 tablespoons (30 ml) corn syrup. Cut dough into 9 slices and place flat in pan. Allow to rise until doubled, about ½ hour. Bake at 375°F (190°C) for 20 to 25 minutes. Allow to cool 5 minutes in pan, then invert pan over a rack and lift from the buns. Complete cooling on rack.

Yield: 30 dinner rolls and 9 butterscotch rolls

Hot Weiner Rolls

A tasty weiner roll that makes a hot dog something special.

> sugar   *1 teaspoon (5 ml)*
> lukewarm water   *1 cup (225 ml)*
> dry yeast   *1 tablespoon (15 ml)*
> shortening   *½ cup (110 ml)*
> salt   *3 teaspoons (15 ml)*
> sugar   *1/3 cup (75 ml)*
> eggs   *2*
> skim-milk powder   *½ cup (110 ml)*
> water   *1½ cups (335 ml)*
> flour   *7 cups (1.57 l)*

Dissolve the sugar in the lukewarm water and sprinkle the yeast over. Let stand for 10 minutes. Beat the shortening, sugar, salt, and eggs until creamy. Add milk powder and water, stirring until blended. Stir in 2 cups (450 ml) of flour and beat well. Add dissolved yeast, stirring until mixed. Beat in 2 cups (450 ml) flour. Then work in approximately 3 cups (675 ml) more flour, kneading until smooth and elastic. Set aside in a warm place to rise until doubled, approximately 1½ hours. Punch down and divide into two portions. Divide each portion into 18 equal pieces. Form each into a long finger. Place well apart on greased baking sheet if crusty rolls are desired, or 1″ (2.5 cm) for soft-sided rolls. Let rise, covered, until doubled, about ½ hour. Bake at 400°F (205 °C) for 12 to 15 minutes. Cool on rack. Freeze in family-sized quantities.

Yield: 3 dozen rolls

Oat Yeast Rolls

This is an unusual variation for an ordinary dinner roll — very light and moist.

> rolled oats   *¾ cup (170 ml)*
> boiling water   *¾ cup (170 ml)*
> sugar   *1 teaspoon (5 ml)*
> lukewarm water   *½ cup (110 ml)*
> dry yeast   *1 tablespoon (15 ml)*
> shortening   *1/3 cup (75 ml)*
> sugar   *¼ cup (55 ml)*
> molasses   *3 tablespoons (45 ml)*
> salt   *1½ teaspoons (7.5 ml)*
> egg   *1*
> water   *¾ cup (170 ml)*
> flour   *4¾ cups (1.06 l)*

Pour the boiling water over the oats and set aside to cool. Dissolve the sugar in the lukewarm water and sprinkle with the yeast. Set aside for 10 minutes. Beat the shortening, sugar, molasses, salt, and egg into oatmeal mixture. Stir in the ¾ cup (170 ml) water and 2 cups (450 ml) flour. Beat well. Stir in the dissolved yeast. Add rest of flour. Turn out on floured board and knead until smooth; the dough will still be slightly sticky. Allow to rise in a warm place for 1½ hours or until doubled. Punch down, form into 30 rolls, and place on a greased baking sheet. Allow to rise in a warm place for ½ hour or until doubled. Bake at 400°F (205°C) for 18 to 20 minutes. Brush with melted butter. Cool on racks.

Yield: 2½ dozen rolls

Whole-wheat Dinner Rolls

A tasty brown roll that rises well.

> lukewarm water   *1 cup (225 ml)*
> sugar   *1 teaspoon (5 ml)*
> dry yeast   *1 tablespoon (15 ml)*
> shortening   *1/3 cup (75 ml)*
> brown sugar   *1/3 cup (75 ml)*
> egg   *1*
> salt   *1½ teaspoons (7.5 ml)*
> scalded milk   *1 cup (225 ml)*
> whole-wheat flour   *3 cups (675 ml)*
> all-purpose flour   *3 cups (675 ml)*

Dissolve the sugar in the lukewarm water and sprinkle the yeast over the top. Set aside for 10 minutes. In the meantime cream together the shortening, sugar, and egg. Add the salt and milk. Mix in the whole-wheat flour and beat well. Add the dissolved yeast, again mixing well. Add enough of the remaining all-purpose flour to make the dough slightly sticky. Turn out onto a floured board and knead for 8 to 10 minutes until the dough is smooth and elastic. Place in a large bowl and set in a warm place, covered with a cloth, until it rises double in bulk — about 1½ hours. Punch down and form into small rolls. Place on a greased baking sheet and put in a warm place to rise until doubled again — about ½ to ¾ hour. Bake in a 375°F (190°C) oven for 15 minutes. Cool on racks.

Yield: 2½ dozen rolls

Buttermilk Buns

A light and flavourful dinner roll.

dry yeast   *1 tablespoon (15 ml)*
sugar   *1 teaspoon (5 ml)*
lukewarm water   *½ cup (110 ml)*
sugar   *1/3 cup (75 ml)*
shortening   *1/3 cup (75 ml)*
salt   *1½ teaspoons (7.5 ml)*
baking soda   *¼ teaspoon (1 ml)*
egg   *1*
lukewarm buttermilk or sour milk   *1½ cups (335 ml)*
flour   *4¾ cups (1.06 l)*

Dissolve the sugar in the lukewarm water and sprinkle the yeast over the water.
Set aside for 10 minutes. Beat together the shortening, sugar, salt, baking soda,
and egg. Warm the buttermilk or sour milk and gradually stir in. Add 2 cups (450
ml) of the flour and beat well. Stir the yeast to be sure it is dissolved and mix into
the flour mixture. Add the rest of the flour. Knead on a lightly floured board until
smooth and elastic. Set aside to rise in a warm place for 1½ hours or until doubled
in bulk. Punch down and form into rolls. Place on a greased baking sheet and set
aside in a warm place for an hour or until doubled in bulk. Bake at 375°F (190°C)
for 15 minutes or until cooked. Cool on a rack.

Yield: 2½ dozen rolls

● **YEAST COFFEE BREADS, SWEET ROLLS, AND FRUIT LOAVES** ●

Sally Lunn

A coffee cake that rises high and bakes golden. Sally Lunn was named after the
woman who made them famous in Bath, England, several hundred years ago.
Serve it warm or cold with jam or honey for breakfast.

sugar   *1 teaspoon (5 ml)*
lukewarm water   *½ cup (110 ml)*
dry yeast   *1 tablespoon (15 ml)*
margarine   *½ cup (110 ml)*
sugar   *1/3 cup (75 ml)*
salt   *1½ teaspoons (7.5 ml)*
cardamom   *1 teaspoon (5 ml)*
eggs   *3*
milk, scalded and cooled   *1 cup (225 ml)*
dried lemon peel   *½ teaspoon (2.5 ml)*

or
fresh grated peel   *1 teaspoon (5 ml)*
currants   *½ cup (110 ml)*
flour   *4 cups (1 l)*

Dissolve the sugar in the lukewarm water and add the yeast. Allow to sit for 10 minutes. Cream the margarine, sugar, salt, cardamom, and eggs. Stir in the milk and dissolved yeast. Add the peel and currants. Beat in the flour. Let rise in a warm place for 1½ hours or until doubled. Stir down and spoon into a greased 10″ (3 l) tube pan. Let rise again until doubled, about 1 hour. Bake at 350°F (175°C) for 40 to 45 minutes or until golden brown.

Basic Fruit Bread Dough

Enough dough to make 12 Butterscotch Rolls and two small fruit loaves in the two following recipes.

sugar   *1 teaspoon (5 ml)*
lukewarm water   *1 cup (225 ml)*
dry yeast   *1 tablespoon (15 ml)*
shortening   *1/3 cup (75 ml)*
sugar   *½ cup (110 ml)*
egg   *1*
milk   *1 cup (225 ml)*
salt   *2 teaspoons (10 ml)*
grated orange rind   *1 tablespoon (15 ml)*
ground mace   *¼ teaspoon (1 ml)*
grated nutmeg   *½ teaspoon (2.5 ml)*
cinnamon   *2 teaspoons (10 ml)*
mixed candied fruit   *½ cup (110 ml)*
sliced maraschino cherries   *¼ cup (55 ml)*
raisins   *½ cup (110 ml)*
currants   *¼ cup (55 ml)*
flour   *5 cups (1.13 l)*

Dissolve the sugar in the water and sprinkle the yeast over it. Set aside for 10 minutes. Beat the shortening, sugar, and egg until creamy. Add the milk, salt, rind, mace, nutmeg, cinnamon, and fruits. Beat in 2 cups (450 ml) flour. Add the dissolved yeast and stir well. Work in the remaining flour and knead on a lightly floured board until smooth. Put in a warm place to rise for 1½ hours or until doubled. Use dough to make Butterscotch Cloverleaves and Fruit Bread, following.

197

Butterscotch Cloverleaves

A candy-glazed, fruit-filled dessert roll that can be served at any time.

Balls of Basic Fruit Bread dough 36 ¾″ (1.9 cm)

    butter, melted   2 tablespoons (30 ml)
    brown sugar   2 tablespoons (30 ml)
    corn syrup   2 tablespoons (30 ml)
    raisins, nuts

Mix the butter, sugar and syrup together and divide equally among 12 greased muffin cups. Place a few raisins and nuts in each cup. Place 3 fruit balls in each cup. Set aside in a warm place to rise for 45 to 60 minutes or until doubled. Bake at 375°F (190°C) for 15 to 20 minutes. Allow to rest for 5 minutes when taken from the oven. Then turn the pan upside down on a large plate and allow to rest for another 2 to 3 minutes. Remove the muffin pan, making sure the cloverleaves have all loosened. Serve warm or cold.

Yield: 12 cloverleaves

Fruit Bread

A moist fruit bread — use it as a breakfast treat as well as a dessert bread.
    Form the remaining fruit dough into 2 loaves and place in 2 greased loaf pans. Set aside in a warm place to rise until doubled, about 1½ hours. Bake at 375°F (190°C) for 40 minutes. Brush top with melted butter or ice with butter icing as desired. Serve sliced with butter.

Yield: 2 small loaves

• STEAMED BREAD •

Steamed Boston Brown Bread

This bread is a must with baked beans. Originally it was steamed in one large dish, but I find three small rolls a better size to manage and easy to slice.

    all-purpose flour   1 cup (225 ml)
    baking soda   1¼ teaspoons (6 ml)
    baking powder   1 teaspoon (5 ml)
    salt   1 teaspoon (5 ml)
    cornmeal   1 cup (225 ml)

shortening   *1/3 cup (75 ml)*
seeded raisins   *½ cup (110 ml)*
graham flour   *1 cup (225 ml)*
thick sour milk   *1½ cups (335 ml)*
molasses   *½ cup (110 ml)*

Sift together the white flour, soda, baking powder, and salt. Stir in the cornmeal. Cut in the shortening and add the raisins. Stir in the graham flour. Mix together the milk and molasses and stir in only until combined. Spoon into 3 oiled 19-ounce (540 ml) cans, (each will be 2/3 full). Cover tops with waxed paper and tie. Sit on a rack in a deep saucepan and pour in boiling water to a level halfway up the sides of the cans. Cover and steam 2½ hours. Cool partially. Cut bottoms from cans and gently push out the bread. Slice and serve warm with butter.

Yield: 3 round loaves

● MUFFINS ●

Muffins are like biscuits but much easier to make, since there is no rolling or cutting. The variety in muffins is even greater than in biscuits. I have a real problem with myself when making biscuits and muffins. The success of one's efforts lies in having enough will-power to stop mixing at the precise moment the dry ingredients are moistened by the liquid ingredients. I find myself wanting to give it just "one more stir to be sure", and muffins with holes and tough biscuits are the result.

Banana Muffins

flour   *2 cups (450 ml)*
baking powder   *2 teaspoons (10 ml)*
sugar   *1/3 cup (75 ml)*
salt   *¾ teaspoon (4 ml)*
raisins   *½ cup (110 ml)*
beaten egg   *1*
milk   *2/3 cup (150 ml)*
mashed banana   *1 cup (225 ml)*
vegetable oil   *3 tablespoons (45 ml)*

Sift together the dry ingredients, and stir in the raisins. Mix together the egg, milk, banana, and oil, then mix with the dry ingredients only until moistened. Fill greased muffin cups 2/3 full. Cook at 400°F (205°C) for 15 to 20 minutes.

Yield: 14 muffins

Bran Muffins

Bran muffins are the most popular muffins of all, but their ingredients vary widely. Serve these warm with honey for a treat on Sunday morning. I make them beforehand, freeze them, then reheat them.

bran   1 cup (225 ml)
milk   ¾ cup (170 ml)
shortening   3 tablespoons (45 ml)
brown sugar   1/3 cup (75 ml)
egg   1
raisins or dates   ½ cup (110 ml)
flour   1 cup (225 ml)
salt   ½ teaspoon (2.5 ml)
baking powder   3 teaspoons (15 ml)

Stir together the bran and milk and let soak until moisture is taken up. Beat in the shortening, sugar, and egg. Add the raisins or dates. Sift together the dry ingredients and stir into first mixture only until just moistened. Fill greased muffin pans 2/3 full and bake in a 400°F (205°C) oven 25 minutes.

Yield: 12 medium muffins

Honey Bran Muffins

A moist and fluffy muffin that browns well because of the honey.

sifted flour   1¼ cups (280 ml)
baking powder   3½ teaspoons (17.5 ml)
salt   ¾ teaspoon (4 ml)
bran   1½ cups (335 ml)
raisins   ½ cup (110 ml)
honey   1/3 cup (75 ml)
egg, well beaten   1
milk   1 cup (225 ml)
cooking oil   4 tablespoons (60 ml)

Sift together the flour, baking powder and salt. Stir in the bran and raisins. Mix together the honey, egg, milk, and oil and stir lightly into dry ingredients until just moistened. Fill well-greased muffin pans 2/3 full. Bake in 400°F (205°C) oven 15 to 20 minutes.

Yield: 14 medium-sized muffins

Molasses Bran Muffins

Molasses make these a beautiful brown and moist in texture.

    sour milk   ½ cup (110 ml)
    molasses   ½ cup (110 ml)
    bran   1 cup (225 ml)
    egg   1
    shortening   4 tablespoons (60 ml)
    raisins   ½ cup (110 ml)
    flour   1 cup (225 ml)
    baking powder   2 teaspoons (10 ml)
    baking soda   ½ teaspoon (2.5 ml)
    salt   ½ teaspoon (2.5 ml)

Combine the milk, molasses, and bran. Let stand until moisture is taken up. Add the egg and shortening and beat well. Mix in the raisins. Sift together the dry ingredients and stir into bran mixture only enough to moisten. Fill greased muffin cups 2/3 full. Bake at 400°F (205°C) for 15 to 20 minutes.

Yield: 12 muffins

Cornmeal Muffins

A moist, tasty muffin that rises well.

    flour   1 cup (225 ml)
    sugar   1/3 cup (75 ml)
    baking soda   1 teaspoon (5 ml)
    baking powder   2 teaspoons (10 ml)
    salt   ¾ teaspoon (4 ml)
    yellow cornmeal   1 cup (225 ml)
    egg, beaten   1
    sour milk   1 cup (225 ml)
    vegetable oil   ¼ cup (55 ml)

Sift together the flour, sugar, soda, baking powder, and salt. Stir in the cornmeal. Beat together the egg, milk, and oil. Mix with the dry ingredients only until moistened. Spoon into greased muffin tins, filling them 2/3 full. Bake at 400°F (205°C) for 15 to 20 minutes. Serve cold or warm.

Yield: 12 medium muffins

Plain Muffins

Here is another recipe that can be made ahead into a mix if desired. Let your imagination take over and vary with added fruit, spices, or peels. But they're good just plain, served hot with butter.

Mix thoroughly together:
flour   2 cups (450 ml)
sugar   2 tablespoons (30 ml)
baking powder   4 teaspoons (20 ml)
salt   ½ teaspoon (2.5 ml)
powdered milk   1/3 cup (75 ml)
When ready to bake add:
egg, beaten   1
water   1 cup (225 ml)
cooking oil   ¼ cup (55 ml)

Stir just until dry ingredients are moistened. Spoon into greased muffin pans, filling 2/3 full. Bake at 400°F (205°C) for 20 to 25 minutes.

Yield: 12 medium muffins

Graham Gems

To Scots, gems and muffins are synonymous. These would be good with dates added for a change. This recipe originally called for butter and lard instead of oil.

graham flour   1½ cups (335 ml)
all-purpose flour   ½ cup (55 ml)
baking powder   2 teaspoons (10 ml)
baking soda   1 teaspoon (5 ml)
salt   ¾ teaspoon (4 ml)
sugar   1 tablespoon (15 ml)
sour milk   1 cup (225 ml)
molasses   1 tablespoon (15 ml)
egg, beaten   1
cooking oil   2 tablespoons (30 ml)

Thoroughly mix together all the dry ingredients. Measure the molasses, egg and oil into the milk and mix thoroughly. Make a well in the centre of the flour mixture and pour in liquids all at once. Stir with a fork only until the dry ingredients are dampened. Spoon into well-greased muffin tins, filling them ¾ full. Bake at 400°F (205°C) for 15 minutes.

Yield: 12 medium muffins

Oatmeal Muffins

These muffins are a golden yellow and the aroma, when baking, will bring the whole family.

flour   1 cup (225 ml)
brown sugar   3 tablespoons (45 ml)
baking powder   3 teaspoons (15 ml)
salt   ¾ teaspoon (4 ml)
cinnamon   ¼ teaspoon (1 ml)
shortening   4 tablespoons (60 ml)
minute oatmeal   1 cup (225 ml)
finely chopped dates or raisins   ½ cup (110 ml)
egg, beaten   1
milk   1 cup (225 ml)
molasses   2 tablespoons (30 ml)

Sift together all the dry ingredients except the oatmeal. Cut in the shortening. Mix in the oatmeal and dates. Stir together the egg, milk, and molasses and pour all at once into dry mixture, stirring with a fork just until moistened. Spoon into 12 greased muffin cups, filling them 2/3 full, and bake at 400°F (205°C) for 20 to 25 minutes.

Yield: 12 muffins

Honey-Cinnamon Muffins

Honey makes these muffins bake to a beautiful brown.

sifted flour   2 cups (450 ml)
baking soda   ½ teaspoon (2.5 ml)
baking powder   2 teaspoons (10 ml)
cinnamon   1 teaspoon (5 ml)
salt   1 teaspoon (5 ml)
brown sugar   ¼ cup (55 ml)
egg, beaten   1
honey   3 tablespoons (45 ml)
sour milk   1 cup (225 ml)
cooking oil   2 tablespoons (30 ml)

Sift together the flour, baking powder, soda, cinnamon, and salt. Stir in the sugar. Combine the egg, milk, honey, and oil. Stir liquids into the dry ingredients until just moistened. Spoon into greased muffin cups, filling them 2/3 full, and bake at 425°F (220°C) for 20 to 25 minutes.

Yield: 11 muffins

Molasses Gems

Spicy and full of flavour.

    flour   2 cups (450 ml)
    salt   ½ teaspoon (2.5 ml)
    baking powder   2 teaspoons (10 ml)
    baking soda   ¼ teaspoon (1 ml)
    sugar   3 tablespoons (45 ml)
    ginger   ½ teaspoon (2.5 ml)
    cinnamon   1 teaspoon (5 ml)
    cloves   ¼ teaspoon (1 ml)
    cooking oil   3 tablespoons (45 ml)
    egg, beaten   1
    molasses   ½ cup (110 ml)
    sour milk   ½ cup (110 ml)

Sift together the dry ingredients. Combine the egg, milk, oil, and molasses. Add all at once to the flour mixture, stirring with a fork only until moistened. Spoon into greased muffin tins, filling them 2/3 full, and bake at 375°F (190°C) for 15 minutes.

Yield: 12 muffins

Pumpkin Muffins

Golden, moist, and spicy!

    flour   1½ cups (335 ml)
    baking powder   2 teaspoons (10 ml)
    salt   ½ teaspoon (2.5 ml)
    sugar   2/3 cup (150 ml)
    cinnamon   ½ teaspoon (2.5 ml)
    nutmeg   ¼ teaspoon (1 ml)
    ginger   ½ teaspoon (2.5 ml)
    cooking oil   1/3 cup (75 ml)
    egg   1
    cooked pumpkin   ¾ cup (170 ml)
    milk   ¼ cup (55 ml)
    seedless raisins   ½ cup (110 ml)

Sift together the dry ingredients. Stir together the liquids, pumpkin, and egg. Add the raisins to the dry ingredients, then stir in the liquids just until moistened. Spoon into greased muffin tins, filling them 2/3 full. Bake at 400°F (205°C) for 15 to 20 minutes. Serve warm or cold.

Yield: 12 muffins

Whole-wheat Muffins

Quick to mix up at the last minute for a special touch to your meal.

> all-purpose flour   ¾ cup (170 ml)
> wheat germ   ¼ cup (55 ml)
> whole-wheat flour   1 cup (225 ml)
> baking powder   4 teaspoons (20 ml)
> salt   ¾ teaspoon (4 ml)
> sugar   1 tablespoon (15 ml)
> egg, well beaten   1
> melted butter or oil   4 tablespoons (60 ml)
> milk   1 cup (225 ml)
> molasses   2 tablespoons (30 ml)

Sift together the dry ingredients. Stir the liquids together and mix all at once and quickly into the dry mixture until just moistened and still lumpy. Fill greased muffin tins 2/3 full and bake at 375°F (190°C) for 20 minutes.

Yield: 12 medium muffins

Orange Cranberry Muffins

Red berries peep out from a golden brown biscuit.

> fresh cranberries, halved   1 cup (225 ml)
> powdered sugar   ½ cup (110 ml)
> flour   2 cups (450 ml)
> baking powder   2 teaspoons (10 ml)
> sugar   ¼ cup (55 ml)
> salt   1 teaspoon (5 ml)
> egg, beaten   1
> orange juice   ¾ cup (170 ml)
> vegetable oil   ¼ cup (55 ml)

Mix the cut cranberries with the powdered sugar and set aside. Sift together the dry ingredients. Thoroughly combine the egg, juice, and oil and pour into the dry ingredients, stirring with a fork until just moistened. Fold in the sugared cranberries. Spoon into greased muffin tins, filling them 2/3 full, and bake at 400°F (205°C) for 20 minutes. Serve warm or cold.

Yield: 12 medium muffins

Applesauce Muffins

These are one of my family's favourites.

    flour   1½ cups (335 ml)
    baking powder   2 teaspoons (10 ml)
    salt   ½ teaspoon (2.5 ml)
    cinnamon   ½ teaspoon (2.5 ml)
    nutmeg   ¼ teaspoon (1 ml)
    sugar   2/3 cup (150 ml)
    cooking oil   1/3 cup (75 ml)
    egg   1
    sweetened applesauce   ¾ cup (170 ml)

Sift together the dry ingredients. Thoroughly beat the oil, egg, and applesauce and stir into the dry ingredients only until moistened. Bake in greased muffin tins, filled 2/3 full, at 375°F (190°C) for 15 to 20 minutes.

Yield: 12 muffins

Cinnamon Muffins

This recipe came from the recipe book of the late Mrs. E.H. Wright of Conway, Ontario. The original recipe called for butter or drippings, but I find cooking oil is as good and is handy. These muffins rise high and cook to a golden brown.

    flour   2½ cups (560 ml)
    salt   1 teaspoon (5 ml)
    ground cinnamon   1 teaspoon (5 ml)
    baking soda   1 teaspoon (5 ml)
    brown sugar   1 cup (225 ml)
    egg   1
    sour milk   1½ cups (335 ml)
    vegetable oil   ½ cup (110 ml)

Sift together the flour, salt, cinnamon, and soda. Stir in the sugar until well blended. Beat the egg and add to the sour milk and oil. Pour into the dry mixture all at once and blend with a fork only until dry ingredients are moistened. Spoon into greased muffin pans (rings, as our grandmothers called them), filled 2/3 full, and bake at 400°F (205°C) for 15 to 20 minutes. Serve warm or cool on a rack.

Yield: 16 medium muffins

Tea biscuits were very popular among the settlers because they were quick to make and could be popped into the oven just before the meal was served. At first they were just plain biscuits, but all kinds of variations have been developed. They used to be made with cream of tartar and baking soda, but baking powder is easier to use.

English Tea Biscuits

Currants give a special flavour to these biscuits. For added interest, try cutting them with a donut cutter.

    flour   *2 cups (450 ml)*
    baking powder   *3 teaspoons (15 ml)*
    salt   *2/3 teaspoon (4 ml)*
    sugar   *½ cup (110 ml)*
    shortening   *¼ cup (55 ml)*
    currants or raisins   *½ cup (110 ml)*
    egg, beaten   *1*
    milk   *½ cup (110 ml)*

Sift together the dry ingredients and cut in the shortening. Add the currants or raisins. Mix the milk and beaten egg together. Stir, lightly, into the flour mixture. Roll out on a lightly floured board to ¾″ (2 cm) thickness. Cut with doughnut or biscuit cutter. Brush with milk and sprinkle with sugar. Bake on ungreased cookie sheet at 425°F (220°C) for 20 minutes. Serve hot or cold, buttered.

Yield: 14   2″ (5 cm) biscuits

Soda Biscuits

They rise high and light and are good warm, served with soup and stews.

    flour   *2 cups (450 ml)*
    baking soda   *½ teaspoon (2.5 ml)*
    salt   *½ teaspoon (2.5 ml)*
    shortening   *4 tablespoons (60 ml)*
    sour milk   *¾ cup (170 ml)*

Sift together the dry ingredients and cut in the shortening. Stir in the milk to make a stiff dough. Turn onto a floured board and knead slightly. Roll ½" (1.25 cm) thick and cut with a biscuit cutter. Bake on an ungreased baking sheet at 425°F (220°C) for 15 minutes or until lightly browned. Serve warm with butter.

Yield: 12 biscuits

Cheese Straws

These golden-brown straws are the perfect accompaniment for soup. I prepare the dry mixture ahead of time, then about 20 minutes before serving, add the water, roll and cut them, and pop them into the oven. They come out piping hot with a delicious aroma of cheese, just in time to be eaten with the soup. You can reheat any leftovers for another day. Freeze them in the meantime.

> flour   *1 cup (225 ml)*
> baking powder   *1 teaspoon (5 ml)*
> salt   *2/3 teaspoon (4 ml)*
> dry mustard   *½ teaspoon (2.5 ml)*
> cooking oil   *2 tablespoons (30 ml)*
> finely shredded Cheddar cheese   *1½ cups (335 ml)*
> water   *6½ tablespoons (98 ml)*

Sift together the dry ingredients and rub in the oil until it resembles fine crumbs. Stir in the cheese. Add enough water to make a dough that can be rolled. Roll ¼" (0.5 cm) thick on a floured board and cut into strips 3" X ½" (7.5 X 1 cm). Bake on ungreased cookie sheets at 425°F (220°C) for 10 minutes or until light brown. Serve hot.

Yield: 2½ dozen straws

Baking Powder Biscuits

Quick to make and good with almost anything. Serve them hot from the oven with lots of butter.

> flour   *2 cups (450 ml)*
> baking powder   *2 teaspoons (10 ml)*
> salt   *2/3 teaspoon (4 ml)*
> shortening   *¼ cup (55 ml)*
> milk

Sift together the dry ingredients. Cut in the shortening. With a fork, stir in enough milk to make a soft dough — about ½ cup (110 ml). Roll out lightly on a floured board and cut with a biscuit cutter. Bake on ungreased sheets in a 425°F (220°C) oven 20 to 25 minutes.

Yield: 10 biscuits

Buttermilk Herb Fingers

    sifted flour   *2 cups (450 ml)*
    baking powder   *3 teaspoons (15 ml)*
    baking soda   *¼ teaspoon (1 ml)*
    salt   *1 teaspoon (5 ml)*
    thyme   *¼ teaspoon (1 ml)*
    savory   *1/8 teaspoon (0.5 ml)*
    oregano   *¼ teaspoon (1 ml)*
    shortening   *1/3 cup (75 ml)*
    sour milk   *¾ cup + 2 tablespoons (190 ml)*

Sift together the first four ingredients and stir in the herbs. Cut in the shortening and add the milk, stirring with a fork only until dry ingredients are moistened. Knead gently a few times on a lightly floured surface. Cut into rounds or strips. Bake on ungreased sheets 10 to 12 minutes in a 425°F (220°C) oven.

Yield: 15 biscuits or 24 fingers

Bran Scones

    flour   *1 cup (225 ml)*
    salt   *½ teaspoon (2.5 ml)*
    baking powder   *4 teaspoons (20 ml)*
    brown sugar   *¼ cup (55 ml)*
    shortening   *3 tablespoons (45 ml)*
    bran   *1 cup (225 ml)*
    milk   *½ cup (110 ml)*

Sift together the flour, salt, and baking powder. Stir in the sugar. Cut in the shortening and add the bran. Stir in the milk to make a dough that can be handled. Turn out on a lightly floured board and roll or press out to ½″ (1.5 cm) thickness. Cut in diamond shapes and bake on a greased and floured baking sheet at 425°F (220°C) for 15 minutes. Serve warm with butter.

Yield: 12 scones

Scotch Scones

These are delicious served warm with fresh strawberry jam. If you have sour milk to use up, this is a great way to do it.

    flour   3 cups (675 ml)
    baking powder   4 teaspoons (20 ml)
    salt   1 teaspoon (5 ml)
    sugar   ½ cup (110 ml)
    shortening   2/3 cup (150 ml)
    currants or raisins   2/3 cup (150 ml)
    egg, beaten   1
    sour milk   1¼ cups (280 ml)
    baking soda   ½ teaspoon (2.5 ml)

Sift together all dry ingredients except soda. Cut in the shortening. Add the currants or raisins. Add beaten egg, saving a little to brush over the tops. Dissolve the soda in the sour milk and add to first mixture, mixing just until moistened. Press out on lightly floured board and cut into diamond shapes. Brush with reserved egg. Bake on ungreased cookie sheets in a 425°F (220°C) oven for 12 to 15 minutes.

Yield: 3 dozen scones

Raisin Sugar Scones

These scones are one of my happy memories of afternoon tea at my aunt's, Mrs. F.B. Wright, of Conway, Ontario. They will melt in your mouth, hot from the oven, with butter. The original recipe calls for a mixture of lard and butter, but margarine or shortening work equally well.

    flour   2½ cups (560 ml)
    sugar   ¾ cup (170 ml)
    salt   ½ teaspoon (2.5 ml)
    baking powder   4 teaspoons (20 ml)
    shortening   2/3 cup (150 ml)
    raisins   1 cup (225 ml)
    egg, beaten light   1
    sweet milk

Sift together the dry ingredients. Cut in the shortening until fine and crumbly. Add the raisins. Add enough milk to beaten egg to make 1 cup (225 ml). Stir in with a fork only until dry ingredients are moistened. Turn out on a floured board and roll ½″ (1.25 cm) thick. Cut in diamond shapes and place on an ungreased baking sheet. Sprinkle lightly with sugar. Bake at 425°F (220°C) for 12 to 15 minutes. These may be reheated for later use.

Yield: 3 dozen scones

Chelsea Biscuits

These biscuits have many names and are sometimes called Railroad Biscuits. They are a good change from cookies and cake, along with fruit, for dessert.

    flour   *2 cups (450 ml)*
    salt   *2/3 teaspoon (4 ml)*
    baking powder   *2 teaspoons (10 ml)*
    shortening   *½ cup (110 ml)*
    milk
    butter, melted   *1 tablespoon (15 ml)*
    brown sugar   *¼ cup (55 ml)*
    cinnamon   *¼ teaspoon (1 ml)*

Sift together the dry ingredients. Cut in the shortening until crumbly. Mix in about ½ cup (110 ml) milk, lightly, to make a dough. Roll out and spread with butter. Sprinkle sugar and cinnamon over all. Roll up like a jelly roll. Slice in ½″ (1.25 cm) slices and place on greased baking sheet. Bake at 400°F (205°C) for 18 to 20 minutes.

Yield: 1 dozen biscuits

Butterscotch Biscuits

These are a variation of the preceding recipe, a little more trouble but well worth it.

    flour   *2 cups (450 ml)*
    salt   *2/3 teaspoon (4 ml)*
    baking powder   *2 teaspoons (10 ml)*
    shortening   *½ cup (110 ml)*
    milk
    soft butter   *4 tablespoons (60 ml)*
    brown sugar   *5 tablespoons (75 ml)*
    corn syrup   *5 tablespoons (75 ml)*

Make up the biscuit dough as instructed in the recipe preceding and roll ¼″ (0.5 cm) thick. Blend the butter, sugar, and corn syrup, and put half this mixture in the bottoms of 12 muffin cups. Spread the other half over the rolled dough. Roll as a jelly roll and cut into 12 slices. Place one slice in each muffin cup. Bake at 400°F (205°C) for 20 to 25 minutes. Allow to cool 5 minutes. Then invert pan over a rack and remove biscuits. Complete cooling on rack.

Yield: 12 biscuits

Jelly Biscuits

Quick to make, nice to look at, and good to eat.

    flour   *2 cups (450 ml)*
    baking powder   *3 teaspoons (15 ml)*
    baking soda   *¼ teaspoon (1 ml)*
    salt   *¾ teaspoon (4 ml)*
    cinnamon   *¼ teaspoon (1 ml)*
    sugar   *¼ cup (55 ml)*
    egg   *1*
    cooking oil   *1/3 cup (75 ml)*
    sour milk   *¾ cup (170 ml)*
    jam

Sift the dry ingredients together. Beat the egg and reserve 1 teaspoon (5 ml) for glazing tops. Mix the egg, milk and oil together. Add to flour mixture, stirring only until moistened. Knead lightly on a floured board. Roll out ½″ (1.25 cm) thick, cut with biscuit cutter, and place on a greased pan. Mix reserved egg with 1 teaspoon (5 ml) water and brush tops. Make deep indentation in the middle and fill with jam. Sprinkle lightly with sugar. Bake at 425°F (220°C) for 8 to 10 minutes.

Yield: 14 biscuits

Jam Bran Scones

Golden triangles filled with jam or jelly!

    egg   *1*
    sour milk   *1 cup (225 ml)*
    cooking oil   *1/3 cup (75 ml)*
    bran   *¾ cup (170 ml)*
    flour   *2 cups (450 ml)*
    salt   *1 teaspoon (5 ml)*
    baking powder   *3 teaspoons (15 ml)*
    baking soda   *¼ teaspoon (1 ml)*

brown sugar   *1/3 cup (75 ml)*
jam or jelly

Beat together the egg, sour milk, and oil. Mix with the bran and allow to stand while sifting together the dry ingredients. Stir the brown sugar into the flour mixture, then stir into the bran until just moistened. Turn out on a well-floured board and press out in a rectangle ¼" (0.5 cm) thick. Cut in 3" (7.5 cm) squares. Place 1 teaspoon (5 ml) jam or jelly in the centre of each and fold over. Seal edges with a fork. Place on a greased baking sheet. Bake at 425°F (220°C) for 12 - 15 minutes.

Yield: 1½ dozen scones

Oatmeal Fruit bars

These scone-like bars are delicious with coffee or milk. The original recipe called for "raw oatmeal" and "rolled wheat".

oatmeal   *3 cups (675 ml)*
whole wheat flour   *4 cups (1 l)*
sugar   *1½ cups (335 ml)*
baking soda   *1 teaspoon (5 ml)*
salt   *1½ teaspoons (7.5 ml)*
seeded raisins   *1 cup (225 ml)*
melted butter   *1 cup (225 ml)*
water   *1 cup (225 ml)*

Mix together all the dry ingredients. Add the raisins and melted butter and stir until mixture is in coarse crumbs. Add enough water to make a stiff dough. Turn out on an unfloured board and roll to ½" (1.25 cm) thick rectangle. Cut in 1" X 3" (2.5 X 7.5 cm) bars and lay on greased tins. Bake at 375°F (190°C) for 10 minutes or until lightly browned.

Yield: 4 dozen bars

• QUICK FRUIT AND NUT BREADS •

Nut Loaf

My mother used to make this with the hickory nuts that we gathered each year on our farm.

```
shortening    2 tablespoons (30 ml)
sugar    ½ cup (110 ml)
eggs    2
flour    2 cups (450 ml)
baking powder    4 teaspoons (20 ml)
salt    ¾ teaspoon (4 ml)
milk    1 cup (225 ml)
chopped nuts    ½ cup or more (110 ml)
raisins or currants, if desired    1 cup (225 ml)
```

Cream the shortening; add the sugar, beating until fluffy. Add the eggs and beat well. Sift together flour, baking powder, and salt and add to the creamed mixture alternately with milk. Dust nuts, and fruit if used, with flour. Fold in gently. Turn into a greased loaf pan and let stand for ½ hour. Then bake at 350°F (175°C) for 40 minutes. Cool and serve in slices with butter.

Yield: 1 loaf

Date Bread

This bread is even better the second day after baking. Serve it sliced and buttered.

```
dates    1 pound (455 g)
baking soda    2 teaspoons (10 ml)
boiling water    1 cup (225 ml)
sugar    1 cup (225 ml)
butter    1½ tablespoons (22.5 ml)
flour    1¾ cups (395 ml)
egg    1
salt    ½ teaspoon (2.5 ml)
vanilla    1 teaspoon (5 ml)
```

Chop the dates, sprinkle soda over them, and pour on the boiling water. Let stand till mixture is just warm. Add the sugar and butter, and blend in 1 cup (225 ml) flour. Add the egg, blend well, then add rest of flour and the salt; mix in the vanilla. Turn into a well-greased loaf pan, 2/3 full as batter rises well. Bake at 350°F (175°C) for 40 minutes.

Yield: 1 loaf

Bran Raisin Bread

Moist and delicious any time of the day, from breakfast through afternoon tea.

    flour   2 cups (450 ml)
    sugar   1 cup (225 ml)
    salt   ¾ teaspoon (4 ml)
    shortening   3 tablespoons (45 ml)
    bran   2 cups (450 ml)
    raisins, floured   1½ cups (335 ml)
    egg   1
    molasses   ¼ cup (55 ml)
    either
    sour milk   2 cups (450 ml)
    and
    baking soda   2 teaspoons (10 ml)
    or
    sweet milk   2 cups (450 ml)
    and
    baking powder   4 teaspoons (20 ml)

Sift together the flour, sugar, salt, and either soda or baking powder depending on type of milk used. Cut in the shortening. Add the bran and floured raisins. Beat the egg and add with the molasses to the milk. Add the liquids to the dry mixture and mix well. Place in a well-greased loaf pan and let stand 20 minutes. Then bake at 350°F (175°C) for 45 minutes. Remove from pan to cool on rack. Brush the top with melted butter. Serve sliced with butter.

Yield: 1 loaf

Cranberry Bread

Cut the baked loaf in two and freeze half to have on hand for unexpected coffee company.

    halved cranberries   1½ cups (335 ml)
    sugar   1 cup (225 ml)
    flour   3 cups (675 ml)
    baking powder   3 teaspoons (15 ml)
    baking soda   1 teaspoon (5 ml)
    salt   1 teaspoon (5 ml)
    grated orange rind   1 tablespoon (15 ml)
    egg   1
    sour milk   1½ cups (335 ml)
    cooking oil   4 tablespoons (60 ml)

Mix ¼ cup (55 ml) of the sugar with the halved cranberries. Set aside. Sift together the dry ingredients and stir in the orange rind. Mix together the egg, milk, and oil, then stir into the dry ingredients only until moistened. Fold in the sugared fruit. Bake in a greased loaf pan for 1 hour at 350°F (175°C). Cool and serve, sliced, with butter.

Yield: 1 loaf

Mixed Fruit Bread

This is a pretty bread when sliced and is better the second day when the flavours of the fruits have penetrated it.

    flour   *2 cups (450 ml)*
    baking powder   *4 teaspoons (20 ml)*
    salt   *1 teaspoon (5 ml)*
    sugar   *¾ cup (170 ml)*
    shortening   *½ cup (110 ml)*
    rolled oats   *1 cup (225 ml)*
    snipped dried mixed fruit   *1 cup (225 ml)*
    chopped walnuts   *½ cup (110 ml)*
    egg   *1*
    milk   *1½ cups (335 ml)*

Sift together the flour, baking powder, and salt. Stir in the sugar. Cut in the shortening until texture is of coarse crumbs. Stir in the rolled oats, nuts, and mixed fruits. Beat the egg and mix with the milk, then add all at once to the dry ingredients and stir lightly only until moistened. Pour into a greased loaf pan. Bake at 350°F (175°C) for 1 hour. Cool and serve sliced with butter.

Yield: 1 loaf

Pumpkin Bread

Early housewives made a delicious bread from cornmeal and pumpkin. The cornmeal gives this bread a slightly crunchy texture.

    cornmeal   *1/3 cup (75 ml)*
    boiling water   *1/3 cup (75 ml)*
    sifted flour   *1-1/3 cups (300 ml)*
    baking soda   *1 teaspoon (5 ml)*
    baking powder   *2 teaspoons (10 ml)*
    cinnamon   *½ teaspoon (2.5 ml)*
    nutmeg   *½ teaspoon (2.5 ml)*
    ginger   *½ teaspoon (2.5 ml)*

216

salt   ¾ teaspoon (4 ml)
vegetable oil   ½ cup (110 ml)
sugar   2/3 cup (150 ml)
eggs   2
cooked pumpkin   2/3 cup (150 ml)
raisins   2/3 cup (150 ml)

Pour the boiling water over the cornmeal and allow to cool completely. Sift together the dry ingredients except for sugar. Add the oil, sugar, and eggs to the cornmeal and beat thoroughly. Stir in the dry ingredients alternately with the pumpkin, saving a little flour mixture to dust the raisins, which are added last. Grease a loaf pan, dust with flour, and line the bottom with waxed paper. Pour in the batter and bake at 350°F (175°C) for 50 to 60 minutes. Serve sliced with butter.

Yield: 1 loaf

Raisin Loaf

A spicy, moist loaf that rises well. Eat one now and freeze one for later.

seedless raisins   1½ cups (335 ml)
boiling water   1¾ cups (395 ml)
shortening   ½ cup (110 ml)
sugar   1½ cups (335 ml)
eggs   2
flour   3 cups (675 ml)
cinnamon   1 teaspoon (5 ml)
nutmeg   ½ teaspoon (2.5 ml)
cloves   ¼ teaspoon (1 ml)
baking soda   1 teaspoon (5 ml)
baking powder   2 teaspoons (10 ml)
salt   1½ teaspoons (7.5 ml)
nuts, chopped (optional)   1 cup (225 ml)

Pour the boiling water over the raisins and set aside until cool. Blend together the shortening, sugar, and eggs until creamy. Sift together the dry ingredients and mix alternately into the creamed mixture with the raisins and water. Add the nuts if desired. Pour into two greased loaf pans. Bake at 350°F (175°C) for 50 to 60 minutes. Cool and serve sliced with butter.

Yield: 2 loaves

Graham Loaf

This recipe came from the cookbook of the late Mrs. E.H. Wright of Conway, Ontario. It is a delicious, moist bread with a nut-like texture, nice to serve as a breakfast bread with jam or as a first-course accompaniment.

cornmeal   1 cup (225 ml)
water   1¼ cups (280 ml)
graham flour   2 cups (450 ml)
baking powder   2 teaspoons (10 ml)
salt   1 teaspoon (5 ml)
sugar   ½ cup (110 ml)
eggs   2
cooking oil   ½ cup (110 ml)

Pour the water over the cornmeal and set aside for 5 minutes. Thoroughly combine the flour, baking powder, salt, and sugar. Beat the eggs well and stir in the oil. Add the flour mixture to the cornmeal mixture, then add the egg mixture, stirring until just moistened. Turn into a greased loaf pan and bake at 375°F (190°C) for 40 minutes. Cool and serve sliced with butter.

Yield: 1 loaf

Banana Bread

Banana bread is an old-time favourite. This loaf rises high and is moist and tender.

shortening   1/3 cup (75 ml)
sugar   ¾ cup (170 ml)
eggs   2
sifted pastry flour   1-2/3 cups (375 ml)
salt   ½ teaspoon (2.5 ml)
baking soda   1 teaspoon (5 ml)
baking powder   1 teaspoon (5 ml)
chopped nuts   ½ cup (110 ml)
mashed bananas   1 cup (225 ml)

Thoroughly cream the shortening, sugar, and eggs. Sift together the dry ingredients and dust the nuts with 1 teaspoon (5 ml) of the mixture. Mix the dry ingredients into the creamed mixture alternately with the banana. Fold the nuts in last. Bake in a greased loaf pan at 350°F (175°C) for 60 to 65 minutes.

Yield: 1 loaf

Upside-down Prune Cake

A delicious coffee cake that's good warm or cold.

> butter   *2 tablespoons (30 ml)*
> brown sugar   *½ cup (110 ml)*
> chopped nuts   *¼ cup (55 ml)*
> pitted, cooked prunes
> sifted, pastry flour   *1 cup (225 ml)*
> baking powder   *1 teaspoon (5 ml)*
> salt   *½ teaspoon (2.5 ml)*
> egg   *1*
> sugar   *½ cup (110 ml)*
> milk   *¼ cup (55 ml)*
> vanilla   *1 teaspoon (5 ml)*
> cooking oil   *2 tablespoons (30 ml)*

Melt the butter in an 8″ (2 l) square cake pan. Sprinkle the brown sugar and chopped nuts evenly over butter. Cover with drained, pitted prunes and set aside. Sift together the flour, baking powder, and salt. Beat the egg until light and add the sugar, beating until creamy. Add the dry ingredients to the creamed mixture alternately with the milk, beating well. Add the oil and vanilla and combine completely. Pour over the prune mixture in pan and bake at 350°F (175°C) for 35 to 40 minutes.

Yield: 6 servings

● **DOUGHNUTS** ●

In early days "fried cake" and "doughnut" denoted two different types of cakes. Just as the names imply, fried cake meant a cake made of stiff cake batter, fried. A doughnut was made of yeast dough, fried. Lard was used for frying, as it was usually in good supply.

Old-fashioned Fried Cakes

This recipe originally called for "one granite cup of milk, one tea cup of sugar and four tablespoons of drippings".

shortening   1/3 cup (75 ml)
sugar   1 cup (225 ml)
eggs   2
flour   3-2/3 cups (825 ml)
baking powder   4 teaspoons (20 ml)
nutmeg   1 teaspoon (5 ml)
cinnamon   1 teaspoon (5 ml)
salt   1¾ teaspoons (9 ml)
milk   1 cup (225 ml)
fat for frying

Thoroughly cream the shortening, sugar, and eggs. Sift 2 cups (450 ml) of flour with the nutmeg, cinnamon, salt, and baking powder. Add alternately with the milk to the first mixture. Mix in the rest of the flour to make a soft dough. Roll out lightly on a floured board to ¾" (2 cm) thickness. Cut with a floured doughnut cutter. Fry in deep fat at 365°F (185°C) for 3 to 4 minutes, turning only once. The fried cakes will darken slightly after they have been removed from the fryer. Drain well on absorbent paper.

Yield: 1½ dozen large cakes — 1½ dozen "holes"

Potato Fried Cakes

A deliciously moist and light cake.

shortening   3 tablespoons (45 ml)
eggs   2
sugar   1 cup (225 ml)
milk   1/3 cup (75 ml)
mashed potatoes   1 cup (225 ml)
flour   2¾ cups (620 ml)
baking powder   3 teaspoons (15 ml)
salt   1 teaspoon (5 ml)

Thoroughly cream the shortening, sugar, and eggs. Add the milk and potatoes. Sift together the dry ingredients and stir well into potato mixture. Roll on a lightly floured board to ½" (1.25 cm) thickness. Cut with a floured doughnut cutter. Fry in deep fat at 365°F (185°C) for 2 to 3 minutes. Drain on absorbent paper.

Yield: 1½ dozen large fried cakes

Prize Doughnuts

These doughnuts, made with yeast, rise high and fry to a golden brown.

    warm water   ½ cup (110 ml)
    sugar   1 teaspoon (5 ml)
    yeast   1 tablespoon (15 ml)
    shortening   1/3 cup (75 ml)
    sugar   1/3 cup (75 ml)
    egg   1
    salt   1¼ teaspoons (6 ml)
    warm milk   1 cup (225 ml)
    flour   4 cups (1 l)
    chocolate or vanilla butter icing

Dissolve the 1 teaspoon (5 ml) sugar in the warm water and scatter the yeast over.
Set aside for 10 minutes. Thoroughly cream the shortening, sugar, salt and egg.
Stir in the milk and 2 cups (450 ml) of the flour. Add the dissolved yeast, mixing
thoroughly, then work in the remaining flour. Allow to rise in a warm place until
doubled in bulk, about 1½ hours. Knead down and roll out on a lightly floured
board to 1/3″ (0.75 cm) thickness. Cut with a floured doughnut cutter. Allow to
rise again in a warm place until doubled and very light, about 30 to 45 minutes.
Fry in deep hot fat at 365°F (185°C) for 3 to 4 minutes, turning once. Drain on
absorbent paper. When cool, ice with vanilla or chocolate butter icing.

Yield: 2½ dozen large doughnuts — 2½ dozen "holes"

American centennial
cake pan, disassembled

CANDY

CANDY IS ALWAYS a treat. In England it is usually called sweets or boiled sweets, but in America it has become known as candy. Candied fruits, made with honey, have long been made in the Orient. Medieval physicians very often used some form of candy to disguise unpleasant medicines. Marzipan, one of the oldest candies known, seems to have been generally made throughout Europe, and in the Middle Ages was sometimes molded into fancy shapes. By the 17th century, sugarplums, made of boiled sugar, were known in England but it was not until the 19th century that candy was made in any quantity. The Great London Exhibition in 1851, displayed large quantities of sweets and soon other countries became interested in the making of candy. By the mid 1850s there were a good many candy factories in North America although most fine candy was still imported. With the rise in mechanization and the increase in the availability and quantity of sugar, candy-making has become an important industry in Canada as well as the United States. It is interesting to note that one of the merchants listed in 1857 in Cobourg, Ontario, was a confectioner who sold candy as well as pastries.

222

The early settlers made maple-sugar candy, often at sugaring off parties. Sap was boiled until it threaded in cold water; then the syrup was drizzled over white snow and turned into taffy, sometimes known as "jap wax". A mid-1850 recipe for Maple Sugar Sweeties calls for a little of the thick sugar from the sugaring off to be placed in a saucer and stirred with a very little flour, a small bit of butter, and flavoured with lemon or peppermint or ginger. It was allowed to cool and cut into little bricks about 1" (2.54 cm) long.

Molasses was also used for candy, and almost any early recipe book carries a recipe for molasses taffy — a mixture of molasses, sugar, vinegar, butter, soda, and salt. When it is cool enough to handle, it is pulled until it is firm and light in colour and then cut into pieces. It may be flavoured with peppermint.

Chocolate Fudge

brown sugar   3 cups (675 ml)
sweet milk   1 cup (225 ml)
unsweetened chocolate   2 ounces (58 g)
butter, size of walnut
vanilla   1 teaspoon (5 ml)

Put sugar, milk, melted chocolate in saucepan. Boil, without stirring, until mixture forms a firm ball in cold water or soft-ball stage. Add butter and vanilla, stirring and beating rapidly until the mixture grains like honey. Pour at once into buttered 8" (1.2 l) square cake pan. Cut when partially cooled.

Maple Cream

A delicious, creamy candy — one piece tastes like more.

brown sugar   3 cups (675 ml)
cream or milk   ½ cup (110 ml)
butter   1 dessertspoon (10 ml)
vanilla   1 teaspoon (5 ml)
nuts or dates   ½ cup (110 ml)

Bring sugar and milk or cream to a boil. Add the butter. Boil 15 minutes or to soft-ball stage (234°F to 240°F, about 114°C). Remove from heat and add vanilla and nuts or dates. Beat briskly 5 minutes and put in buttered 8" (1.2 l) square cake pan. Cut when partially cooled.

Caramel Candy

Cocoa and molasses make this one a real taste treat.

butter   3 tablespoons (45 ml)
molasses   3 tablespoons (45 ml)
cocoa   3 tablespoons (45 ml)
white sugar   1½ cups (335 ml)
milk   ½ cup (110 ml)
vanilla   1 teaspoon (5 ml)
chopped nuts   ½ cup (110 ml)
raisins   ½ cup (110 ml)

Mix first five ingredients together in a saucepan and stir over heat until the sugar is dissolved and it comes to a boil. Allow to cook, without stirring, until it reaches soft-ball stage, 236°F (114°C). Remove from heat and stir in vanilla, nuts, and raisins. Beat until creamy and stiff enough to pour into a buttered 8″ (1.2 l) square cake pan. Allow to partially cool. Cut into pieces and allow to set for several hours in refrigerator.

Patience Candy

A creamy caramel toffee with a rich texture.

white sugar   3 cups (675 ml)
cream   2 cups (450 ml)

Caramelize 1 cup (225 ml) sugar by melting over medium heat until golden brown. Slowly add 1 cup (225 ml) cream, stirring constantly until dissolved. Add remaining sugar and cream, and stir until mixture comes to a boil. Cook, unstirred, to 236°F (114°C), soft-ball stage. Remove from heat and beat until smooth and glossy and thick. Pour into a buttered 8″ (1.2 l) square cake pan and set in a cool place to harden. Cut before completely cool.

Mocha Cream

Coffee lovers will like this glossy candy with its hint of chocolate.

coffee   1 cup (225 ml)
unsweetened chocolate   2 ounces (58 g)
brown sugar   4 cups (1 l)
cream   ¼ cup (55 ml)
vanilla   1 tablespoon (15 ml)
raisins or nuts

Over medium heat, dissolve the chocolate in the coffee. Add the sugar, stirring until dissolved. Raise heat and continue stirring until mixture comes to a boil and reaches 236°F (114°C), soft-ball stage. Stir in the cream and boil again until it reaches 236°F (114°C) again. Remove from stove and stir in the vanilla and raisins or nuts. Beat until glossy and thick. Pour into a buttered 8″ (1.2 l) square cake pan and cool partially before cutting.

Baking Powder Candy

A little like maple cream, but with its own flavour.

> brown sugar   *3 cups (675 ml)*
> flour   *1 tablespoon (15 ml)*
> baking powder   *1 teaspoon (5 ml)*
> milk or cream   *1 cup (225 ml)*
> butter, size of an egg
> vanilla   *1 teaspoon (5 ml)*
> chopped nuts   *½ cup (110 ml)*

Thoroughly mix together the sugar, flour, and baking powder. Add the milk and butter and stir over heat until it comes to a boil. Allow to cook until mixture reaches 236°F (114°C), soft-ball stage. Remove from heat and add the vanilla and nuts. Beat until creamy and pour into a buttered 8″ (1.2 l) square cake pan. Allow to cool for several hours. Cut before completely cool.

Sea-foam Candy

My mother had five sisters, and I think that is the only way they could have had enough elbow power to beat this creamy candy long enough. I find my mixer does a good job.

> brown sugar   *2 cups (450 ml)*
> water   *½ cup (110 ml)*
> egg white   *1*
> salt   *¼ teaspoon (1 ml)*
> vanilla   *1 teaspoon (5 ml)*

Mix the sugar and the water together and bring to a boil, stirring. Allow to boil until mixture reaches 260°F (128°C), hard-ball stage. In the meantime, beat the egg white very stiff. Drop the syrup very slowly into the egg white, beating well until all is mixed in and cooling. Add the salt and vanilla. Drop in mounds from a teaspoon on buttered waxed paper about 2″ (5 cm) apart. Set in a cool place to harden.

225

Cocoa Fudge

A creamy, rich candy that you may add nuts to if you wish.

> white sugar   1 cup (225 ml)
> cocoa   1½ tablespoons (22.5 ml)
> milk   ¾ cup (170 ml)
> brown sugar   1 cup (225 ml)
> salt   ½ teaspoon (2.5 ml)
> butter   1 tablespoon (15 ml)
> vanilla   1 teaspoon (5 ml)

Stir together all the ingredients except the vanilla. Bring to a boil, stirring only until the first bubbles appear. Allow mixture to boil until it reaches 236°F (114°C), soft-ball stage. Remove from heat, add the vanilla, and beat until smooth and creamy. Pour into a buttered 8″ (1.2 l) square cake pan. Cut in squares before it fully hardens.

Popcorn Balls

My mother always made a large supply of these to hand out on Hallowe'en night.

> corn or maple syrup or molasses   ¼ cup (55 ml)
> sugar   1 cup (225 ml)
> water   ¾ cup (170 ml)
> baking soda   ¼ teaspoon (1 ml)
> hot water   1 teaspoon (5 ml)
> butter   2 tablespoons (30 ml)
> salt   ¼ teaspoon (1 ml)
> vinegar   ½ teaspoon (2.5 ml)
> vanilla   ½ teaspoon (2.5 ml)
> popped corn   6 quarts (6.78 l)

Put sugar, corn syrup, and water in a saucepan and boil to 260°F (128°C), hard-ball stage. Dissolve baking soda in 1 teaspoon (5 ml) hot water, then add to syrup along with butter, salt, vinegar, and vanilla. Cook until mixture again reaches 260°F (128°C). Pour slowly over popped corn, mixing thoroughly with greased hands, and form into balls. Allow to cool.

"Laura Secord" Chocolates

This recipe was given to me by Mrs. Blake Allen of Toronto who originally came from the Napanee area. It was given to her by her aunt. These candies used to be a must at Christmas when I was a teen-ager.

> eggs 3
> butter, melted *¼ pound (113 g)*
> icing sugar *3 pounds (1.4 kg)*
> flavouring, fruit, and/or nuts

Beat the eggs and butter for 15 minutes. Then add the icing sugar, a little at a time, until all sugar is combined. Divide into as many bowls as there are flavours desired. Add any flavouring, fruit, or nuts as desired. Form into varied shapes and sizes. Refrigerate ½ hour before dipping.

COATING

> unsweetened chocolate *7 ounces (198 g)*
> paraffin *½ cake*

Melt chocolate and paraffin in top of double boiler. Dip each piece in mixture by running a toothpick or fine skewer through it. Keep adjusting the heat; if coating is too warm, it will run off, and if too cold it will make too heavy a coating for the candy. Cool on waxed paper.

Molasses Taffy

My family enjoy both eating this candy and having the fun of a taffy pull.

> molasses *1 cup (225 ml)*
> brown sugar *½ cup (110 ml)*
> vinegar *1 tablespoon (15 ml)*
> butter *2 teaspoons (10 ml)*
> baking soda *1/8 teaspoon (0.5 ml)*

Combine the molasses, sugar and vinegar and boil to soft crack stage, 280°F (138°C), stirring occasionally. Remove from heat and add the butter and soda, stirring in quickly only to blend. Pour into a well-buttered pan. When taffy is cool enough to handle, pull it with buttered fingers until light-coloured and firm. Cut with scissors into desired sized pieces onto waxed paper. Wrap to store.

CANNING & PRESERVING

MEANS OF CANNING produce had not yet been discovered when our forebears first came to Ontario. It was not until the latter half of the 1800s that canning was begun in the United States and was gradually introduced to Canada. Up until that time, people depended on ice houses to keep food fresh as long as possible. Our forebears devised many ways of preserving foods for the winter season, and adopted many of the Indian methods, as well.

Any and all wild berries that were edible were gathered and used in many ways. The Indians preserved these fruits for winter use by making fruit cakes out of them, and the settlers adopted this method, too. Fruit cakes were made by boiling blueberries, raspberries, currants, cherries, green gages or any kind of plums or small fruit, for half an hour. The fruit was then spread out on pans and dried near heat or in the sun. When partly dry, it was cut into squares, turned over, and sprinkled with sugar. Lacking pans, the Indians spread their fruit on large leaves to dry completely, and the cakes were then stored away in boxes in a dry place for later use. These fruit cakes could be reconstituted by stewing, when they resembled a preserve.

Cranberries could be preserved for a long time simply spread out in a dry place, or they could be put in containers and covered with cold water. Just as today, cranberry sauce and jelly were the chief uses made of them, although they were also made into pie.

Because apples were grown in orchards in the Niagara area by 1791, they quickly formed part of the staple diet. Many were the rural apple-paring bees; apples were peeled, cored, strung on thread, and hung around the walls of the cabin to dry, then stored in bags. They provided food all year and so many ways of using them were found — apple jelly, preserves, pies, and tarts, as well as apple syrup, butter, sauce, and cider. Sometimes apples were buried in sand-filled barrels to retain their freshness.

The root cellar kept many vegetables fresh for winter use, but they were very often pickled, if possible, or dried.

Most meats were preserved by salting away in a brine solution or by a combination of smoking and salting. Fish and beef were also dried. Ice-houses provided short-term preservation only.

Because the early settlers in Upper Canada relied heavily on pickled cucumbers and vegetables for their winter food, vinegar was an important commodity. It was made from birch or sugar maple sap; when the sap became poor for sugar, it was boiled down to about 1/3 to 1/5 of its volume. When it had cooled to lukewarm, yeast was added, then the mixture was set in a warm place, usually beside the fireplace, to ferment. In a few weeks it was ready to be used. Good cider vinegar could be made by exposing cider to the air for several months. Vinegar was also made from beets, noted for its specially fine colour, and red or white currants.

Canning revolutionized food habits and diet. A wide variety of foods became available for use, and cooking methods changed accordingly. In fact, this year 'round availability of a wide assortment of foods was partly the cause of the over-rich eating habits of the early 1900s, when tables were lavishly laid with very rich food. Today's freezing facilities have again changed our methods of food preservation, and the variety of food for year 'round use is almost endless.

When glass sealers were first introduced, and for many years after, they were expensive and so were not replaced unless absolutely necessary. Cracks were patched with a home-made cement. I can still recall seeing some jars of my great grandmother's patched with this dark compound:

229

Cement For Jars

> plaster of paris   *1 pint (565 ml)*
> resin   *1 pound (455 g)*
> lard   *2 tablespoons (30 ml)*

Mix all together and apply to crack on outside of jar. Allow to harden.

Since the pork barrel was an important part of every home, a good brine to pickle it in was essential. Here is the one that's marked "excellent" in our family book.

Brine To Cure Pork

To 100 pounds of meat, make a brine to cover it strong enough to carry an unpeeled potato about 3″ in diameter. Add to brine 1 teaspoon saltpetre, 4 cups brown sugar and ½ pound bulk pepper.

● JAMS ●

I have only included three recipes for jams as I do most of my jam, fresh, in the freezer.

Heavenly Jam

A tasty and pretty jam, almost like a marmalade.

> peaches, peeled and chopped   *2 cups (450 ml)*
> pears, peeled and chopped   *2 cups (450 ml)*
> crushed, canned pineapple   *2 cups (450 ml)*
> lemon juice   *1/3 cup (75 ml)*
> oranges   *2*
> maraschino cherries and syrup   *6-ounce bottle (170 ml)*
> sugar   *14 cups (3.15 l)*
> liquid fruit pectin   *6-ounce bottle (170 ml)*

Squeeze the juice from the oranges and put the pulp through the food chopper. Mix together all the ingredients except the pectin, and bring to a rolling boil for 1 minute. Add pectin and stir in well. Let stand for 5 minutes and bottle in sterile jam jars. Cover with melted paraffin.

Yield: 16 9-ounce (252 ml) jars

Peach Jam

    peaches, peeled and cut up   *20*
    apples, peeled   *6*
    oranges   *4*
    maraschino cherries   *6-ounce bottle (170 ml)*
    sugar
    powdered fruit pectin

Cut up the cherries. Put the apples and oranges through the coarse cutter of the
food chopper. Make into jam using the following proportions: to 4 cups (1 l)
prepared fruit, add 5 cups (1.13 l) sugar and 2-ounce box (58 g) of powdered fruit
pectin. Make up following the directions in the fruit pectin box.

Yield: 14 9-ounce (252 ml) jars

Wild Plum Jam

Native to North America, the wild red plum grew in abundance along streams and
in thickets. It was used by the Indians, who ate it raw, cooked, and dried. Early
settlers also used the wild red plum, and dried, it was a staple article of diet. Plum
butter was made from it. Here is the jam recipe from my mother's book:
    Boil plums with plenty of water until skins begin to break. Pour off water and
juice and drain in a colander. Boil plums again in a smaller quantity of water until
quite soft before adding the sugar, pound for pound.

    For more detailed canning instructions, consult Ontario Government Bulletin
No. 468, on canning, or consult your provincial government for a similar
publication.

● FRUIT ●

Rhubarb And Pineapple

This is a delicious combination of fruit.

    cooked, sweetened rhubarb   *12 large cups (2.93 l)*
    large pineapple   *1*
    sugar   *3 cups (675 ml)*

Cook rhubarb in very little water until tender. Sweeten to taste. Pare pineapple, cut in thin slices, and put it through the food chopper. Add the sugar and cook, adding no water, until clear. Mix with the rhubarb and bring to a simmer. Can in sterile jars or cool and freeze in desired quantities.

Yield: 5 to 6 quarts (5 to 6 litres)

Grapes

My mother used to serve a large spoonful of these preserved grapes in the middle of a dish of applesauce. The flavours complement each other.

> purple grapes   *6-quart basket (7 l)*
> water   *3½ cups (785 ml)*
> sugar   *7 cups (1.57 litre)*

Wash the grapes twice. Separate skins and pulp. Add 3 cups (675 ml) water to the skins and boil for 1 hour or until tender. Cook pulp with ½ cup (110 ml) water for 10 minutes; put through colander and if necessary add ½ cup (110 ml) water to seeds and cook again and put through colander. Add sugar to pulp. Boil 5 minutes. Add pulp to cooked skins and boil 5 minutes more. Seal hot in sterilized jars.

Yield: 4 quarts, 1 pint (4 litre, 565 millilitres)

Gooseberries

Since freezing gooseberries is so easy, I would strongly recommend that method of preserving them rather than canning.

Clip stem and blossom ends from gooseberries. Wash and drain very well. Put in freezer containers in required quantities. A little sugar may be added if desired but it is not necessary. Freeze at once.

Raspberries

For each quart jar (1.13 l) allow 1 quart (1.13 l) fruit. For each 1 quart (1.13 l) fruit allow 1½ cups (335 ml) water and 1-1/3 cups (300 ml) sugar boiled together for 5 minutes and skimmed. Fill each jar to the top with berries, shaking gently to settle while filling. Fill with boiling syrup to base of neck of jar. Place lid on jar, adjusting metal ring to barely tighten. Process in boiling water bath for 20 minutes for quart jars (1.13 l). Remove to cool on a rack, tightening metal ring to seal.

Use this syrup in the following two recipes to can plums, gages, peaches, and pears.

Allow 2 cups (450 ml) syrup to 1 quart jar (1.13 l) — 8 cups (1.8 l) water plus 10 cups (2.25 l) sugar for 6-quart (6.78 l) basket of fruit.

Gages And Plums

For either gages or plums, wash the fruit and prick with a fork to prevent bursting. Fill jars with raw fruit and fill with boiling syrup, leaving a headspace. Process in a boiling water bath, pints (565 ml) 15 minutes, quarts (1.13 l) 20 minutes.

Peaches And Pears

For either peaches or pears, peel fruit, halve, and core or pit. Place in a brine bath to prevent fruit from turning brown. Drain well and pack in jars, cup-side down. Cover with boiling syrup, leaving headspace. Process in boiling water bath, small jars 20 minutes, large jars 25 minutes.

• MEATS AND FISH •

Here are two interesting old recipes for canned meat and fish.

Canned Beef

Before freezers were available our meat was always canned. It came out of the jars red and juicy and was simmered gently in its own juices.

"Fill jars to within 1″ of the top with raw beef, cut to proper size, adding 1 teaspoon salt to each jar. Place a piece of suet on top. Add no water. Boil 3 hours in a boiling water bath and seal jars with paraffin."

Canned Fish

This was nice made up in fish cakes and then fried to a golden brown. The vinegar softened the bones.

"Clean, wash and halve fish along back bone; cut off tails. Pack in jars. Add 1 teaspoon salt and 2 tablespoons vinegar to each jar. Cook for 3 hours in a boiling water bath. Do not add water and do not bone fish."

Our ancestors enjoyed a variety of relishes and pickles with their meats; I have included only a few recipes here. Green tomatoes were featured in many recipes.

Sweet Green Tomato Pickle

green tomatoes   *1 peck (8 l)*
vinegar   *1 small quart (1 l)*
salt
whole allspice   *1 tablespoon (15 ml)*
pepper   *½ tablespoon (7.5 ml)*
whole cloves   *1 tablespoon (15 ml)*
brown sugar   *3½ cups (785 ml)*

Slice the green tomatoes, sprinkle with salt, and let stand overnight. Drain and cook very slowly in water, keeping shape of slices. Drain and add the vinegar and remaining ingredients. Simmer until pickle pretty well absorbs liquid. Seal hot in sterilized jars.

Green Tomato Catsup

I prefer this catsup to red catsup.

green tomatoes   *1 peck (8 l)*
large onions   *4*
dry mustard   *½ cup (110 ml)*
vinegar   *1½ cups (335 ml)*
coarse salt or to taste   *1/3 cup (75 ml)*
sugar   *4 cups (1 l)*
cloves, whole   *1 teaspoon (5 ml)*
allspice, whole   *1 teaspoon (5 ml)*
cinnamon stick   *1 tablespoon (15 ml)*
water
cayenne pepper to taste

Slice the tomatoes and onions, sprinkle liberally with salt, and let stand overnight. Drain and chop, cover with boiling water, and cook until very tender. Put through colander. Blend the mustard with a little water until smooth. Add mustard, vinegar, salt, sugar, and spices tied in a bag to tomato mixture. Boil gently until thick and bottle hot in sterilized jars.

Bordeaux Sauce

This recipe came from Mrs. Mary Kennedy, a cousin on my father's side, and she says it is good.

green tomatoes   *1 gallon (5 l)*
cabbage   *1½ heads*
onions   *10*
green peppers   *4*
turmeric   *1 tablespoon (15 ml)*
mustard seed   *1 tablespoon (15 ml)*
cinnamon   *1 tablespoon (15 ml)*
celery seed   *1 tablespoon (15 ml)*
coarse salt   *¾ cup (170 ml)*
sugar   *2 pounds (910 g)*
vinegar

Chop the vegetables and sprinkle with salt. Let stand for 2 hours. Drain. Mix in the seasonings, coarse salt, and sugar. Add enough vinegar to cover pickle. Seal. Do not cook.

Indian Apple And Tomato Sauce

This recipe is also one of Mrs. Mary Kennedy's and is one of my paternal grandmother's. I have not tried it, but she was an excellent cook.

ripe apples   *4½ pounds (2.25 kg)*
green tomatoes   *4½ pounds (2.25 kg)*
brown sugar   *3 cups (675 ml)*
vinegar   *3 cups (675 ml)*
cinnamon   *1 teaspoon (5 ml)*
turmeric   *1 teaspoon (5 ml)*
red pepper   *¼ teaspoon (1 ml)*
coarse salt   *¼ cup (55 ml)*

Put the tomatoes and apples through the food chopper. Add the rest of the ingredients and boil until thick. Bottle, hot, in sterile jars.

Indian Sauce

Here is another variety of this sauce, my mother's recipe, made with ripe tomatoes.

ripe tomatoes   *12*
ripe apples   *12*
onions   *6*
green peppers   *2*
ginger   *1 tablespoon (15 ml)*
mustard, dry   *2 tablespoons (30 ml)*
sugar   *1 pound (500 g)*
coarse salt, or to taste   *¼ cup (55 ml)*
blended vinegar   *1 cup (225 ml)*
water   *1 cup (225 ml)*
cayenne and black pepper to taste

Chop vegetables very fine and add remaining ingredients. Simmer until thick. Seal, hot, in sterilized jars.

Green Tomato Marmalade

Both the green and the red variety that follows are delicious.

large green tomatoes, sliced   *12*
white sugar   *3 pounds (1.5 kg)*
raisins   *1 pound (500 g)*
lemon, sliced thin   *1*

Pour boiling water over the tomatoes and let stand ½ hour. Drain and add the remaining ingredients and boil until mixture reaches marmalade consistency, approximately 40 minutes to 1 hour. Bottle, hot, in sterilized jars.

Red Tomato Marmalade

large ripe tomatoes   *15*
root ginger   *½ ounce (14 g)*
sugar   *4 pounds (2 kg)*
lemons, sliced thin   *3*

Peel and slice the tomatoes. Let stand in a colander ½ hour to drain juice. Place in saucepan, add ginger in a bag, and boil ½ hour. Add sugar and boil 40 minutes longer. Add lemons and cook another 20 minutes or until thick. Remove ginger. Bottle hot.

Marion's Pickle Relish

This recipe came from my aunt, Mrs. H. Hough of Sillsville, Ontario.

large cucumbers   *12*
small cucumbers   *12*
large onions   *12*
mustard seed   *2 ounces (58 g)*
celery seed   *2 ounces (58 g)*
brown sugar   *7 cups (1.57 litre)*
salt   *1 tablespoon (15 ml)*
vinegar   *3 pints (1.70 litre)*
flour   *½ cup (110 ml)*

Peel the large cucumbers and chop them by hand. Leave the small cucumbers unpeeled and slice thinly. Slice the onions thinly. Boil together all the ingredients except the flour. When cooking well, mix the flour with a little of the vinegar, stir into the pickles, and cook till thick. Bottle, hot, in sterilized jars.

• VEGETABLES •

Tomatoes

Wash and blanch tomatoes. Peel and remove stem and core. Pack into jars, pressing down so fruit is covered with its own juice. Use a knife blade to work out all air bubbles. Leave ½″ (1.25 cm) headspace. Add 1 teaspoon (5 ml) salt per quart (litre) jar. Process in a boiling water bath — small jars, 35 minutes, large jars, 40 minutes. Remove to rack to cool and complete seal of metal ring at once.

Corn

Here is an interesting old recipe for canning corn. I do not recommend its use but have included it for interest only.
   "Cut off a 10 quart pail of corn from the cob. Add a small handful of salt. Pound with a wooden spoon until milk rises to top. Fill jars, put tops on sealers, place in boiler and cover with hot water. Boil 3 hours. Tighten up tops when done."

237

THIS & THAT

HOUSEKEEPING FOR OUR pioneer grandmothers was a very different story from today. Even the first brooms had to be made by hand from the materials that were readily available, usually cedar or hemlock boughs tied to a stick for a handle. In Scarborough Township some Scottish settlers imported the Scottish broom plant, although brooms made of this were used mainly for their favourite winter sport, curling. Later brooms were made of corn.

Early housekeepers made use of both sand and lye to clean floors and furniture. Their "washing machines" were barrel arrangements, not unlike a churn, in which the clothes were pounded, and some people managed to construct various kinds of wringers.

Soap had to be made at home. When hardwood trees were burned to clear the land, the ashes were saved, and every home had a "fat box" in which were placed all the rinds, drippings, and grease from meat; bones were boiled down in strong lye, the lye improving the soap quality. Into a barrel or hollowed-out log went a layer of straw, and ashes were well pounded down on top. Lye, two quarts to the barrel, was either placed in the bottom of the barrel, dissolved in

238

water and mixed through the ashes, or put on top. Hot water was poured in, followed by cold soft water from time to time. Within two to three days a deep red liquid soaked out the holes in the bottom of the container and was carried by means of a grooved board to a large iron kettle that held all the bones and fat of the previous winter. The lye dissolved the bones and fat, and a soft soap was the result. When salt and resin were added and the boiling process continued, a hard soap was obtained, which was moulded in boxes, cut into bars, and dried out behind the kitchen stove. I can remember my mother lining the box with an old cloth before pouring in the soap so that it could be lifted out more easily when hardened. Here are some old recipes from our family book for soap and washing aids, as well as some household hints and old-time medicines. I have included them for interest only and do not recommend their use.

Hard Soap

1 pound borax, 16 pounds rendered tallow, 1 pound resin, 5 pounds lye, 8 gallons water. Boil slowly 2 hours, let stand until firm. Cut and pack.

Bleaching Solution or Javelle Water

½ pound chloride of lime, 2 pounds washing soda, 2 quarts boiling water. Put lime and soda in a basin, add the water and stir until all dissolved. Strain through cheesecloth, doubled, and bottle tightly. When fresh, dilute with 3 or 4 times the quantity of hot water; when old, use it at its full strength. Afterwards use a strong solution of vinegar to counteract the effect of the alkali; then rinse the fabric in several clear waters. Use only with white cottons or linens.

Soap Bark

¼ cup soap bark, 2 cups boiling water. Let bark steep in water 10 to 15 minutes; then strain through cheesecloth. Sponge material well after brushing it thoroughly. Brush it again after sponging, pressing also if necessary.

To Remove Wall Paper

Use 1 heaping tablespoon saltpetre to 1 gallon of hot water and apply freely several times with a brush. Keep water hot.

To Keep Cheese Fresh

Wrap in a cloth previously steeped in vinegar and water. Re-steep cloth from time to time.

Stove Polish

To keep iron and steel stoves from rusting, dissolve ½ ounce camphor in 1 pound of lard. Remove scum and mix black lead to make a good iron colour. Apply and leave 24 hours. Then rub with linen cloth. Will keep stoves clean for months.

Crack Filler

1 pint turpentine and 2 quarts boiled oil. Thicken with corn starch until like strained honey.

To Mend Hot Water Bags

Apply several coats liquid court-plaster allowing each coat to dry before adding the next.

Copper Cleaner

Your copper boiler or reservoir on the kitchen range will look like new if cleaned with a paste made of kerosene and coarse salt or kerosene and powdered bath brick.

Healing Salve

Melt equal parts beeswax, mutton tallow, resin and linseed oil. Heat only enough to mix. Very healing.

Zinc Ointment

6 pints of lard, mix with 1 pint zinc.

For A Cold In The Head

Sniff powdered borax up nostrils.

Onion Poultice

6 or 10 onions, chopped fine. Place in frying pan over a hot fire. Add about same quantity of rye meal and vinegar to form a stiff paste. Stir thoroughly and simmer about 10 minutes. Put into large cotton bags and apply as hot as can be borne. Change every 10 minutes, reheating and applying until relieved. Do not let patient get chilled in changing poultice.

● OLD-TIME MEDICINAL USES FOR SOME SPICES AND HERBS ●

Because settlers were usually far from doctors, they relied heavily on home-made medicines. Spices and herbs were widely used for cure-alls. The roots, stems, leaves, and seeds were made into a tea. Boneset and hemlock teas were taken for colds as well as spearmint tea and a tea made from the roots of the May-apple. Ailing children were given catnip tea. Poultices were made from crushed plantain leaves.

Salt was used for cure of infections, to stem bleeding, etc.

Sage was used for poultices in cleansing old sores, also as a diuretic.

Tansy was believed to relieve kidney problems, as was parsley.

Garlic was recommended for whooping-cough, coughs, colds, asthma, and worms.

Cayenne pepper was a useful stimulant in paralysis, fevers, etc.

Cinnamon was used to relieve vomiting, colic, and diarrhea, or oil of cinnamon used to relieve toothache.

Ginger was also used to relieve colic and indigestion.

Mustard was used as an emetic.

Sage was believed to be an excellent remedy for colds or night sweats.

Red pepper mixed with molasses was considered one of the best remedies for delirium tremens and sea-sickness.

● RELISHES SERVED WITH MEATS ●

Roast beef	Horseradish, grated
Roast veal	Tomato or horseradish sauce
Roast mutton	Currant jelly
Roast pork	Applesauce
Roast lamb	Mint sauce
Roast turkey	Cranberry sauce
Roast goose	Applesauce (steamed apples)
Roast duck	Black currant jelly, orange salad
Roast chicken	Bread sauce
Fried chicken	Corn fritters, cream gravy
Cold boiled tongue	Olives, pimientoes, sweet peppers
Pork sausage	Applesauce
Corned beef	Mustard

INDEX

242

244

247